WHISPERS IN THE TALL GRASS

NICK BROKHAUSEN

CASEMATE
Philadelphia & Oxford

Published in the United States of America and Great Britain in 2019 by
CASEMATE PUBLISHERS
1950 Lawrence Road, Havertown, PA 19083, USA
and
The Old Music Hall, 106–108 Cowley Road, Oxford OX4 1JE, UK

Hardback Edition: ISBN 978-1-61200-775-5
Digital Edition: ISBN 978-1-61200-776-2

A CIP record for this book is available from the British Library

Printed and bound in the United States of America

Typeset in India for Casemate Publishing Services. www.casematepublishingservices.com

For a complete list of Casemate titles, please contact:

CASEMATE PUBLISHERS (US)
Telephone (610) 853-9131
Fax (610) 853-9146
Email: casemate@casematepublishers.com
www.casematepublishers.com

CASEMATE PUBLISHERS (UK)
Telephone (01865) 241249
Email: casemate-uk@casematepublishers.co.uk
www.casematepublishers.co.uk

I'd like to have two armies, one with lovely guns, tanks, little soldiers, staffs,
with distinguished and doddering Generals and dear little regimental officers,
concerned over their General's bowel movements or their Colonel's piles;
an Army to be shown for a modest fee at every fairground in the country.

The other would be the real army, composed entirely of young enthusiasts
in camouflage uniforms, who would not be put on display
but from whom impossible efforts would be demanded and
to whom all sorts of tricks would be taught.
That is the Army in which I should like to fight.

Jean Larteguy (Jean Pierre Lucient Osty)
The Centurions

This book is dedicated to those men who shared the crucible of war with me, and to those who to this day uphold the honor and fidelity of the Special Forces Regiment.

Most of all it is dedicated to the fallen, to whom we owe today.

Contents

Acknowledgements

Thank you to Casemate for republishing *We Few* and with assistance in paring down the stories for *Whispers in the Tall Grass* to be more in tune with what the public can digest.

I especially acknowledge and thank the staff in Oxford for helping me to weave through the bureaucracy of publishing. They say an army runs because of the NCOs, well a publishing house runs with well-organized communicators called editors.

This is also the time to acknowledge my very special sister, Sandy Alvstad, a retired English teacher/professor, and Carol my soul mate. Their vocal and written surgery on the manuscript made it readable and reaffirmed the reasons I slept through those classes in school.

Finally, thank you to the men with whom I served. Brave men are awarded the Medal of Honor; exceptional and valorous units are awarded the Presidential Unit Citation. The attrition rate in CCN, in South Vietnam, was one in three. Most men survived only a few months running missions. They did it for their team, they did it for their country. Their families should be very proud of them; I know I am and was proud to serve with them. The tribute from our government is included overleaf.

The Presidential Unit Citation (Army) for Extraordinary Heroism to the Studies and Observations Group, United States Military Assistance Command, Vietnam

The Studies and Observations Group is cited for extraordinary heroism, great combat achievement and unwavering fidelity while executing unheralded top-secret missions deep behind enemy lines across Southeast Asia. Incorporating volunteers from all branches of the Armed Forces, and especially, U.S. Army Special Forces, Special Operations Group's ground, air and sea units fought officially denied actions which contributed immeasurably to the American war effort in Vietnam. Military Assistance Command, Vietnam–Special Operations Group reconnaissance teams composed of Special Forces soldiers and indigenous personnel penetrated the enemy's most dangerous redoubts in the jungled Laotian wilderness and the sanctuaries of eastern Cambodia. Pursued by human trackers and even bloodhounds, these small teams out-maneuvered, out-fought and out-ran their numerically superior foe to uncover key enemy facilities, rescue downed pilots, plant wiretaps, mines and electronic sensors, capture valuable enemy prisoners, ambush convoys, discover and assess targets for B-52 strikes, and inflict casualties all out of proportion to their own losses. When enemy counter-measures became dangerously effective, Special Operations Group operators innovated their own counters, from high altitude parachuting and unusual explosive devices, to tactics as old as the French and Indian War. Fighting along their Montagnard, Chinese Nung, Cambodian and Vietnamese allies, Special Forces-led Hatchet Force companies and platoons staged daring raids against key enemy facilities in Laos and Cambodia, overran major munitions and supply stockpiles, and blocked enemy highways to choke off the flow of supplies to South Vietnam. Special Operations Group's cross-border operations proved an effective economy-of-force, compelling the North Vietnamese Army to divert 50,000 soldiers to rear area security duties, far from the battlefields of South Vietnam. Supporting these hazardous missions were Special Operations Group's own United States and South Vietnamese Air Force transport and helicopter squadrons, along with U.S. Air Force Forward Air Controllers and helicopter units of the U.S. Army and U.S. Marine Corps. These courageous aviators often flew through heavy fire to extract Special Operations Group operators from seemingly hopeless situations, saving lives by selflessly risking their own. Special Operations Group's Vietnamese naval surface forces—instructed and advised by U.S. Navy SEALS—boldly raided North Vietnam's coast and won surface victories against the North Vietnamese Navy, while indigenous agent teams penetrated the very heartland of North Vietnam. Despite casualties that sometimes became universal, Special Operations Group's operators never wavered, but fought throughout the war with the same flair, fidelity and intrepidity that distinguished Special Operations Group from its beginning. The Studies and Observations Group's combat prowess, martial skills and unacknowledged sacrifices saved many American lives, and provide a paragon for America's future special operations forces.

Author's Note

Whispers in the Tall Grass is a first-person record of the impressions of tumultuous times and events. It is not for those with delicate sensitivities, or those who are unfamiliar with military vernacular and the macabre sense of humor that helps to blunt the reality of life and death struggles.

I started to write as a catharsis to rid myself of my demons while illuminating some of the history and valor of the individuals with whom I served. The view is not one derived from the lofty heights of evaluation of the combat reports, archives of official orders, or the military's vast trove of dry, tepid accounts of battles devoid of the suffering of the participants. It is my reflections as a participant and as an observer. It is harsh, profane, and littered with the rough humor of those of us that survived. It is not always written chronologically, for that I apologize. There are other great books out there that fit those historical parameters.

My challenge was to let you, the reader, see what the daily war looked like when we were out there trying to survive it, both physically and mentally, and yet not make the book a continuous string of missions from which we didn't expect to return.

All of us tended to get banged up on every mission. Sometimes we could only be on the ground for 20 minutes before we had to be removed or be annihilated. Sometimes it was the trip home that wasn't survived. We had incredible air support from brave pilots; the chopper pilots flew to get us knowing not "if" but "when" their helicopters would be shot up.

Through writing *Whispers* I have found a deeper appreciation of our great Republic, the times, and the incredible resiliency we possess as a people. Vietnam was an era of great turmoil and dissention within our society, yet tempered with an ethos of Duty, Honor, and Country, that shaped my generation.

Those core values are with us today. We imparted them to our children and they still surface wherever our progeny are put in the crucible of war.

The greatest tragedy to befall any people is the loss of the spirit of "WE," that sharing of ideals and culture. My generation was witness to just such disintegration and where it can lead, as we watched a country tear itself apart through division. We came home to the rot that had started in ours.

In conclusion, these are the tales of my youth, written nearly forty years ago when my recollections were fairly fresh. The book was never intended to be literature, nor is it scholarly. *Whispers in the Tall Grass* is a tribute to the unit, its record of accomplishment, and to the gallant, quirky characters that exhibited raw courage and dedication to the missions and each other under fire. Those characters and events will always remain vivid in my memory.

Prologue

Whispers in the Tall Grass is the second book detailing my recollections of events and people that served with me in Military Assistance Command Vietnam, Studies and Observations Group (MACVSOG), Command and Control North (CCN). CCN was the progeny of Delta, Command and Control Central (CCS) was the progeny of Omega, and Sigma begat Command and Control South. Our task at CCN was deep penetration reconnaissance in the enemy's hinterland and within his forward battle area. We followed the orders given to us through the chain of command in Saigon under direction from the Joint Chiefs of Staff and the crowd over at Langley, Virginia. We reported ground activity of the enemy… wherever directed. As a responsibility and tribute to each other, we retrieved our own when a mission did not go well. We pulled as many of these Bright Light missions as we did the reconnaissance inserts.

The book starts where the first book, *We Few*, left off. I have been with my teammates Mac and Cook long enough that we have become "one animal" in regard to our ability to survive and complete the missions assigned to us. Mac is a product of Alabama, with a wealth of combat knowledge, and is the leader of our team, Recon Team Habu. Both Cook and I outrank him, but he is the leader, our One-Zero by virtue of experience. Cook is also from the South and has a prior combat tour. In addition, he has attended Ranger school along the way and we constantly tease him about his "Rangerness." He is fondly tagged as Commando Head. Cook is our One-Two and I am the One-One. We, as a unit, in reality are everything that the Rangers want to be and more, but the tag fits Cook like a layer of military paint.

Habu operates out of Da Nang, at a base called Marble Mountain. This is our garrison and logistics point, but we also use forward operating bases called launch sites where we marry up with the air assets and launch our missions.

The teams normally run with two Americans and six Montagnard soldiers who we affectionately call Yards, or "little people," from the tribal areas, as well as the Chinese Nungs and some Vietnamese. Usually the individual teams will be all from one tribe. They are drawn from the indigenous people of the individual hill tribes. They are battle hardened veterans with a warrior culture. We have teams that are Bru, Sedang, Rhade, and other ethnic groups. All of the Americans are non-commissioned officers, or officers, and our bond with each other is more of a brotherhood than a standard army structure. In the main, we are Special Forces, with few exceptions, and the unit is all voluntary. We are a prime example of peer pressure in that regard, as the missions are near impossible without luck, skill and superior firepower … all of which need to be there on the same timeline. We are constantly surrounded, by virtue of the fact that we operate in and amongst the enemy's forward troop concentrations.

Ours is a strange peerage system as all the SOG teams are true meritocracies. Whatever the rank of the most experienced man is, he is the team leader, so you might have a lieutenant or a captain subordinate to a junior sergeant. To the uninformed, we would seem to be much too casual in our relationship to our officers, but it is quite the opposite as we embrace them as brothers and co-conspirators in our mutual survival. Military discipline hasn't degraded as might seem to be the case by our sometimes antics. Instead, military discipline has been enhanced through our shared suffering. The system promotes the talented, and keeps our attrition levels low enough that we think we have a chance to survive. The first is a sterling idea, the second is an illusion.

We are bonded by our trust in each other and tempered by having survived, on numerous occasions, near extinction as a cohesive fighting force. The team is everything. We are family, and we are, by extension, Montagnard or whatever ethnic group the "little people" stem from. More importantly, we are a major thorn in the side of the PAVN, People's Army of Vietnam. Our operations are tying up thousands of enemy troops in their efforts to thwart us. We cause far more damage to his battle formations and ability to wage war than conventional units. In order to contend with us, they have to use their radios, and they have to deploy troops to encircle and destroy us, which creates a target-rich environment for the air assets.

At the point where the book begins, I have survived to see the war and the missions get more difficult. The enemy has begun to use special anti-recon formations to hunt us when we are discovered in their territory. The missions are beginning to be one-way tickets for many and our losses are mounting.

We watch as the war becomes an open sore to the public, and an unfinished task for us. As a functional combat intelligence unit, we are the top of the food chain. As NCOs and junior officers, we organize and conduct combat operations that in other circumstances would take much higher command structures, and their staffs, to replicate. With teams consisting of a few Americans leading Montagnards we have intuitive, indigenous fighting teams that despise the NVA and are a true asset.

CHAPTER I

The Frying Pan

When the grass whispers, the lion stalks the land...

ASHANTI PROVERB

The serenity of the South China Sea, splashed with the hues of the sunset, provides the backdrop to my musings. I am sitting on one of the bunkers on the sea side of our base in Da Nang with a bucket of beers, occasionally lowering their body temperature with a CO_2 fire extinguisher before popping one open. I wanted some privacy to sort out the demons in my head.

We have been at this for nearly a year and my thoughts are not on home or even surviving, but rather on my family here. The members of this cabal of the deranged, this pool of the homicidally talented have become my brothers and, at this point, my kin.

We have just returned from a much-deserved in-country "R&R." During our absence, the bombing campaign has intensified up north. Due to the Cookie's indiscretions we are in double jeopardy.

A soft rain starts to fall and the air takes on that electrical excitement ahead of a storm coming from inland, across the marshes south of Da Nang. It is pensive and yet charged, fitting my mood as I recall the past and steel myself to get back into harness. The past is just that. I try to put it all in perspective and prepare for the new beginning.

The two Yards manning the machine gun on top of the bunker begin to laugh and chatter away in Bru about the camp dog, Ugmo. Ugmo is a cross between several breeds, including some Chinese breed that looks like a wrinkle factory, and possibly another species or two. He is built like a midget mastiff and has an overactive libido. If it isn't mechanical, Ugmo tries to reproduce with it. I look over and see that he has chased down one of the camp ducks and has it pinned; he's trying to mate with it, while the duck keeps pecking at his equipment in self-defense. The Yards find it tremendously amusing and are calling out encouragement to the duck. I find it somehow philosophically relevant. We are the duck, and circumstance is a big ugly dog with its own agenda.

* * *

After a tumultuous R&R, we are back at Marble Mountain, our "home" in Vietnam. It is also the home to 15–20 partial or whole Recon teams and everybody is acting like they know some dark secret that is yet to be revealed to me, a poor mortal. This would be the secret of what exactly was the social atrocity which the Cookie had committed while on R&R in Saigon. Now we wait.

My teammates are Mac (with nearly eighteen months running Recon), and our "new" guy, Cook (who had been with the team for nearly five months), a package of pent up militarism that will someday do him well—that is until this last sojourn in Saigon, where he had committed some horrible infraction that leaves us marked as social lepers. The team is under a dark cloud since those misdeeds appear to be worthy of excommunication and castration, just for a start. In the wisdom of the military, we all will pay for our collective sins against good order.

We had earned this trip as we were due for one. Each year, we are authorized one in-country and one out-of-country R&R or as we called it "I & I," Intoxication and Intercourse. You would be lucky to get one R&R a year unless you were a Remington Raider in Saigon. Although in-country R&Rs were normally three days, we had wrangled an extra three days because of injuries sustained in a ruckus along the main hardball coming back to the camp from Da Nang the week before. Some deserters and other trash in a three-quarter-ton had pulled up behind us, tried to pass, and when there wasn't room they pulled back and fired an M 79 grenade at our jeep. There never was a true escape from the war.

Cook sustained broken ribs from where the shell hit the back of the seat he was sitting in. Luckily, it had not armed itself. Mac sustained a sprained wrist and back. I escaped injury, but since the team was not able to run missions until we were healed up, I went along because I didn't want to straphang with another team while we could be tearing up the rug in Saigon. I should have stayed back.

We'd had almost a week away from running Recon and Bright Light missions. Mac stayed with Cook in Saigon the first part of the R&R but I had elected to go to Vung Tau the old seaside French resort. I enjoyed a blissful four days of beach, alcohol, good food, and new acquaintances, before Mac showed up to tell me that we needed to get back to Da Nang and we would pick up the Cookie en route.

On the last day in Vung Tau, relaxing at a café, I witnessed a bombing. After the dust dissipated, I had lost one of my new friends and another was now without her legs. I was ready to go back up north where you knew where the threat would come from and were prepared for the carnage.

As planned, Mac and I retrieved Cookie on our way back from Vung Tau. Cookie had hung around in Saigon with Rocky the Ranger. Rocky is another Special Forces type, who is assigned to an A camp somewhere in the outback. A former Mobile Guerilla or Mike Force alumnus, he is unsafe to be around, especially anywhere that involves explosives or a proliferation of folks that go by the book.

When we get back to House Ten, which is the Saigon nerve center and safe house for projects, both Cook and Rocky are already considered unhealthy to be around. They had caused enough trouble in Saigon that there was a regular dragnet in force trying to locate them for questioning and recriminations, followed by swift incarceration. The MPs in Saigon staked out House Ten and have already made two sweeps in an attempt to ferret them from their hidey hole. Both times their luck held and they were able to escape the long arm of the law. The staff at House Ten now wants nothing to do with them, and, though hiding them from scrutiny, are tiring of the subterfuge.

Rocky has now fled to wherever he is hiding out, no doubt with pleasant memories of the mayhem he caused. I am sure that he is safe, comfortably tucked into some remote outpost of the exiled. He and the rest of his A team are probably so far out in the boonies, they are grateful to be surrounded by the NVA just for the company.

We no sooner are reunited with the Cookie than we are quickly bundled out the door of House Ten, bag and baggage. We are taken to the airfield, with the admonishment to wait six months before coming back.

On the bird back to Da Nang, Mac and I listen to Cook's tastefully edited version of the sordid events. Even the air crew is studiously avoiding us. Evidently they too have heard some hideous aspect that Cook is leaving out of our briefing, or they only know we have become persona non grata. I am starting to feel socially syphilitic. Apparently, Rocky had slipped the bonds of common sense, so much so that even Cook was thinking of ditching him in Saigon. The warm glow of finding another Ranger buddy to hang out with has dissipated.

Cook and Rocky are both permanently barred from Mama Bics, our unofficial Rest and Recuperation headquarters downtown. That, in itself, is a record. I don't think anyone has ever done that before.

* * *

The trip to Da Nang takes about ninety minutes and the sound inside the bird, limits the talking. I enjoy the time to think. As a group, Special Forces could exist as the mobile insane asylum for the army. It is chock full of type-A personalities with anger issues, ex-wives, and a predilection for violence. There also is a certain class of us that have been here for too long. These men have figured out how to manipulate the manpower shortages and the reluctance of the mentally balanced to jump into projects that involve signing a suicide pact as a procedure for acceptance. They move from project to project with no break other than a thirty-day extension leave, and then strap on their gonads for another tour. If you show up at some A camp, or the Mike Force or some other acronym, they are always glad to have fresh meat. By the time you have been reported as AWOL from the shipping depot, you are too valuable and essential to the mission to be released. Saigon will forgive almost any sin as long as you are willing to do the work.

There are examples of the envelope if one wants to push it. Jerry "Mad Dog" Schreiber was a prime example. He was individually quirky, introverted, and deadly efficient in the bush. He was also burned out. He knew that his number was getting smaller and his chances of survival were almost nil. He wanted to quit, but he didn't. One day, he went out as a straphanger with one of the hatchet companies at Command and Control Central, and never came back. He was last seen advancing on the enemy and is now officially listed as missing in action. Now he is a myth, a legend that haunts this war. The "bush" had just swallowed him up.

I am trying not to be like that. Once you take this war personally, you sever the bond that held you to following orders dispassionately. There is something fascinating about that, something akin to the moth and the flame. You have assumed a role that ensures your own destruction, but it flits around the edges of your conscience until it becomes more real than the thought of returning to a society that most of us have abandoned as surreal.

I try to remember the faces and names of the seven people that arrived here with me. Only three of us are still running missions; the rest are either dead or so badly wounded that they were sent to the States. I can't remember their names, and only brief snatches of their faces. I can't think about quitting though: it seems dishonorable, not to the army or even Special Forces, but to my peers here in this theater of the macabre. These are my brothers, my kin.

My reverie is broken by our landing in Da Nang where we will drive to our base at Marble Mountain. It is one of the "particularly demented" category who arrives to pick us up at the airbase, in the form of the incredibly talented and emotionally twisted, Captain Robb.

As we make our way over to air operations, we spy Captain Robb motioning for us to get in his vehicle. We load our stuff in the back of his beat-up Land Rover which looks like it barely survived WWII. No telling where he acquired it. There isn't a non-dented surface on it and there are obvious bullet holes in the body as well. There is, however, the faint remnant of a USAID "hands across the sea" emblem on one door. It looks like a wreck but runs like a raped ape.

Dai Uy Robb may be wearing captain's bars, but I am sure that outside of his twisted peers in Recon, the rest of the Army wants nothing to do with him. He has been over here for four years already. He got his start in the Phoenix program, which was designed to eradicate the cellular structure of the Viet Cong. This was, in the main, accomplished by selective assassination. One normally conjures up a mental picture of assassins as Italian gentlemen in sharkskin suits, whereas the good Captain looks like a New England schoolmaster, until you look into his eyes. He is also one of the few men I know that are perfectly comfortable with the thought that his, or your, existence is only momentary.

He doesn't say much and keeps looking at us and chuckling to himself, as if he is in on some secret joke. Cook and I are sitting in the back seat, with Mac up front with Captain Marbles. Robb keeps peeking at us in the rearview mirror and continues the chuckling. He turns out of the gate at Gunfighter, the sprawling airbase in Da

Nang and into the evening traffic. For sure, Cookie has committed some terrible act that he hasn't told us about yet, since no one wants to discuss the details.

I am not all that worried about any recriminations, since I have an excuse: I had escaped to Vung Tau before the horror story started. All in all though, there is bound to be some sort of team counseling session. Mac was involved in part of it, but I can see that he is getting foggier about the details and is trying to distance himself from Cook. Robb listens to Mac and me laying the groundwork for Cook's plunge into the prime suspect slot. He looks in the rearview mirror at me and half sneers his first comment since he picked us up.

"Did you guys kill someone?" The thought seems to amuse him and he breaks out laughing. Mac and I look at him with the faces of two choirboys, and answer almost in unison.

"*We* didn't, *Dai Uy*, but no telling what *Cook* may have done," making sure to emphasize his name. Robb just snickers into the wind.

"It won't do you any good," he cautions, "he is *your* man." But then he sighs and adds, "At least you guys have each other." Now there is an understatement. Robb has always been a loner. Even when he was running targets, he ran light, just him and four little people. When he was transferred to NKP, his little people quit to a man. They just walked out the gate after discharge. If they couldn't run with our mad captain, then they wouldn't run at all. Joss, or luck as some would name it, is a river that we all swim in. I can't help it; I use his isolation as a means to get back on track.

"You don't have anyone, *Dai Uy*, because you are basically unlovable." He just snickers at that. He jerks the wheel and we careen past a minibus with frightened faces peering out the mud-splattered windows at us. Mac looks at him and me before quipping,

"Rumor has it, *Dai Uy*, that your little people quit because you had taken to giving your weapon a woman's name." We both laugh at that until Cook chimes in from the back seat.

"I give my grenades names sometimes."

"What?!" we both say in unison. He stares back as if it was a common thing and that we do it also. I make a note to check his gear when we get back to see if he has chalked something on his grenades, like some sort of weird bomb art from WWII. Mac just looks at me and makes the universal screw loose motion with his finger next to his right ear.

Robb downshifts and slides around the corner to the outer bunker line and the gate manned by the Yards from Security Company. They rush out and remove the barrier, all the while grinning like baboons. The Yards like Robb; to them he is the ghost that walks. They treat him like he was one of their tribal elders. As we wait for the wire to be moved back, he wags a finger at us.

"Now that you guys are back, they have something special planned for the three of you. I hope that you are healed up because it doesn't look like you're going to get any convalescence time." He cackles about that before careening the last hundred meters to the main gate and bunker line.

"In fact, there are conversations going on right now about the three of you and your immediate future." He hisses through a wolf-like grin. "There was supposed to be a special reception for you that I imagine included leg irons and handcuffs; but Captain Manes and SMAJ Waugh were diverted to more pleasurable pursuits and since I was in the neighborhood, I decided to pick you up myself and save you and the army that embarrassment. Something more important has come up, I imagine. You know how the war is." He adds a few more interesting observations about "new concepts" possibilities.

What could Command have in mind beyond raids, ambushes, prisoner snatches, and running for your life? I am musing that over when Robb adds that if we need a straphanger he would be available, as if he was an addition to the equipment list. That would be just what we need, an armed nuke to remind us of the severity of our sins. We pull up in front of Recon Company. He drops us off, puts the rover in gear and cackles as he drives away.

As we walk over to our hut, I am mulling over the possibility that we are now so socially stunted, that only Robb wants to hang out with us. I look at Mac as we put our stuff in the hut, and we both eyeball Cook. Even with my highly developed sense of the bizarre, I cannot fathom what he has done that could possibly attract this kind of attention. We finish up and needle him into going over to the club with us, but not before tossing his web gear to see if he has chalked names or slogans on the side of his grenades. He has.

The club is relatively quiet, with only about fifteen guys there. It is our personal retreat from the reality of what we do. It has all the charm and ambience of a honky tonk, combination biker bar and the trappings of pool table and war art. In the back is a stand up bar and a kitchen where they do fries, burgers and mystery dishes. Behind the bar is a velvet painting of a very supine, very naked lady as a talisman against mortality. As we walk in everyone goes quiet, then everyone starts laughing.

Laurent pops into view, and he howls at us, "You guys have been baaaaad!" As if it were a revelation from the Catholic Church. I look at him: Yup, he's drunk. He emphasizes, "Baaaaad," like your little brother would, after you convince him to pee on an electric fence while standing barefoot on a metal pole barn. You can't help but like Laurent, he looks like everyone's idea of the typical kid brother. Behind him is his running mate Bernie. Bernie has obviously been feeding his charge alcohol again. Laurent gets drunk on a shot glass, so Bernie has him on an alcohol training program. As a result, he has thrown up on everything over the last few months.

He even threw up on Captain Manes one night. That was entertaining. Mac and I get oblique to him since his reputation for projectile vomiting is legendary. Bernie holds up a container of the French fries they make in back. Christ, they are so greasy you could oil a machine gun with them. He makes a motion indicating that Laurent has already consumed a fair amount of heave ammo.

Laurent lurches toward us and we deftly avoid him since at this stage his time reaction and depth perception are about that of a ground sloth. Cook hisses something about getting him to throw up on us but we are past before he gets the opportunity. As we make our way to the bar, I hear the wet splashing sound of regurgitation behind us. Lovely.

Cliff is working the bar. He had gotten all shot to pieces and had retired from running missions. He was one of the most experienced One-Zeros and won the coveted Browning Hi Power for one particular mission; now he is running the club and helping out until they find a slot for him. This is a special category of convalescence in place, as a concept, to preserve the talent. We sidle up to the bar and he looks at the three of us and asks Mac and me what we would like. He studiously ignores Cook.

"You two," he intones, "need to drink heavily, since rumor is," he punctuates the next comment with a finger stabbed in Cook's direction, "that HE has committed something that will guarantee your being either chained to him on a Georgia road gang, or sent somewhere that alcohol is not on the menu for a number of years." He gets our drinks and finally gives Cook one but refuses to take our money, saying merely, "It's on the house; I want to tell my grandkids someday that I actually saw the three of you before you were dragged off to purgatory."

We try again to pull the story out of Cook, but he is still sulking over our checking his web gear for autographed grenades. He wanders off after an hour or so. The rest of the chimps close in on us with the grace of a Gestapo interrogation, trying to pull details out of us. So, we are not the only ones in the dark; only the Command appears to know. We start to make things up, just to test the waters. No matter how outrageous, we get no believers; everyone assumes that we are covering for the Cookie.

We stumble back to the hooch a couple of hours later. Cook is curled up in his sack, with a look on his slumbering face as if he were an acolyte in the order of peace and tranquility. I want to pour lighter fluid on him and set him on fire in the hope that in the few minutes before cognizance kicks in we might get some details. Mac points out the pitfalls of that plan, and we both are soon wrapped in the warm embrace of slumber land.

Whatever Cook did, it is probably the only thing still secret in the war.

CHAPTER 2

Justice Must Be Blonde

"Gooooooooood Moooooorrrrning Vietnam!" The radio alarm clock on Mac's bedstead blasts the morning ritual greeting from Adrian Cronauer, a slightly demented zoomy, as he begins his morning show. He is the Air Force disc jockey from Armed Forces radio. This brings stirrings of life from the two shrouded figures on the bunks across from me. Mac tries a grab at the button that shuts down this infernal noise maker, only to be intercepted by a jungle boot thrown from Cookie's corner that slams into the radio and kicks it off the stand and onto the floor, along with a mini grenade and a half can of Black Label beer.

The radio shuts off through disconnection, luck, or divine intervention, and Mac mumbles a terse "Thanks" from under the sheets. He rolls tighter into his nest as Cook mutters from the other bunk: "I hate that sombitch, someday I'm gonna go to Saigon and erase his loud little ass." Then he too shifts, farts, and tries to grab a few more minutes of sleep. I light up a cigarette and cough the first two puffs as my throat rejects the smoke. The light on my bedstead has done its duty in keeping the cockroach population massed behind the walls and not crawling all over us. You can hear their scratches and movements when you listen for them, and the walls are perforated here and there with .22 holes where the Cookie has blasted away at the unseen foe behind the walls with the silenced High Standard pistol. If he keeps it up, we will suffer when the rains come.

I lay there enjoying the cigarette and stretching out the sleep kinks, steeling myself for the harsh sunlight. Dawn doesn't just creep up quietly in this country, it virtually explodes. The radio suddenly blasts back to life from its new position on the floor, with the crescendo from Iron Butterfly or some other heavy rock spirit-blaster. Cook raises his head and I see his hand reaching for the silenced pistol in his web gear.

Mac has One-Zero ESP though, because he growls "Don't shoot my radio Cook!" with his back still to both of us. Cook stays his hand on the pistol and instead eases himself over to the edge of the bed. He lifts the covers slightly and a stream of urine jets out to pool on and around the source of the latest top ten. The radio shorts out with a brief spark and sputter.

The radio was Mac's pride and joy. He had bought the thing over in Saigon and has that unique attraction to radio—stereophonic, dial-less, whatever—that made him glow at the thought of being its owner.

Cookie, on the other hand, viewed it as both an annoyance and a possible candidate for target practice. As the radio sputters its life out, Mac turns over and looks over the bed at the corpse of his new toy in a pool of urine. He looks over at me as if by virtue of the fact that I am there, I am somehow involved. I reach over and pick up a canister of mace.

"Before you do something rash, remember that you, the all-powerful midget God of combat, were the one who picked him." I nod in Cook's direction, noting that he is edging his hand towards the Taser perched on the top of the mini refrigerator.

"And you might remember that escalation over this can only result in more problems from the head shed. We are in enough hot water over his antics in Saigon." I get up and grab my shaving kit, never letting go of the mace can in the process. I look at both of their feral little mugs and start for the door. "I am going to go shower. You and Skunk Boy here can work things out after I am gone. Personally, I need a shower, and you two need to be held in a fire hose bath for about an hour, and now," I pause and look at the radio, "this place needs a bleaching. If you do it with the urine still pooled, it will create chlorine gas, and it might kill off some of the cockroach population in the process." I look at Mac, he looks at Cook, and both realize that the solution involves a victim to be successful, so both start to get up as well. No bleach in the hootch, ergo the first one that can find some will be off the victim list.

Outside our hootch, Mac's pet monkey is perched on a pole like some Neolithic tribal totem; the fur-covered abscess lets out a banshee shriek. I keep a baleful eye on the little chancre, since the monkey loves to piss or defecate with amazing accuracy. Maybe that's where Cookie learned his latest ballistic talents.

The monkey is a gibbon monkey that Mac had picked up and was fattening up for some special holiday feast with the Montagnards. Cook and I were hoping that the Yards would kill it, and we would all be invited to the feast, then get happy drinking Mampei. But until this day could arrive, the monkey lived on a pole outside our hooch and we fed it. In return, it screamed like a banshee and would shit in its hand and throw it at anyone who passed by, very entertaining. On top of that, every dog in the camp hated the bloody thing. But worse, the monkey hated Cook, and the feeling was reciprocated. In fact, the monkey would devise ways to break into the hooch. It could always find a way in, and when it got inside, it went to Cook's stuff and trashed it. It even shit in his boot one time. Cook hated the thing. Hell, I hated the thing.

I am halfway through a shower when Mac and the Cookie stumble in and seek the same jump start for the day. There are about eight of us in the shower, an equal number shaving at the sinks, and a few more in the toilet stalls and at urinals. The steam from the showers compacts the atmosphere into a combination of soap, shampoo, aftershave and farts. Another lovely morning in the army.

I finish and grab my kit. I am reasonably sure Mac and Cookie didn't have time to either clean up or, more importantly, booby-trap anything while I was gone, so I head back to the hooch and get dressed so I can go to the mess hall and see what the master of the ptomaine, Rickard, the mess sergeant, has dreamed up this morning. I am pushing on the door as the two renditions of the Hatfield McCoy feud come up the walk in their dainties.

"See you at the mess hall," I fling at them as I step off into the sand. At that moment, the fur cannon launches a wad of rolled-up monkey shit and a stream of urine and feces, which splatters onto Cook's head and shoulders. The monkey howls and Mac splits a rib laughing at the Cookie, who now looks like the splash wall on a pigeon roost. Cook shoots the monkey a promise of murder and retribution, and heads back towards the shower.

"See I *told* ya, ya'll shouldn't have ruined mah radio!" Mac calls after his retreating back. I am going to the mess hall; this will only get worse and I need food to have the strength to participate.

The only thing that will end the escalating world of quid pro quo will be our getting a mission. We will probably get one this morning and have to move into isolation—that is, after we get whatever ass-chewings we have missed or accumulated during our brief absence. When we get alerted for a mission we go into isolation and physically move to a fenced-in set of buildings where we will prepare the mission, by going over all the old target folders for that area, latest aerial and intelligence on the area. We will also prepare the team for movement to the launch site usually in a day and a half. At the launch site, we will wait until it is our turn to be inserted. Upon launch, our Bright Light team will go airborne and circle to be prepared to be immediate support if we get into trouble.

Today, Mac and Cookie have to get Doc Wang to look them over and stamp them fit for duty. This is a formality, because unless you are unconscious, limbless, or delirious with fever or madness, you are considered fit for duty.

When I get to the mess hall, it is already filling with the remnants of the company that are not actively engaged in running missions or at the launch site. I fill my plate with a lumberjack portion, find an unoccupied table and settle in. I am halfway through with my breakfast when Mac and Cookie come in. A discernible hush accompanies their arrival. Mac sashays his way through the chow line, making inane comments loud enough that all can hear, as if he hasn't a care in the world. No brains, no headaches. Cookie looks like he used half a roll of toilet paper to stopper the blood flow from what was either a bad shaving exercise or a suicide attempt. Either way it will do him no good, since Captain Manes gives all of us the eyeball and an evil smirk.

A few people make the sign of the cross and chuckle at their witticism. No bother, because with this crowd, odds are that someone will probably have committed some misdeed last night that will make us look like amateurs by comparison. Mac and Cookie consume their meal and belch in unison.

"Mac, do you notice that we seem to be the center of attention?" He looks at me and then over at the Cookie.

"Yep. What's new about that? Bet we are going to finally learn what Cookie did in Saigon." He snickers and Cook just scowls at both of us.

"I bet we get a mission," is all he says. No shit Sherlock, I am thinking. Just how dangerous beyond the usual will be testimony to whether Cook's offence was a normal infraction of good order and discipline, or whether it approached the reprehensible.

It is rare to see so many of us here at the base in Da Nang. Usually the majority are up at the launch sites in Phu Bai or Quang Tri. There they would be busy waiting to launch, or already at the target running for their lives with the NVA hot on their trail, or running Bright Light missions to save their fellow teams from annihilation. My sphincter alarm is starting to go into the red zone. Obviously, there is a lull in the war effort or the weather has turned to mush out in the target areas. A lull can only spell disaster for us since it means that someone has found time to come up with a new mission for CCN. Since what we do now borders on the suicidal, anything new has to be truly terrifying.

Manes stands up and growls out a terse, "Let me have your attention." This is followed by a few mumbles and the crowd goes quiet.

"There will be a company formation in the theater at oh-nine-hundred. Be there, and make sure your playmates are there, as it is mandatory." He then turns towards our table. "You," he points at Mac and me and Cookie, "will be in the CO's office with me as soon as you are done filling yourselves, which would be now. Pick it up gents, time is a-wastin'."

We follow him out. Once we are outside, Mac asks him what this is all about. Manes just chuckles.

"You three had better not have created some horrible situation that the colonel has to answer for." He gazes dourly at Cookie. "Did you shave yourself my man, or did you let these two help you? No matter. I had a lot of high hopes for you being a sobering and soldierly influence on these two." He jabs a finger in my direction, "But it seems that they have corrupted your senses and you have sunk to their level." He grins and turns on his heel and we all pile into his latest jeep from the stolen vehicle inventory.

All this business about our seeing the Colonel is starting to make me nervous. I have the sneaking suspicion that the use of blackmail, wrapped up in a motivational exercise called the threat of incarceration, has ratcheted up my nervousness a few notches, and my survival gene is starting to glisten. Cookie's crimes must have approached the truly hideous.

We go into the TOC and find Colonel Donnie waiting for us, accompanied by the S2 and S3, and an Air Force colonel. He looks us over with a wince of displeasure at the toilet art on Cookie's face and waves us to be seated, then turns to the Air Force colonel.

"This is RT Habu." The S3 goes over to the situation map and starts reading from a file that is obviously a target folder.

"Gentlemen, you were operating in Hotel Five, on an area reconnaissance, when you encountered a coaxial cable running east to west along this ridgeline here." He takes a pencil and points to an area inside the target box on the map indicating the ridge. "RT Habu did not have a wiretap device so you followed it laterally for about two hundred meters to see where it led." He points again at the map, "At this point, you discovered a box attached to the cable with three junctions going off with leads to the north and west, and continuing on again to the east. RT Habu took photographs of the box and moved tactically for another four hundred meters, before making contact and having to be extracted under heavy fire." He pauses.

I am starting to pull the memories of the mission from my store of nightmares. Hotel Five is a ball buster as a target. We had inserted by using a Nightingale device that simulates a firefight, then inserting the team on an alternate site so it looks like they haven't landed. It requires a deft hand by the air assets, inserting you with a quick roll onto a patch big enough to drop into quickly without choking power on the bird. Not an easy task; it requires a lot of experience to pull off effectively. If it is done correctly the landing will go unnoticed and the team gets off in a mad rush in a couple of seconds. The enemy will go towards the sounds of the firefight, which is the device detonating the cherry bombs and firecrackers connected by time fuse in sequence. It sounds just like automatic weapons and grenades.

We had, for once, been able to stay overnight and it was on the next morning that we found the cable. The area was full of NVA; we had avoided contact for most of the day, and were trying to ease closer to the source of the cable to pinpoint whatever it ran to. I remember Mac taking pictures of the box and the cable. Coaxial meant major headquarters, but even without that we knew we were close to something because we could hear truck engines to the west and the place was full of signs that indicated a lot of folks were in the area. We had tried to mix our tracks in with the rest whenever possible; we were wearing the NVA-issued Bata boots, and had mixed our tracks real well. But, still I was pissing my pants every time Mac squeezed the button on the Pen Double E camera. It sounded like a gunshot to my frayed nerves.

We had continued on from the box location and our luck ran out about four hours later, when we ran head-on into what appeared to be a platoon-size element. The contact lasted about three minutes and we were on the run after that for most of the afternoon trying to grab a high point we could defend with air support. We had gotten lucky and they managed to pull our gasping asses out of an LZ almost as little as the one on which we had inserted.

Cookie, ever the collector of odd kit, had taken a green case from one of the dead NVA as we had run through them. It had some sort of device inside with

Russian markings and we had turned it in at the launch site when we got back. It was apparently some sort of optical device used for coordinating fires from AA batteries. Usually, they were used on the heavier calibers such as the 37 mm anti-aircraft gun. We had noted it and dismissed it since Hotel Five was notorious for its AA coverage. Big deal, a 37 mm, they were getting to be as common out there as the 12.5 mm.

The S3 goes over to an object on the table and pulls the cover off it. It looks just like the box we saw in the bush, painted in that weird Soviet shade of pea green. It is the same type of box, of that I am sure. The Air Force type is eyeballing us as if we had stepped off an alien spaceship, which would be humorous except I am getting the nagging feeling that Hotel Five is in our future. I would like to soil myself, but it wouldn't slow the slide into the abyss that I am sure we are about to be shoved into. Whatever Cook did in Saigon, I want to take full responsibility for it, and maybe they will send me to Long Binh Jail. I look at Mac; he shakes his head as if he could read my mind, indicating that it won't save us.

The S3 continues.

"The Air Force is sure that this type of relay is part of an integrated air defense and communications system that is employed to coordinate triple A targeting as well as secure transmissions between Headquarters and subordinate commands." Now there is a news flash. Who the hell do they think carries coaxial cable around out there, some low-ranking Nguyen? So that he can call his girlfriend? They use hard line so that we can't RDF their locations like when they use the radio. Cookie is staring at the box as if he could intimidate it into revealing it's secrets. Wouldn't that be nice? Then, we wouldn't have to go back to Hotel Five, as I am sure that is where this briefing is leading. The S3 finishes and looks at us.

"Is this the device that you came across?"

Everyone is now looking at us. Mac has that look on his face he uses when he is buying time. Cook is staring at the box on the table, as if he could track it right back to where it was made and who made it. He probably actually knows what it is, from one of the many DOD books on Soviet Ordnance Recognition that he has sequestered in his Ranger nest back at the hootch. Being the One-One, my job is emergency situations. That's what an assistant team leader does, pick up the trash and try to keep us alive. Lie! The first thing that comes to mind is always the most logical. No, *that* isn't the box we saw, it was smaller, fatter, had a big red sign that said "Don't report me or you'll be sorry!" and could pick up Radio Hanoi. In fact it *looked* more like a radio. Yeah, that's it. If it was a radio, they could fly one of the Blackbirds over it and do it all remotely at 20,000 feet while having a highball. Yeah, it's a radio.

I never get the chance to speak before Cook blurts out: "Yes sir, that's it, a Soviet dash fourteen communist something, something, five. I was sure that's what it was when I passed by it." I *knew* it! I am going to have to get faster or Mac and I will have to leave him in his cage when we have to come up here. Mac just nods and I just sit there dumbfounded. We are sunk, toast, kaput, finished. Cook looks like he won the spelling bee; I want to slit his throat. The Colonel nods at Manes, and says simply:

"That will be all. You're dismissed."

We rise and follow the square back of Manes outside. The sunlight is like a visual electroshock when we turn the corner of the blast wall. I am numb. That was too easy. For sure we are about to be cooked. Why are all the running teams back here? I have to have a chat with Mac about the Cookie. Right now I want to sell him to a Turkish boys' club. That would be too good for him. I want to strip him, handcuff his arms behind him, put him on roller skates, and leave him in the Tenderloin district to be used as a pull toy. He is a dark spot in my soul right now. There is such a thing as gung ho, but the English translation means "work together." For Christ's sake!

We proceed to the theater, which is actually a telephone-pole-and-corrugated-tin architectural masterpiece in the center of the compound. It is also the aiming point for the VC home guard mortar crew, hidden on Marble Mountain, if they see a bunch of us, and they happen to be doing their bit for the cause that day. Manes goes out in front and gives us the briefing about what is happening. It's a real slim diet of information though. Basically we, that would be us, the suspicious, will make ourselves busy ensuring that we are up to snuff, with a lot of range work etc. This is followed by the chunky threat about the consequences of causing trouble or mayhem, and making him work for a living. We are dismissed and everyone starts to drift away. Captain Manes doesn't even give us a second glance before roaring off in his stolen automotive asset.

The panic sweats are overtaking me. For sure, this briefing bodes no good for us. I am walking with Mac, and Cook is lagging behind us a few steps with a dejected look on his face. I hope he is suffering. He probably thought that Manes was going to call us up out of the crowd and tell the rest of the chimps that we were off on some hellish adventure that involved blowing up a dam, killing thousands with only an entrenching tool, and having streets named after us. He is actually kicking the dust like some petulant nine-year-old. I want to see if he is fireproof.

"You know Mac, we are going to have to do something about Commando Head back there or he is going to get us into serious trouble. In fact, you could say, since *you* are the one who *picked* him, that it is your responsibility as the team leader to do something about his education." Mac doesn't answer he just turns his head and grins at me. That says it all. We are back. Home is where the heart is in this place. It does have charms though, if you like the bizarre and twisted. Try to be the observer to your own participation in someone else's mad opera. Down on our level there are no lofty arguments one way or the other.

The monkey shrieks another howling welcome at us as we shoot past it into the hootch. A splat of thrown monkey feces hits the grenade wall behind us. I suspect that Cook has been feeding the damn thing Darvon pain killers in its diet to destroy its aim.

* * *

Around 1600 we get the news to saddle up and move into isolation. As soon as we get settled in, Mac links up with the AST and comes back with the bad news. They want us to go back and see if we can do a wiretap. They have the line that they want tapped all picked out. That friggin' box, I should have set fire to the bloody thing. The target area is an ass-kicker just in regard to the terrain, it's full of NVA and we will have maybe two hours before we are running for our lives. That doesn't leave much time to install a tap and get any traffic on tape.

We start going over the target folder and the overlays for the suspected enemy units. After you overlay that on the map, you can't see the gridlines that show elevation. Why don't they just bomb the snot out of the area? Of course that won't work since the terrain is not conducive to carpet bombing. That's why the NVA are hiding in there and dug in to their eyeballs no doubt. We keep at it and start to come up with a twist that might buy us time when we get in. We need two, maybe three days on the ground if we are to get any traffic that will help the think-tank figure out how to get at them.

It is late evening before we decide to call it a night. Sweet dreams.

CHAPTER 3

Someone is Listening

The vegetation of the old bomb scar is weeping humidity where I am lying prone on the jungle floor, my head down and looking off to the side. The sweat is beading on my eyes and nose, from the humidity that is soaking my little spot on the planet. My heartbeat is like a bass drum in my ears and it isn't from running. I am completely motionless and holding my breath, trying to be nonexistent at that moment. What I am trying not to alert is the North Vietnamese soldier who is about forty-five meters from me. He is part of a three-man trail watcher team and they are doing their twice-daily line walk. They are checking the trail and, more importantly, they are periodically checking the communications line that runs parallel to the trail.

They had come around a bend in the trail downhill from me, and I had heard the three klicks on the URC-10 we were using to communicate without breaking squelch. I had just enough time to quit moving and freeze as they walked up into range. The old saying that if you can see the enemy, they can probably see you, comes to mind. I keep as still as I possibly can. At that level of fear, the senses heighten to where they are screaming at your brain receptors and your brain wants to recoil in terror from your spinal column. I am watching the man closest to me from the corner of my eye, trying not to move my head. Mac and Cook, along with the rest of the team, are about forty meters behind me in the thick trees on the slope. My area is all cut back under the upper canopy and fairly open, with small underbrush about two meters high. Where I am lying is an old bomb scar probably a couple of years old. Thank God for nature. Here it regenerates in a matter of months. Everywhere except where those ninnies are using Agent Orange, that is. Where they spray that shit, nothing wants to come up and the forest takes on a cancerous look.

If the NVA discover me I am truly fucked. There is no cover, just enough brush to provide some concealment but not real cover. The only comfort is that I know that these three NVA have eight guns trained on them right now, which is some measure of backup; but it is scant comfort as I am alone in the open pretending to be dirt.

This mission is a part of the massive effort to find the logistics system Command suspects is tucked in these hills and canyons. Since building and maintaining a logistics depot requires *beaucoup* construction and maintenance folks, there are also a horde of other pissed-off, alert and dangerous types running around looking for bloody trespassers. The trespassers would be us. We had come here with the express intent to tap into their commo-lines and get some tapes of their traffic. We, the hunter-gatherers of the intelligence, would not listen but would merely sneak in, drop the tap on the line, run the lead line out, camouflage everything and come back. Oh yes, and replace the tape every twenty-four hours. I had just done that and had commenced my stealth run back to the hide, where the rest of the team was in a defensive perimeter with two on the backside security.

The initial information dump we'd gotten in isolation was a jumble of intelligence on the area, last patrol reports, estimates of concentrations, and of course the usual stumble through the S4 to find a wiretap that worked. Theirs were all defective in one way or another so we had gotten one from Castillo, aka Castro, aka the Beaner. The Cuban always has a spare set of everything stashed somewhere. I had never done a wiretap; Mac had helped out with one, months before. We had spent two days working with the thing until all three of us could do it in the dark.

We had watched the line for half a day before I went down with Mac and we put the tap on. Now it is tape changing time. We had timed the line checkers, and I should have had plenty of time to accomplish the tape change and get back in position. But these guys just showed up unannounced. I am trying to remember if I followed the "tips" that came with the package. If you did the sequence correctly there was no load loss, thus no one from Hanoi Bell getting suspicious. I am waiting for these assholes to move on and being *very* still.

I hear more voices from the direction they had come from. Lots of voices. The only thing that isn't making me spoil my britches is that they sound like any group of GIs grab-assing and "smoking and joking," so there isn't any great "Hey look, a gringo!" I can only lie there and try to be part of the scenery.

The second group comes up to where the first three have stopped. The leads we had placed to the box are about seventy-five meters up the trail from them. I move my head ever so slightly as they come up, since the other three have relaxed and are focusing their attention on the larger group. I can only see about eight of the total from where I am, but double that number strung out around and back down the trail. As they come up they take off their little packs and sit down on them.

One guy is carrying what looks like an old-fashioned mine detector, with earphones. He starts talking in Vietnamese and I suddenly realize what is going on. This is some kind of class for Christ's sake. I can't make out the words or understand any of it, but I have sat in enough field classes to know what this is. Some of the privates in the rear have already got that sleep-eyed look.

The guy goes on for about ten minutes on what appears to be the proper operation and deployment of the device. Meanwhile, one of his two companions has dug up a portion of the commo-line and attached what appear to be leads and a meter to the wires. The principal instructor now puts the device on audio. There is an audible squawk as he passes over the two leads leading away from the main line and to the meter. The meter shows something but I can't see it, and I'm more worried about pissing my pants and shorting out everything anyway. This is great. Not only am I out here with my britches down, but I am right in the middle of the NVA field training school. I am starting to think that God may have been a bit peeved at our recent social activities and this was some kind of warning order.

I can't do anything. I am thinking about getting one of the soap dish claymores out, but they are in my rucksack, back up the bloody hill. At least I have my CAR-15 and my normal kit. I ease the gun up where I can use it while Charlie Techno drones on below me. My mouth is so dry that I can't even work up a good drool, which would befit my position of being the idiot in the wrong place at the wrong time.

There is a loud slapping noise followed by a moment of dead silence. I can't see what is going on; all I know is that everything has gone silent. I hear someone screaming in an authoritarian voice, then a timid but dutiful litany of phrases and rote answers from what sounds like two other voices. I have no idea what is happening; I just hope that someone doesn't come pushing up slope to take a piss, or I will be training aid number two.

This little interlude is followed by another ten to fifteen minutes of what appears to be rote instruction, with the troops coming up to the front to perform one task or another. The two assistants are now busy packing up the meter and stowing the line back into the soil where they had excavated it. The whole drill has lasted some twenty minutes, but seems like hours.

There is another voice from off to the left and all the NVA that I can see stand up, pick up their packs and put them on to move off down the trail in the direction they came. The clinking and rustle of their movement fades off to the south. I wait for the bush to return to its normal hubbub and then begin to cautiously move back up the slope to where the team is waiting. It takes me about fifteen minutes to get back in position. One of us will have to make this route again and we don't want to make it a beaten path that even the blind can tell was not supposed to be there. That is the hardest part, of course, leaving the bush seemingly undisturbed. Too many trips and you are going to leave a sign. That's always bad when dealing with the trail watchers: they have a set portion of the line to check and know every detail of the bush. You come along and break or bruise a plant next to the trail and they will pick it up sure as spit.

I slip into the team's perimeter and am greeted by Loi who gives me a wan smile. I crawl over to Mac and settle in beside him. I have the tape in a sealed baggie, made from the plastic shipping cover for the radio batteries, and take it out to show Mac that I have swapped the old out for a new one. He nods and pulls me closer. He whispers, "They came up too fast for us to warn you."

"I figured that out when the URC-10 clicked. What the hell was going on? I thought my ass was cooked when they first walked up." I take my canteen out and gulp several ounces to hydrate what I had lost through time and fear.

"Near as I can figure, they were giving the troops some sort of class on checking the line. The first three were cadre of some type; there were about twenty-five in the group that came up with the officer." He wipes his face with a cravat; we are all sweating in the steam-bath atmosphere. "I got about ten pictures of the group and the device they were carrying. I couldn't get a good shot of you, just your foot and part of your leg that were exposed. I thought for sure that one of those privates was going to look up and spot you."

"What the hell was the commotion about halfway through?" I ask him as I am screwing the cap back on my canteen. I ease up to where I can stand and Mac does the same. From where I am now, I can see Cuman, the leader of our indigenous team members, and the rest of the Yards spread out to the right and left and slightly forward. All are intent on looking off towards the trail. Mac looks at me and makes a wry face before answering.

"One of the cadre Jap-slapped two of the privates that were talking in the back and made them stand at attention until the class was over. He had the little pinheads jacked up in the rear. I don't like this; if they come back they are going to eventually discover the tap. I'm thinking that we ought to pull up stakes and move to a better location than here in the little red school house."

I nod and am thinking out the logistics of doing that. We will need to follow the line, which is always dangerous, or we can make a SWAG (Scientific Wild Ass Guess) and see if we can pick it up again where it goes off to the west. Either way it would be best to pull it as it gets close to dark or pull it now and find a Remain Over Night or RON position. We had stayed last night, some seventy-five meters to our rear in the thick brush of the undergrowth. We never like to use the same hide twice, although on a wiretap your choices are limited. You want to be close enough that you can monitor the foot traffic but not too close that you disturb the bush.

"I agree, Mac, that was too damn close. Let's give it until just before first light then we will pull the tap and see if we have any better luck to the west." He nods and looks at the map he has pulled out of his cargo pocket. He points with a twig to an area that denotes the direction we think the trunk line runs.

"We can try and work our way into here. It's probably where the HQ is and will be crawling with troops, but it is an option. There is shitty terrain there though. They can canalize us in that direction. Trouble is they will have the most traffic flow on that line." He never gets to finish the thought because Cook starts clicking his fingers to get our attention and when our eyes lock he makes the hand signals for movement to our front and indicates it isn't just someone out for a stroll. We snap back down to a squatting position with some deadfall to our front.

Mac and I ease up to where we can see the trail. The Yards are all tensing up. I can see the trail and I am very unhappy about what I see. The three line checkers are back and they have brought another group with them. This group is *not* a student formation. These guys move up, establish security and are scanning the bush on both sides of the trail—but more so in our direction. The guys with the equipment point towards the spot where I had been, or at least the general area, and accompanied by a squad they begin running the line check, going up the trail in the direction of the tap.

Mac is quietly trying to get Covey, our air support, up on the air. I mean *real* quietly because these guys are all business. I am holding my breath, wondering what tipped the bastards off or if it is just a coincidence. The group that is moving up the trail reaches the point where we have the tap, and I wait for them to appear on the other side of the bramble. They don't. Two things happen simultaneously. The squad to our front moves upslope and one stumbles onto the minute track I had left leaving the tap and finds the spot where I had lost eight lives, breathlessly waiting. Also there is a concussive boom from where the tap was. The boom is produced by the two toe popper mines we had placed around the device, in case it was discovered. It has definitely been discovered.

The crowd that was getting ready to move uphill freezes for a moment, then whips their attention back in our direction. They are pros and they will know that the sign is fresh. They go into a crouch. Mac has finally gotten Covey up on the air. The squad below us start moving up and Cook lets them get about ten meters, then detonates his claymore. The Yards on either side of him throw two grenades as well. I see that most of the group that was below us is down.

"Let's go," Mac says, "We have to grab some ground so we can hold out until the air gets here!"

"Mac, you want we grab one of the wounded down there?" Cook shouts over the moaning coming from below. Mac shakes his head and starts making hand signals for Cuman to get the team up and start moving higher up the slope. We had reconned a few rally points on the way in; all were defensible for a limited amount of time. I wait for the team to get moving. There is a sudden blast of automatic fire from below, but it is only a couple of AKs and is hitting all over the place. They still aren't sure we are here since we had not engaged them with direct fire, only grenades and a claymore, but the rest of the mob is going to come running to help with the casualties. I get a brief glimpse of the carnage that the claymore has created: a swath of the underbrush has been chewed up. I can't see that many bodies but the squad that was moving up is all gone. There are a couple of folks hunkered down, and they are the ones firing up the real estate. We move out as fast as we can without making a lot of noise.

It takes us about twenty minutes to get to the first rally point. We pile into a defensive position and the three of us go into a quick conference. There is no argument about the fact we are compromised. No more wiretap: the two toe poppers and the detonation cord have eliminated the wiretap and turned it into shrapnel. The only thing they might find is the lead wires. Either way they won't need a forensic team to figure out what happened. We haven't fired a shot but they will have trackers on our asses before the hour is out. Even if it starts raining we won't have enough lag time to lose them and use the rain to cover our track, so we cannot hope to stay in. The mission is scrubbed at this point. What we need to do is survive until the cavalry gets here. The rally point is not as good as the second one higher on the ridges. We waste no time in getting back up and moving off in the direction of the one higher. We can hear signal shots behind us, from down in the valley and off to the south.

It takes us a good hour to reach the second rally point. By the time we get there, Covey has shown up and is moving about a kilometer off to our east. A line of green tracers tracks him from the ground and he banks to the left and dives then cooks off a white phosphorus rocket and flits back up to altitude. Almost on his tail a set of fast movers comes in almost vertical and drops their ordnance.

I can hear Covey since I am right next to Mac where we had plopped down after the grueling climb. As I am getting my breath I hear him relay that the choppers are on their way and that we have a bunch of folks moving our way. No point in subterfuge at this point; they know we are here. When Covey showed up they knew we were still on the ground. I get up and start shoving the Yards into where I want them. Cook is tying in the other half. This is as good of a place as any to make a stand. We have steep slope on two sides with trees and dense scrub, with car-size boulders at our backs going uphill. There is no high-speed trail above us that we know of so we will have time before they can work their way above us. This is as good as it gets in this business.

The NVA are bloodied and pissed and for sure are doing all they can to try to squeeze us and kill us. With air on station, that is going to be a tough task but we aren't home free; the NVA specialize in tough tasks. They will try to run us to ground, then mass on us and get on top of us before the Air Force shows up in numbers. We just have to hold until the air assets get here. We are laying out claymores and tightening up our position.

We are screwed for an extraction LZ. Covey will either have to blow one for us with ordnance, or we might be able to take down a few trees with the two ring mains we have with us. The damn trees are too thick for that to be all that effective, but if we shift slightly and take down two big ones, it might give the birds enough room to get in. We are looking at the trees to determine which ones to use without adding any of our supply of claymores to the charges, in case we need them for defense. Covey comes back on station to tell us there is a small clearing and overflies us to get a mark on our location. Mac manages to signal him with the mirror so he gets us oriented from the clearing. It's about seventy-five meters to our north, further out on the ridge spine we are on. The clearing sucks for a defensive position but Covey thinks he can lay enough fire power to get us out. We have no choice but to move.

We get there at the same time the NVA do. They know every open hole out here, so they have sent a force to close up any LZs. Trouble for them is, they didn't send enough troops. We hit four who have heaved themselves up the ridge and are out of breath. We kill two and the others scramble off downhill and start peppering us with controlled fire. We go through the same drill again in tightening up the perimeter. I take an earmuff charge and knock down a bigger tree upslope that drops and gives us room for the blades to get in. The LZ is just big enough for one bird at a time and the way it sits, we can bleed off to the north instead of to the east where all the bad guys are coming from.

There is no need to be quiet at this time. They know we are here and where we are. Now it's a race to see if we can get out before they mass. Covey comes back over and marks some target down slope, and a set of fast movers come in and drop what appears to be a rack of 250-pounders on the slope below us. The AK fire is picking up, so apparently there are more folks moving our way and getting set. When they have enough they will rush us. They will initiate with RPGs.

A set of A1Es comes in and drops napalm below us, then comes back to work over the slopes above us with the same. Apparently we have movement above us as well. These big prop-driven relics from the Korean War can hang around long after the jet jockeys have pissed through their fuel and leave.

Mac yells over that the air package is five minutes out and to get ready with the first lift. It will take us three birds to get everyone out, because of the altitude, and Covey is stacking them off at the orbit point. About the time I hear the blade snap of the gunships; the ground fire is picking up. The fixed wing assets move off as the choppers get on station. A Cobra comes in across our front, with its chin turret spitting 40 mm. The shells are making a meat grinder in their path and the ground fire drops off just as the first slick arrives. Cook and two Yards scramble up on the felled tree laying with its crown downhill, quickly pile themselves onboard the first slick that arrives; it lifts off and gains altitude.

We have to climb up on the horizontal carcass of the tree I dropped, to get on the slick. I am the next one to go. A Cobra comes in and makes another pass with his guns and rockets, taking a shitload of ground fire in the process. The second slick comes in and balances with one skid on the log. I scramble aboard with my three Yards. We are shoved to the floor by the pilot piling on power and vaulting into the air. The ship tilts to the left and, nose down, gains speed and altitude. I am looking out the side and back to see the third slick come in and Mac, Thua and Cuman scramble aboard. There is a lot of ground fire and another Cobra comes in right across their windscreen and tears up the terrain with his minigun, then Mac is up and away.

The last Cobra is spewing smoke and yet still makes it up with the rest of us. They are to our front about a hundred meters and the other birds are all keeping a weather eye on it. The Cobra is losing altitude and we watch as it settles itself into a flat-topped roundel that looks like an old battery firebase. It continues to lick its demise into the heavens in a greasy black cloud of smoke, as a second Huey comes in and two figures scramble from the stricken bird and into the second. The slick lifts off and gains altitude. I am listening on the headsets, and Covey is getting ready to have a set of fast movers hit the hill to destroy the bird which is still burning. They never get a chance. The helicopter erupts in a ball of flame and its ordnance cooks off.

Forty-five minutes later, we are settling into the launch site. We disembark and drag our gear off the chopper. I have that sour sweat smell cloaking me from three days in the bush. I grab my rucksack and start towards the TOC.

The mission was blown, but at least we got about a day's worth of traffic before we were busted. I turn the tape over to Budrow, the NCO in charge of our launch site, and we go back to getting the team settled in and fed. We will rearm and get set in case we have to pull a Bright Light for another team, but we are finished here otherwise. We will catch a hop back to Da Nang and maybe get some stand-down time. Whatever the boys in Saigon think, there are shitloads of hardcore NVA running around in the target box. More than likely they will bomb the crap out of it. I hope the tape has something of value, because I crapped about eight lives out of nine back there on that slope.

Mac and Cook and I are trying to figure out how the NVA got onto us. Was it a load loss on the line and the class exercise discovered it, or did the two privates notice something and that's why they were talking? Or was it just plain dumb luck and circumstance? They came back too fast with hardcore ass-kickers for it to be luck. I would rather know in case we have to get another mission like this.

It was my first wiretap, and at least we got something. Mac's photos are sent for developing as well as the tape. Whatever they reveal, it will be out of our hands, although we will get a copy of the photos, thanks to Pappy Budrow. We call him that but not directly unless you like lumps.

It is about four hours later, when we are in the shed having a cold beer, that Mac looks at me sardonically and says, "We shoulda stayed in so you could make a little Recon history." I look at him and reply, "Oh, how so?"

"Well, not all that long ago one of our guys who spoke fluent VN and looked the part, actually sidled into a base camp and brazenly joined the troops in a training course and sat in the bleachers with the troops. Why not, he had the same uniform, same Bata boots, looked and spoke like a VN. He even managed to take pictures. Now that takes balls."

"Yeah? And your point is?"

"Well, you could have stood up and asked a question, when you were lying down there; that would have made you a legend both here and with the NVA." He chuckles to himself.

"I can't speak Vietnamese worth a shit. I have no desire to be a legend, I would have been shot full of more holes than a turkey. And last but not least, I was shatting myself at the time."

"It wouldn't have mattered. Cook wanted you to do something spectacular, so he could brag to all his friends about how cool you are."

"Yeah well, Cookie can crawl down there on the next one, and I will take a BB gun along so I can pepper his furry little ass into doing just what you suggest. Or, better yet, why don't you do it?"

"Can't," he says as he reaches for a cigarette and lights it up.

"Why?" I ask him, taking a slow pull on the beer and relishing the tang. Cook looks at both of us with a bemused look.

"I have to demonstrate leadership restraint." He chuckles again. "Besides, you seemed to be enjoying yourself down there. They probably got onto us when your ass snapped shut when they showed up the first time. I could hear it all the way up where we were. If we do this again I may have to equip you with a Kotex to cover the noise factor."

No denying that. However simplified he is making it, I was scared shitless. At least this is something for my two fellow chimps to have fun with, until something new comes along.

CHAPTER 4

Don't Flush, I'm Coming Out

Why does it have to always rain? It's almost as if the good Lord deduced that he needed to flush this place at least twice a day. I can understand the intent, since under the hot sun it takes on an odoriferous quality that would make a slaughterhouse smell like a flower bed by comparison. There is always a wafting, lingering smell of burnt feces from the daily latrine detail, mixed in with the smell of rotting tissue and cordite. Actually, the cordite I can handle, in fact it is like an aphrodisiac.

I am lying on a bunk in the sleeping huts up at the Quang Tri launch site and trying to get the heavy, used-gym-sock taste out of my mouth that comes from napping in the hot afternoon sun. Gahgh! I hate that taste. I take the cap off my canteen and take a pull on the water. It is lukewarm, and I pour some on my head to rinse it off as I swizzle the first gulp before spitting it out on the floor. That little exercise didn't help all that much.

I stand up, stretch and wander over to the door, to look outside and see if there is any chance that the weather might clear. The rain which has been beating on the corrugated tin roof suddenly stops. I look out across the small compound towards the chopper pad and watch the wall of rain moving off towards the east. As it passes I can see other figures emerging from the huts and staring at the sky. There are three teams up here and we are all scheduled for insertion. We are third on the list so we will be pulling Bright Light for the first two. With the way things are going out in Indian Country, that should guarantee us about a day and a half before our slot comes up.

The average time on the ground for a team has dwindled to a day or less, sometimes a matter of hours. That means we will be living on the edge of hysteria for the next twelve hours, anticipating having to go and help extract whoever ran into the NVA first. When that happens, depending on circumstance, we will either sit waiting for the word to go and help pull our comrades from the meat grinder, or sit praying that they can do it on their own.

I would dearly love to be more optimistic, but that is like pulling your own plunker: an exercise in fantasy at best. I want to go over to the TOC and check to see if Covey has managed to get up over the Area of Operations. If he has, we will have a picture of what the weather looks like out there. This country has the weather patterns of a toilet bowl. Everything seems to be clear, and then you are hit by a deluge. They should have named it Bidet-Nam.

I am about to splash my way over to the TOC when I hear a jeep engine racing, and then a shape comes barreling out of the corner of my eye. It is one of the more battered jeeps in our inventory, basically a dented tub with a motor and a transmission, *sans* all the frills like a windshield or lights. It is also going like a bat out of hell in first gear. I step back instinctively as the jeep flashes past the front door with a spare few inches of clearance.

I get a glimpse of the occupants as it zings by. The one sitting petrified in the passenger seat, with eyes as big as saucers, I recognize as Ti Ti Loi, our tail-gunner. He sees me at the last minute and reaches a hand up, as if to wave at me. It is more likely that he is hoping that I will reach out and snatch him out of the jeep. Sitting behind the wheel, intent on the complicated process of driving, is the epitome of why the Montagnards didn't invent the wheel by their lonesome. It is Cuman, our Zero-One. Holding on for dear life in the back is Bong, who probably is using up every incantation in his shaman litany to wrap himself in some sort of protective aura. He is jammed in with Bang, a former NVA Sapper Company Commander. He was a prisoner that Mac and I had recruited from the big POW camp next to CCN, on the recommendation of Cuman. They were from the same clan. Perched on the rear left of the vehicle is Thua, who is calling out suggestions to Cuman and hiding his eyes from the world behind aviator shades, as usual.

The jeep careens past in the blink of an eye and I hear a resounding crash moments later. This is followed by jabbering in Bru and the sound of the engine being restarted. I glance out the door to see what acted as the brake and see the jeep has run into the side of a hut three buildings down. It is partially buried in the wall.

The three in the back have picked themselves up from where Newton's law had deposited them and are pushing the battered jeep back out of the wall of the hut. There is a jabbering animated discussion between Cuman and Thua, which results in Cuman finally taking the jeep out of first gear, so that they can roll it back.

This is great, I am thinking: between the victims and the driver they have just enough brains to operate the jeep. That is, if each one concentrates on a particular control. One for brakes, one for accelerator, one for shifting, one for lookout, and two left over for shrieking. I look back into the interior of the hut and see that the crash has awakened the Mini Mac. The bunk that Cook had been sacked out in is empty.

Mac and I learn why, when we hear Cook's voice from outside between our hootch and the next hut.

"No, *no*, NO! Don't put it in gear until AFTER you get it started!" We hear the jeep starter laboring and then the engine catches. Evidently the muffler has become a victim as well, for it revs up with a resounding roar. We hear some mumbled shouting and the grinding of gears before the jeep zips off. The roar of its little four-banger recedes in the direction of the chopper pad. Thank God for the fact there are no birds sitting out there, to act as pylons in the Bru demolition derby.

Mac and I watch as the jeep careens past the commo van in a spray of mud, with Loi leaning out the right side as centrifugal force tries to eject him. He could get a spot on some yacht team with his counter-balance move. Cook is running a short distance behind, making poor progress in the soupy mud. Mac looks at me and giggles, then apparently realizes the gravity of the situation and gulps. He is thinking what I am at this moment. Budrow!

We had been warned before that teaching our Yards the art of automotive operations was not only verboten but was, as he put it, directly contrary to any semblance of sanity. The three prior exercises had resulted in his typical punishment for infractions. We had dug piss tubes. These are the metal canisters, in which 155 mm artillery shells are shipped. Mounted at an angle and buried halfway into the sandy soil they function quite nicely. In fact by now, since digging them in was the standard punishment exercise, the camp fairly bristled with piss tubes. They dotted the interior of the camp like a field of blunt punji sticks. You could virtually reach a "urination station" without tiring from the walk. When we were finishing our last penance we had sarcastically told Budrow that the piss tube program accurately located where the bunkers were, because that's where the troops were. He had looked out over his domain and snarled,' You're right, so the next time you two and that tribe of yours screws up, you can dig them all up and put them in a random order."

Our driving instruction program had managed not to destroy anything yet, but that was when Mac and I had been running the drill. With Cook out there, apparently the regard for standing orders and caution had blown away on the same foul wind. If the Buffalo was in camp, we were in deep kemchi. Maybe he is over at the airfield, I am hoping in desperation.

There is more muffled shouting out by the chopper pad and another resounding crash, which abruptly stops the laboring complaint of the jeep engine. This time, there is a small wisp of dirty black smoke. It is coming from the direction of the Conex containers that hold the extra ammo. I am thanking our lucky stars that they protected the TOC from whatever collision trajectory Cuman had been on, when I realize that they are full of all kind of things that go boom if in contact with a heat source. Trepidation is overcome by the thought that if it blows up, the jeep and the Montagnard rendition of the Andretti family will be vaporized at the same time.

It is possible that we can gussy up some fire damage on the hut they hit moments before, and convince Budrow that it was an artillery attack. Let's hope that Cook is uninjured if that cover story doesn't work. At least then we can blame him for everything. Mac is shaking his head and about to verbalize the deep shit we are in, when I realize that the hut the boys had used for the bank shot was Budrow's.

"Goddamnsonofabitchinstupidmotherfuckers!"

This comment comes growling from the direction of the same hut, followed by crashing sounds and the unmistakable ripping of wood being splintered. A couple more splintering sounds are followed by some unintelligible gnashing punctuated by very creative expletives, in the text of which both my name and the Mini Mac's can be distinguished. Not only is Budrow not at the airfield, he is here in camp! Worse yet, he was apparently present at the first accident scene. I am hoping that he was terribly injured, and what we just heard was the last frantic thrashing of his about-to-expire carcass. Mac looks at me and we both scramble to get our hands on some sort of weaponry.

I just lay my hands on my Browning when the screen door is ripped off its hinges behind me. I look over at Mac and he is pointing his finger at me! I notice that he has the beanbag gun in his other hand, partially covered with the bag it was in. The little shit was going to use me as bait so he could get a good shot! From behind me I hear an evil hiss, like some Jurassic raptor, followed by "YOU TWO!" There is no mistake and no hope. Not only has Budrow survived but he has made it out of the wreckage of his hut.

He is standing in the doorway looking just like one would imagine one of the Brothers Grimm's trolls to appear to the three nanny goats. He is dressed in just his underwear and there are bits of hut architecture still clinging to his OD tee shirt and matted in his hair. To make matters worse, Mac starts to giggle behind me. I can't manage levity because I realize that the Browning is unloaded.

Budrow eyes the two of us for a moment and then launches into a first-class tirade, starting with, "I distinctly TOLD you two…" I miss a lot of it because there is some sort of goop that looks like a mix of shaving cream and facial mud, which is slowly sliding off his hair-challenged pate and teetering at the edge of obeying gravity. I can't help being transfixed by it, so I miss most of the recriminations and indictment.

I snap out of it as Budrow is winding down. The end of the tirade comprises instructions for us to go and get whatever remains of our team and our One-Two and get our asses over to his hut to help extract whatever remains of his belongings from where they had been flung after the jeep crashed into the wall. Evidently, he had been taking an afternoon sojourn in the bunk, reading one of the Zane Gray novels he is addicted to, when he, the bunk, and the Old West had been catapulted across the room to land upside down in his toiletries and dirty laundry. It had taken him a few dazed moments to extract himself, as he had overheard the Cookie getting the jeep moving again. Having missed being able to exact his vengeance on the culprits, he had stomped over to corner us. I look over his shoulder and out the door and see Cook and the demolition brigade stumble out from behind the TOC heading our way. They are helping Loi who is limping a bit. They are all smudged and spattered with what appears to be motor oil. Cook glances around furtively, sees the broad back of Budrow filling our doorway, and beats a hasty and prudent retreat in the direction of the Yard mess hall. They just clear the outer door and go inside when

Budrow turns and stomps away. He slams what remains of the screen door behind him for punctuation and splashes back in the direction of his hut.

I look over at Mac and we both burst out laughing. We can't help it. Despite the gravity of the situation, it has been hilarious. I walk back over to my bunk and sit down to lace up my boots. Mac looks at me from the chair in the middle of the hut as he puts the beanbag shit back in the bag.

"Did you think that was going to stop him?" I ask him.

"Nah, but it might have knocked the wind out of him long enough for you to slap a magazine in that pea shooter and wound him, so we could get away." We can't help it: we start giggling and laughing hysterically all over again. I can't hold it back; in fact I get the hiccups from laughing so hard, which causes another round. We hear crashing sounds and then Budrow as he yells over in our direction.

"You two pencil dicks better get moving in there. And when you get done my hut better look like it is brand new!" He splashes past our line of view in the direction of the TOC.

Furtive splashing comes from behind the hut and Cook slips through the doorway seconds later, followed by Cuman and Thua. Both of the Yards look castigated, and Cook looks as if he got spray canned by motor oil. He gets a rag out and wipes the oil off his face before asking the golden question.

"Well, what do we have to do?"

Cuman and Thua hang their heads in dejection. Mac looks at the two of them and says sternly: "Oosh, numbah ten! *Trung Si* Buffalo, *beaucoup* pissed off. Go get *tahans* and come back here rik-tik. We all clean up *Trung Si* Buffalo's hut right now! Thua, you go get hammer and tools. We fix wall and anything else that be fucked up."

The two of them shuffle out the door and head over to the team hut to gather up the rest of the team. As soon as they clear the door we start howling with laughter again. Cook starts to loosen up and then he too joins in.

We have gotten ourselves back into some semblance of seriousness by the time the Yards join us outside of Budrow's severely damaged hut. We enter through the shattered remains of the door that the Buffalo had kicked his way through in getting out. Inside, the place is not all that bad, just jumbled; it's debatable whether the accident caused the mess or whether this is how Budrow normally lives. The place has a feral air to it. We pick all the loose stuff up and move it over under the cover of the awning on the mess hall behind us. We leave Xam Pat with Budrow's belongings and tell him not to let anyone touch them.

After careful analysis over a tepid beer we decide that we can remove the three shattered studs and shore up the roof with some two by fours. Cook finds some ten penny nails somewhere and we set about pulling the wall apart after we have butted the new studs in place. This results in the wall being plucked out and landing in the mud outside. It starts to pour rain again as we stand it up and let the rain remove the mud and debris.

Cook and I wander around the camp until we find a sheet of plywood that will, after being shortened, fill in as the new wall on the Buffalo's hut. During this foray, we wander past the remains of the jeep. It is lodged between two of the Conex containers and is a smashed heap in the front. The engine is pushed back and has ruptured, hence the oil shower on the boys. The smoke came from the oil fire that Cook had put out with the CO2 extinguisher next to the ammo containers. Even with the rain, the jeep is still frosted with the residue.

We go get the front loader that someone had stolen months before and, with the help of a tow chain lift, pull the wreckage loose. In the process the engine drops out, along with whatever held it to the chassis. We load it up and tote it all over behind the latrines, leaving it perched on the backside of the berm.

While Cook and I are doing this, Mac has managed to salvage what can be reused in the old wall and put it back in place. Our fellow chimps are by now gathered under the awning chirping away at our misfortune, until Mac wanders over and tells Xam Pat to shoot anyone that looks like they are too close to Budrow's goods. Since Xam Pat has a reputation for following Mac's orders to the letter, our peanut gallery flees for the safety of their respective huts.

Cook and I find just the right stretch of plywood to finish the job. Unfortunately it is part of the ready room for the pilots. But since they aren't there, we quickly remove it, leaving a stretch of the wall sans cover. It actually will be an improvement when the rain stops since it will help ventilate the place. We don't care; all we want is to get the job done.

We come walking back with our find and in about fifteen minutes have the bloody thing in place. Cuman has found some paint, so we merrily slop that on the exterior and the interior of the hut. It is the usual army pea green, but it will do. Even before it dries we are in the process of moving Budrow's stuff back into the finished hut. In total it has taken us about four hours to put the place back together. None of us has seen the Buffalo since he chewed our asses out.

As soon as Xam Pat leaves the mess area, our contemporaries come drifting back. The catcalls begin shortly after that. Mac and I are tidying the hut when we hear some banging outside and look at each other, perplexed. We step outside to find Cook standing there proudly viewing his addition to the hut's exterior. It is a stop sign. Underneath in red letters he has printed "Or Else!" We all smile at that one. Satisfied with our handiwork, we head over to the mess area and join the rest of the hooting gallery for a cold beer.

This episode has eaten up the day and it is getting towards dusk. The cook is frying up some sort of mystery meat gumbo and the odors are making me realize that I am famished. It starts to pour down again, only this time it is a veritable deluge. We can barely make out the TOC through the downpour, and the ground in between has become a moving mass of water and mud. This may be a safer place than the old camp but the drainage sucks.

* * *

The reason we have been trying to train at least three of the Yards to drive is partially because of a mad scheme that we want to pull off and partially out of boredom. Since Pappy Budrow had forbidden us to use the camp as our motor course, the plan had been to use the most worthless and thus expendable automotive heap we had, but also to conduct the training on the roadway out to the front which had one terminus in the Fifth Mechanized Division and the other out somewhere into the swamp to the east. Cook had been doing fine with the training program until he had walked up the roadway and then turned and motioned Cuman to come towards him. The whole exercise was intended to get him to shift into second. A concept that had so far escaped his understanding.

Cuman had started out a bit jerkily, and then gathered speed. At the point where he needed to make the shift, bad things began to happen. He had turned to tell Thua something just as Woody had come out of the base camp to the west and started towards our front gate. Cuman had turned and, seeing another vehicle sharing the same trajectory as he was on, had panicked. He was barreling towards Cook and at the last second jerked the wheel to the left and diagonally slid just a fraction of an inch in front of Woody, who at the last minute realized who was driving. Woody had slammed on the brakes and, of course, physics and the soupy road surface took over. Both vehicles missed Cook by inches, Cuman looking in horror in the belief that he had hit the Cookie, and Woody swearing a blue streak and waiting for the impact. The jeep had slipped between the TOC and the containers by inches and then roared on past me into Budrow's hut. Woody skidded to a stop twenty feet from Cook, who stood there in the roadway shitting himself and amazed at being alive.

The mad scheme that Mac and I had cooked up was not going to get anywhere unless the Yards were able to grasp the concept of driving. For some time we'd been getting linear recons along the trail. That would be 912, or the Ho Chi Minh, to the layman. It was so heavily populated with NVA and trail watchers that getting close to it was tough enough, much less paralleling it for any distance. Being simpletons, we had come up with a simple plan. Why walk or creep along trying to play Daniel Boone, when theoretically we could just drive down it? The only thing we needed was a vehicle. We were pretty sure that we couldn't lift one in. Even an idiot could add that math up. So we looked at the alternative. Why not steal one? It sounds crazy, but there were a lot of truck parks out there, located just at the right place to potentially have our wheels in them at the same time. We could slip in, lay low, find a truck park, and call in an air strike just as we slipped away in the confusion.

The only other thing we needed was a driver that looked like he wasn't raised on burgers and fries. That meant using one of the little people. Mac and I could pass as Asians at a distance but the Cookie was a whole other problem. The only thing he could pass for was a very large rock ape. We hadn't solved that conundrum, but we were working on it. I was in favor of drugging him and leaving him behind, but Mac pointed out that he would never forgive us. My next suggestion, of trussing him up and putting a few lumps on him and taking him along as our prisoner, was also nixed. Maybe we could find a truck out there with a big crate like one that would haul a SAM missile around in it. Then at least we could hide him from view.

All during the training I had noticed that Bang was acting queerly; he had tried to offer suggestions to Cuman but, like with everyone, Cuman was deaf when it came to suggestions. Now, I am sipping my beer and looking out in the driving rain when I hear a jeep approaching. Someone obviously didn't want to walk or swim over to the mess area, I suppose.

The jeep slowly goes by. Inside is Cuman with his arms folded and sitting on the passenger side. And driving is … Bang. Shit! I start to panic until he deftly shifts the gear and smoothly zips out of sight, but not before flashing me a 1,000-watt smile. The little shit. Not only can he drive but he had been in the NVA, which means that he probably knows how to drive one of their bloody trucks as well. I ask Cookie to get us another round. As he gets up and sidles over to the makeshift bar, I look at Mac and beam.

"What the fuck are you grinning about?"

"Bang can drive," I tell him, and add, "Not only that but he just went by here with Cuman riding in the passenger seat." Mac looks at me for a minute; then it dawns on him. This is perfect. He grins like a coon hound and nods his head at the Cookie's back.

"That only leaves one problem."

"Yep, I'm working on that as we speak." We are both so smug about our turn of luck that when Cook comes back and hands us a beer each, he remarks: "You two look like you just discovered blow jobs."

Before he can get comfortable there is a ripping sound. The bottom of the wall bulges and a tide of water and mud comes rushing in. It is soon up to our boot tops as we pick up our chairs and move up into the mess area. The rest of the Americans are already in there, sitting down to Mystery Meat casserole. We slide over and get a shovelful on a plate each, then inform the rest of our contemporaries that the drinking area is under water.

While we're slopping up the remainder of the meal with some bread, Budrow comes in, grunts some sort of expletive dash approval of our remodeling job and begins to refill his belly. We finish up and decide to head over to the hut. It has been a long day.

Outside, the space between the huts is a moving mass of mud and water. As we are working up the nerve to get back to the hut, I catch a glimpse of something riding on top of the flood. Holy shit! It's the destroyed jeep. It goes by like Tom Sawyer's raft, eddies in the current and then gently bumps on its way.

There is some kind of message here. And whatever it is, as Mac sagely says, we are sure to be blamed for it. We look at Budrow, who glances up at us and shrugs belligerently as if to say, what the fuck do you want? With that we plunge off towards our hut. Mac is right, we will be blamed for it, so we might as well get some rest while we can.

After we reach the hut and dry off, the rain finally stops. It is a small respite, for with the end of the rain, the mosquitoes arrive. I manage to fix a mosquito net over my bunk and lay there smoking a cigarette, mulling over the possibilities of driving down the trail in an NVA truck. Maybe we can figure out a way to airlift it out. Or better yet, we can coax a platoon of NVA to get in the back of it with us and let's see how much bonus money that would be for say twenty prisoners? I drift off to sleep, still working on what to do with the Cookie.

CHAPTER 5

'Twas the Night Before Christmas

We have settled back into the daily routine, preparing for when we go back into isolation. It's a few days before Christmas. The Christmas truce is about to go into effect, but we will still be running missions.

So far there has been no move to assign our team a mission, no briefing, no isolation. So we manage to get off camp and go down to Da Nang to Papa Joe's. An Algerian "Frenchy" runs Papa Joe's. He is a leftover legionnaire from the '54 conflict. The quaint ambience of the place is that you were reasonably sure that someone isn't going to slide a bicycle loaded with plastique up next to where you are enjoying your nuc mam and fish, and blow you and your appetite into the next dimension. We finish up around nine, do a little street trawling at the China Night, and head back in the deuce and a half that has arrived to pick up the late revelers.

The deuce has no headlights. Nada. So we find some white star cluster and white parachute flares that were in the back. Tony, another One-Zero, who still hasn't managed the concept of braking, is driving with his usual aplomb. That means we don't hit anything as large as a building, but we are whistling along at twice whatever the MPs consider safe. On top of that, the headlights on the deuce came on then just as fast suddenly short out. I am in the back and shooting flares out in front of us so Tony won't end all our aspirations by plowing into someone's perimeter wire. We meet several vehicles along the way. They are stopped, with their occupants bailed out and on the side of the road. We are all pretty mellow, having a great time singing "Thunder Road" for all we are worth, riding in a great big black deuce spitting fire into the night. It is like being 12 again and going down suicide hill at night on your brother's bike, with just a burning roll of toilet paper on a stick taped to forks for a light.

By the time we get to within a mile of CCN we managed to put every compound along the way onto full alert. But all that is happening behind us because Tony is driving like a maniac. I've got Cookie helping me with the flares, and we are shooting star clusters low angle and parachute flares high angle. Actually it is pretty effective but we run out of green and white star clusters and resort to the red. That's what starts the alert stuff on the camps to the front. Everyone knows red star cluster means emergency something. We are incapable of being concerned with such trivialities at this time; we are on a mission from God.

Uh oh, here they come, about a dozen MP jeeps with their little blue bars lit up like a K-Mart sale. Screw you, I am thinking, we can't stop for you. We have to get back to the camp to be ready to fight the war. That is one of the benefits of an alcohol-fogged conscience: there are no recriminations.

They get close enough until they are about a hundred yards behind us. Then, I can't believe it; one of the shits leans out the passenger side and starts firing his .45 at us. He hits the tailgate and it clangs resoundingly. Everybody hits the deck. Of course we just roll over and shoot the flares from lying on our back. Great fun. Now the law dog opens up again. He is getting annoying. There is an empty 55-gallon drum in the back; we muscle it over, and two of us sling it out the back. It clangs loudly and we hear the squeal of brakes. We are about half a mile from the camp with an escort of four MP jeeps all with their full display of lights on us so we no longer have to use the flares for illumination. When they start to close in again and the same pinhead opens up on our truck, we can't resist firing one over the tailgate. He fires a shot or two and we dump a star cluster flare at the front of the dragnet behind us, with the reciprocal squealing of brakes; they fall back. We get there ahead of the MPs. We slide in the gate and the Yards manning the machine guns at the gate look at us with bewilderment. As we swing through the gate, Charlie Jay, who is fluent in Rhade and Bru, yells out to close the gate and let no mortal pass, or something to that effect. The Yards take that as their new First General Order, and seal the gate behind us. The MPs try to rush the gate until one of the Yards fires a burst from the machinegun over their heads and into the trash dump across the road. We careen to the second bunker line and tell the Americans from Security Company what has happened.

Everyone is pretty pissed off: go through all we do in the field to get nailed by some overly zealous MP who feels it is his duty to fire you up. The thought is not just incongruous but also ludicrous. Alcohol and circumstance does that to you. I am sure using red flares was bordering on idiocy but seemed logical at the time. Time and penance will hopefully heal that offense. Soon, the front of the compound is bristling with MPs with horrid stories of red tracer rounds being fired at them, which is why they returned fire. They thought we were escaping NVA in a stolen truck, etc. That doesn't wash when examined in the light of the day so we are vindicated, although my ass is raw from being chewed out by everyone except the hootch maids.

Thank Karma for the officers that we have. They are our bulwark against the green machine. They manage to pour oil on the troubled waters of our indiscretions and share our plight at the same time. Hopefully some will survive and rise through the ranks to someday be the spine of the army in some future conflict. Discipline is a tempered blade and in our case necessity overrules our demise.

* * *

The holidays are always rough since the longings for home and hearth are always simmering under the task at hand. Little reminders like Christmas lights and holiday music on AFN lend a surreal air to being in a war zone. We have a Christmas tree in the club, with lights, and scant commercial decorations, Guys have been painting mini grenades in bright colors and hanging them as bulbs, along with off bits of kit. There is a belt of machinegun ammo being used as a tinsel wrap. We had tried to do popcorn strings but ended up eating them. Some wit has stolen Braidow’s shrunken head collection and adorned the tree with their painted visages as a reality check. Braidow is a raw-boned cowboy product who had bought them on some R&R junket with the embassy flight.

I am sitting in our team room cleaning the guns and kit, while listening to some rhythm and blues on the reel to reel, our newest purchase from the big PX. I wonder how long it will last before it becomes collateral damage in some bizarre incident. The smell of weapons, gun oil, and web gear is comforting. The gun oil is the stimulant of the century as far as I’m concerned. I hear voices outside, then the door opens, with Mac in the lead of five or six others. I start covering up anything that might get stolen which is everything that isn’t nailed down. With him is Cook and RT Intruder sans the little people. They have their own Christmas Eve story to share.

Jesse is the One-Zero of Intruder, a methodical, agonizingly slow talking Southerner with his One-One, a fellow denizen of the South who hails from the swamps of Louisiana. Chuck Macdowell, is a red headed, stick of dynamite with a short fuse. It’s like having a hybrid cross between a junkyard dog and a bull gator. Missing is Larson, who is probably still entertaining his liver over at the club. I don’t have long to wait, as Keith Larson comes in at the heels of the others. Larson is from Minnesota and has aspirations of playing professional hockey. He should do well, as he is built like a crash dummy and has a grin that makes him look like a wolf staring at a nice fat marmot. Tagging along is Frank Mariano, a compact version of meat with the charm of a mob enforcer. Frank is a fine example of the Italian community of Detroit, home of the Italian libido.

All are just back from Phu Bai where they completed a sterling mission in the Ashau Valley. It was meant to be a reconnaissance and picture taking expedition. Jesse called it a World Series, which means there are so many enemy troops on and around that you have priority on anything that has ordinance and can assist. The camp had been abuzz with rumors of their mission. They had handed the NVA a mauling but had been chewed on as well.

They all help themselves to a beer, which leads me to believe that someone knew I had made a beer run to Da Nang for Ba Mi Ba, that light lager, aged with formaldehyde. Around here, there is no such thing as personal property, unless you count war toys, but booze, pogey bait, and all else is fair game…everything except the holiday fruitcake from home. You couldn’t even give that to the Yards. There are two on the table and no one is picking at them.

Everyone settles in and the story of their mission begins to unwind, in snatches of tactical and technical debrief, interspersed with "Holy shit, that was close."

"It was the Christmas truce."

"We were abiding by it, but the NVA were using it to move men and material south." In response, we began inserting roadblocks into their holiday merriment.

RT Indigo was assigned a static defense position, on a hilltop with bad approaches for the enemy. You wanted good fields of fire and visual on the trail system you were trying to interdict.

RT Intruder drew a December 24th insert for the reconnaissance. Since our Recon teams didn't exist on the big war board, ergo… technically no violation of the truce. The NVA should have talked to the Hessians, because we will cross a frozen river on Christmas Eve to kill you. We have done it before.

Intruder chose a hilltop on the Laotian side of the border, close to the intersection of Route 922 from Laos and Route 548 through the Ashau Valley. Keith, had flown a visual Recon with a trail FAC three days prior. It was typical weather in the Ashau with fog, so they had slipped through a hole to below to see what was afoot in the target box. When they broke out of the clouds, there were enemy troops everywhere and guns started opening up on them. They took photos of the hilltop and decided it was "fine" for what they had in mind.

Around nine in the morning on December 24th, right on the heels of the fog clearing, the team walked to the waiting choppers. On the way, several soldiers from the 101st took pictures of them. This was natural since our teams all looked like a bad remake of Terry and the Pirates, with all sorts of exotic weaponry and man toys. Mariano had taken their film away from them and exposed it, which started a ruckus until Jesse told the Yards to shoot anyone they saw taking pictures. That settled the chop in the frackus.

Sluggo Murphy was their Covey rider in the O2 Forward Air Control aircraft, hovering over the team and coordinating air support like a mother hen. It was four slicks, with the team on three of them, and Mariano with the Chase Medic onboard the fourth, plus the usual gunships. Keith was listening to Don McLean's "America Pie" on the way in as some weird backdrop to the whole affair. Sluggo was working A1Es out of Thailand as their heavy support as they prepped the hilltop and surrounding area with hard bombs. Whatever NVA that had been on the hill were erased during that strike. Chuck and the remainder of the team had finished off any wrigglers in the wreckage.

I asked Keith what he had done first when they got on the hilltop, in the hope that it would moderate his beer consumption. It doesn't work. My supply of Ba Mi Ba is rapidly diminishing.

Keith answered and continued his story.

First, we oriented on the target, identified two landmarks for the Escape and Evasion route in case we were overrun before we could get dug in proper. But, the more immediate problem was that there was a 12.7 machinegun located below on the slope and it was hammering on the air assets. It was decided to try to knock it out with hand grenades.

Keith lobbed one but it bounced off a tree and landed back in front of the team, exploding in a shower of fragmentation and debris. Chuck, the One-One, crawled over to him to remind him the idea was to kill the enemy not the team. This is called combat counseling.

When we looked out into the valley there were so many people that it looked like someone had kicked over an ant hill. Naturally, they were all pissed off about Jesse's rendition of the welcome wagon. There were so many visible you couldn't count them. We felt like eight black ants on a red ant hill.

The team had brought extra radios so Jesse and I got busy calling in targets to Covey on the horde below. Sluggo was magnificent that day. He had aircraft stacked up over the target and Sluggo was using them up as fast as they came on station, until there were so many they were rapidly running out of fuel. Sluggo was balancing between aircraft that had to either dispose of their ordinance, because they were running out of go juice, and the ordinance they carried versus what was needed and where. Some of the fast movers showed up and would have ten minutes to expend their ordinance before they had to turn back and refuel.

Chuck was coordinating the team to repulse an attack on the west side. The gunships remaining from the insert quickly eliminated that group as a threat. We didn't have to look for targets because they were all around us and out into the valley. Sluggo said that there's a larger group coming up from the south, about a company in strength. He worked a set of A1Es with napalm and that quickly eliminated that threat. As the A1E came in he was so low you could make out his face.

Intruder thought they were screwed. The enemy kept pressing and attacking while the bombers were taking out large numbers on the valley floor and keeping the hordes from massing on the team. The gunships broke up another attack on the west side. RT Intruder had been on the hilltop about two hours and had been fighting since their feet hit the ground.

The gunships, having expended their loads, were shuttling back to the rearm and refuel point. They had plenty of ammo with them as the heavy machinegun started up again, trying to knock out the gunships and bombers along with yet another assault. The team blew some of the claymores when the NVA began to close on that side and the attack faded off.

Sluggo called again and asked us to look at the "Y" in the road out about a klick to see if we could see dust.

Keith was watching when a PT 76 Russian amphibious tank rolled out of the wood line, and they all about crapped themselves because with the main gun the tank could blow their position into snot and regrets. Jesse was looking through the SOI for the code word for TANK. Unfortunately Jesse has the same syndrome as I do that of gasping and stuttering under pressure. McDowell doesn't have this problem because he is too busy smashing things, shooting things, while blowing up the real estate, and other violations of the "be nice" directive. Keith can no longer wait for Jesse because the tank is getting into position to be part of the next assault on the hill. Keith transmits in the clear.

> "WE have a TANK, I repeat we have a TANK."
>
> The radio went silent for a moment then Sluggo asked for confirmation. Shortly afterwards two fast movers obliterated the tank and the surrounding area.

Then, some self important wit came on the air and admonished Keith for using improper radio procedures which could give away the team location. Keith told him that every NVA between their patch of ground and Hanoi knew where they were by now, adding that the wit get off the radio. He did.

Right after that TOC came up and wanted the team to get pictures of the tank or maybe go get pieces of it. The valley is crawling with bombed, pissed off NVA, and the TOC wants war souvenirs? Another logical sounding request if you aren't the one having to do it. The Yards looked at Keith and said we can get to the tank but we will all die. This followed some invectives, profane in nature, and the combat shopping walk was cancelled. Keith said he was afraid Jesse would go if given the order.

Intruder had been fighting for several hours when Sluggo said he had to turn them over because he was out of fuel and marker rockets. They did a transition of Coveys, but before he left, Sluggo made a low pass over their position and did a strafing run with his CAR 15 out the port window. As he passed over he threw something out of the window that landed amongst the team. It was a banana knife. He radioed that they could use that if things got too close, then rolled back up to altitude and was off.

> Jesse told the new FAC they were fine on ammo so he wanted to stay and continue to direct the airstrikes. As long as the team was there the NVA had to dislodge them.

Keith said he contemplated wounding Jesse so they could call it off, but they would need an AK47 for the story to fit.

> The pressure on the team abated somewhat, and they were working the FAC on some of the far targets, when an entire formation of enemy troops showed up moving down the road from Laos. Troops were spread out in a semi-tactical formation as if they were in the Mayday parade in Hanoi. They were about four hundred meters out, so Chuck set his binoculars on zero focus and took pictures with the PEN double E camera, using the binos as a zoom lens.
>
> There were five or six of the enemy troops that stood out, since they were head and shoulders taller than the rest and were together in the middle of the formation. They were wearing gray fatigues and seemed to be of importance. Sluggo came back on station and took over as Covey. He began to decimate this formation in short order, the first strike hitting the group in the gray

fatigues. Sluggo radioed them that the launch site wanted to pull Intruder out as a weather front was moving in, and a resupply or reinforcement was out of the question. The slick package was en route to the orbit point and they would be pulled in the next half hour.

Intruder continued to observe the air assets working the area over as they prepared to be extracted. In the fighting, the team had relocated off the crest of the hill. There were trees to contend with if we hoped to be extracted from where we were. They would have to take down a couple of shattered trunks in order to have a good LZ.

Chuck, taking advantage of being the One-One, said to take some explosives and rid the area of obstructions.

Keith used claymores after he crawled down and set up the charges and linked them with Det Cord. This way, they would go simultaneously.

Sluggo reported that the slicks would follow the last set of A1Es, and they would be rigged with ladders. The slicks asked them if the LZ was secure, which was relative to the situation. Intruder was still receiving small arms fire from pockets around the base of the hill but it was all light arms so they lied and told the slicks it was okay. The slicks, however, knew that it would be a hot LZ since they had delivered them to the hill.

Keith blew the charges and then scrambled up to the denuded area. The helicopters arrived, the dust partially obscured the LZ from the enemy. He and the rest of the team clambered up a ladder and hooked in. Once they cleared the hilltop, the ride back was serene. Everyone was fine except a few leaking holes which, when they got to the launch site, the medics patched up with all the finesse and compassion they were noted for. They had caught a major enemy formation with their pants down and had mauled it with air support. More important they are jubilantly alive.

* * *

With the story completed, we are headed over to the club. The Recon rendition of *Amahl and the Night Visitors*, have drained my beer supply, leaving the mini fridge cracked open and empty as a victim of Butch and Sundance. I let the group go ahead of me and as we get there it's the usual boisterous crowd, a few around the pool table, some playing poker, and the rest playing dead or near zombie from the alcohol. Ah alcohol, the universal lubricant. This is what homecoming parties would be like in Norway in the eighth century.

Some wit has booby trapped the TV room again, usually it's a smoke grenade with a trip wire and it appears that is the case again. Booby trapping is a form of entertainment as a protest to the limited offerings on TV since all we get is AFVN and newsreels. When you come back, one has to be careful of these little treats, as well as the odd wild critter in your hooch usually planted by these same rascals. George the Python makes the rounds on a weekly basis, usually appearing in someone's bed. Cook has added him to the barbeque menu if he ends up in ours.

Since the camp was overrun in 1968, it has been mandatory for all Americans to be armed inside the camp. So, there is a collection of pistols, shotguns—silenced or not—as well as specialty weapons in attendance for the alcohol-fired celebration of Intruder's success. We are clinging to their good fortune and celebrity, in the offhand chance that we will get some brownie points against the 'Thunder Road" incidence. It's slim but you take what you can grasp. All the weaponry here is just so that in the event of an attack you can shoot your way back to the team room where the serious hardware and explosives are.

We have been getting new specialties such as the bean bag gun, which incapacitates the would-be prisoner instead of shooting him in the legs with a silenced .22. The logic is that if he can't walk you have to carry him. Gasping for breath but still mobile is a much better alternative. So far no enemies have been hit with it, but camp dogs, fellow travelers, MPs, and at least one reporter have tested nicely.

I have brought my latest acquisition. A forage through the S4 has produced my Christmas gift to myself. It looks like an oversized 44 magnum revolver: it has a larger frame and cylinder to accept six shells, which look like 410 shotgun shells. Inside are a couple hundred steel darts per shell and the gun uses compressed gas instead of gunpowder. It is almost completely silent and is deadly out to about 30 meters then the shot pattern gets too broad. I show it to Keith and he lights up as if someone bequeathed him a hockey puck franchise. He is drooling over it when I tell him that I got one and five boxes of ammo but there were three left up at S4. I artfully lied that there was more ammo and one pallet that had an HE warhead that was really experimental.

I told him that he should go up in the morning but in case he didn't that Sluggo knew where they were and he was keen to get a pair; the secret warhead ammo especially. Mariano has wandered over as I am finishing. It is almost transparent as I can see them reliving their extraction as well as Sluggo's close air support. They can visualize Sluggo zipping and weaving all over the sky again, zooming and swooping, only this time waving the two superguns and blasting away out the window. Forget the banana knife, he will be like Pecos Bill up there, a danger to everybody. I should have wandered over and told Macdowell that I saw Sluggo picking up two when I picked up mine, but that is treading too close to the abyss. It will be better this way. I have visions of Sluggo being shook down by MacDowell before he is allowed in an aircraft. I don't run Phubai that often so I should be safe from the fall out. Besides, no sense letting them merely bask in their greatness, this will temper the festivities.

CHAPTER 6

Ghosts

Mac, Wesley and I are sitting on the bunker line facing the sea. It is hot but there is a cool and refreshing breeze coming from offshore. We are going over the sort of things that men talk about when there is some slack time. Home. Where are you from? Did you know this guy? We are also discussing the lore of our trade: the lessons that we learn, and the odd twists of fate that may catch up with you. It is not armchair quarterbacking, but rather a careful analysis of things that go bad or things that should have worked but didn't. This is a seminar on learning to think on your feet.

The subject of Doc Watson and Baby San Lloyd comes up, and both Wes and Mac are silent, then reflective. Both were involved, Wes in the original mission and Mac in the Bright Light. Wes starts off since he was on the team.

> By the end of 1970, more and more teams were running heavy, just in terms of overall numbers but also beefing up the number of Americans, either with straphangers from other teams or with new people coming in. Captain Watson had done the same with his team and they had drawn one of our worst areas to do an area Recon in.
>
> Actually it was a linear Recon since it involved the Ho Chi Minh Trail. A section of the trail snakes along the border with Laos and on the top of the Western Wall of the A Shau Valley. This escarpment rises nearly two thousand feet from the valley floor, in a series of steps. If you look at a map of the area the contour lines are so close together, it looks like brown shading. The terrain rises in a series of steep cliffs of gray rock arranged in steps, some very narrow on top, some twenty to thirty meters wide.
>
> The team had picked an insertion LZ that was actually in Laos, but the danger of running into the Laotian border officials was a minor point. Since the PAVN controlled the whole area with their buddies the Pathet Lao, I doubt that running into anybody would result in anything other than a gunfight.
>
> Aerial photos had shown a substantial trail along the top, winding in and out of Laos, following the contours of the land instead of some arbitrary boundary drawn on a map. It was a high-speed trail, probably 6 to 12 feet wide and hard packed, so they were moving troops and supplies along it. Their common practice was to put trail watchers out who would quickly react, along with ground troops, to any suspected incursion or interdiction.

Wes is droning on in the peculiar nomenclature of our trade. Mac chimes in on the lay of the land and undergrowth descriptions, and some bits and pieces of information from other teams that have run the same target. The one thing that was blaringly evident was that the enemy had a lot of troops that could react on you quickly if you managed to insert. Wes takes a pull on his beer and wipes the foam off his upper lip, and continues.

> The team's insertion had gone well and they had RONed for the night after moving quite a distance up the long axis of the ridgeline. The terrain was so steep and twisted, falling off to the east, that as they had surmised the enemy didn't have anything down in the rocks. The team came across no sign as they picked their way stealthily through the underbrush; there were no signal shots indicating that someone was searching out their suspected position. They had been undetected most of that day and had eventually found the trail.
>
> "Trail" conjures up to most people a packed footpath through a deciduous forest. The ones we run across are anything from hard-packed dirt roads to wisps of cleared growth. It all depends on their usage and what moves along them. This trail was a hard-packed clay and rock surface and had communications wire running along both sides of it. It was a heavily used track: there were footprints and cart tracks as well as bicycle tire tracks so thick that you couldn't drive a pin down into it without hitting a print.
>
> The team had set up an ambush and an enemy soldier had come along soon after, pushing a bicycle. Shots had been fired. Both the bicycle and the man were down. They went through his rucksack, pockets, and pouches and found documents indicating that the man was a courier of some sort. Wes had found an NVA flag and had stuffed it in his rucksack. No sense letting some weenie in Saigon get that as a souvenir. Everything, even articles of clothing, goes back because it all gives us intelligence about the enemy.
>
> They stripped the courier and called for an immediate pickup and moved quickly to a place where they could be extracted, knowing that the shots would be investigated and when the NVA discovered the hidden body the hunt would be on in earnest. In fact, the NVA contacted them before they were able to reach the selected extraction point. A running gun battle erupted, with the enemy trying fanatically to pin them down and then overwhelm them. Wes had, at some point, been forced to discard his rucksack and abandon it. They were in a running fight for their lives.
>
> They had gotten the slicks on station and four birds came in and picked up Wes and all of the Yards. Captain Watson, Sammy, and Baby San had remained on the ground, in a position where an inbound ship could get them out by strings.
>
> The slick came shortly afterwards, its blades and power plant straining in the thin air. Wes waited at the orbit point and listened to the team as Covey had vectored another chopper and the support ships in. They had hovered over the team and dropped the strings to them. The three hooked themselves in, and the chopper applied power and started to lift them through the trees. Sammy remembers being pulled through the branches before his rope broke and he fell twenty feet to the forest floor. Banged up but still able to move, he managed to work his way to some ground away from the extraction point. The helicopter with Watson and Baby San continued on for a short distance, then suddenly did an abrupt U-turn and crashed into the cliffs about 100 meters down from the crest.
>
> We listened in shock as Covey and the package reported these events over the radio. They had been receiving ground fire on the extraction. Now evening and weather had closed in, and operations were suspended for the night. Wes was left with the sinking feeling that he was the only American survivor, that luck and bad timing had caught up with the rest.

As Wes finishes the retelling of the story, he sits staring out to sea, taking a sip of his beer, lost in thought. Mac takes over in that slow drawl, telling how RT Habu had been nominated as the Bright Light. Da Nang had been in a buzz over the loss, so SMAJ Billy, and Cliff Newman had come up to Phu Bai on the first thing smoking to beef them up. Waugh was fit to be tied over the fact that he had been specifically ordered not to go on the recovery, but Newman joined Habu and they were to be inserted at first light. Wes added that he insisted he go along— "It was my fucking team, they weren't going to tell me I couldn't go." He is a tough little Bantam; lots of combat time both here and with the 101st Airborne. The kind of person you imagine when someone says "Sarge."

Mac continues, telling the story of his Bright Light team.

> The Bright Light team picked an LZ on top of the ridgeline; from there they could move quickly to the last location of the team and the place where Covey said the wreckage of the chopper had ended up. Jimmy Horton was the One-Zero, and Daart was the One-One, though Wes and the others had more experience. It was Habu's show; everyone else would fall in place and make it happen. They had lifted off and as the package got to the orbit point, Covey located Sammy. They had the chase slick pick him up and took him back to the launch site. He told how when the helicopter lifted up, the ship had pulled them through the trees. His rope broke but he could hear the other two being dragged away through the canopy.
>
> The Bright Light team was in the air when they were informed that Sammy had been picked up. They reached their landing zone, about 400 meters from the lip where they suspected that the aircraft went down, got on the ground and started to move out to the east. En route they found a way to work down to the air crash site by periodically flashing a mirror on to the Covey, then having Covey tell them which way to adjust. Everyone was being super careful knowing that the bad guys could and would move on them, at any time.
>
> Enroute they came upon Wes's rucksack; it evidently had not been discovered by the NVA from the previous day. After checking it for booby traps, they took it with them. Covey got them where they could see him from the ground and then flew over the wreckage of the helicopter, wobbling his wings back and forth. They were only about a hundred meters from the wreck when the unexpected happened.
>
> The Covey aircraft flew over the ridge out of sight. They heard no ground fire but it nosed over and into the cliffs. The crash killed both the pilot and the Covey rider.
>
> Now the team had two crash sites. They finally found the wreckage of the helicopter. Twisted in among the trees, it was torn apart: the craft laid on its roof, the tail boom separated and wreckage compacted in and among the boulders and trees. The aircraft wreckage was still smoldering and the area around showed ample evidence of the fire that ensued as it broke apart and the fuel cells erupted.
>
> It was slow and grisly going as the team went about investigating and documenting the crash site. The pilot and co-pilot, horribly burned, were still attached to their seats. The door gunner, who would normally have been on the left side in the cargo area, was about 15 feet up in a tree and smashed against it. The crew chief was pinned under the wreckage with only one leg visible. All were dead.

> It was evident that the crash had resulted from a lateral twisting as the aircraft plunged into the trees. Pivoting on the bodies entangled in the trees, attached by their ropes. As it rolled, still in the trees, it broke into two pieces with its own rotors and the effect of airspeed. It had thrown the gunner out, slinging him into a tree trunk. In that instant it burst the fuel cells and rolled over on top of the crew chief, pinning him underneath as it continued to burn. Not a pretty end but hopefully quick. Mac and Wes gathered the remains that they could and called for extraction.

Mac stops talking, takes a deep breath, and tells Wes to hand him a beer. We sit there looking at the water and Mac starts in again.

> Horton was trying to coordinate the extraction from the ground. They had found no sign of the missing team members but had all the bodies of the crew accounted for. He was trying to have the first ship that came in drop strings and take two of the Americans over the ridge to the Covey crash site to recover the body of the Covey rider and the pilot. Get everybody out and back before darkness and weather socks the area in. If the other two, Doc and Baby San survived, perhaps they were evading capture, like Sammy had.
>
> About a half hour later, the team learned that a Jolly Green would recover the Covey site. Soon the big UH53 came roaring right over their position and up and over the ridge. They let down their PJ and Lightning Wunderlich, and recovered the two bodies using a jungle penetrator.

This is a winched device on the big birds, like an elevator on a cable; it has a weighted device on the end with two drop seats that fold out and you can strap into.

> The team was still at the helicopter crash site and still waiting for a time window when the package would arrive and the team could extract. They had detected no movement but were getting that funny feeling that tells you that there is a shitload of bad guys around.

After a while you learn that you should listen to that little voice because it is usually right. They had been in with far too many aircraft, and they knew old Mr. Charles was going to come a-looking. It was getting late and Horton was telling the launch site that they needed to do something: get the team out or they would have to stay in the area overnight.

The Launch Site Officer to this day had better be hiding because his comment was that "It won't hurt you guys to stay on the ground for one night with no sleeping gear." Mac says that "This caused Horton to have, as Mac puts it, a "come apart," but he communicated real slow and deliberate over the radio to the idiot that if he gets out of here he is going to come back to Phu Bai and kill him as first order of business. That shut them up.

> Daylight was running out and the team had no options left except to find a better place to spend the night. They decided to move up and away from the crash site and find some defensible ground. They had moved about a hundred meters, expecting to make contact the entire time, when one of the Yards and Mac spotted ropes hanging in the branches at the tops of the trees to their right. These could only be the strings that the two missing team members were suspended on. Twenty meters further, they found Doc and Baby San. Both men were dead, hanging side by side, their weapons slung in front of them and their harness intact, still attached to the ropes

> snaking out through the trees like green umbilical cords. They looked as if they were sleeping, just hanging in the branches. They were chest level with Mac when he stood on the edge of the cliff, but about twelve feet out above a fifty-foot drop straight down. The ropes that were their lifeline were suspending the bodies just out of reach.
>
> The team tried to get the bodies down but it was a no go. So they would have to hole up and come back to try again in the morning. Tomorrow would have its own set of problems, but right now they needed to find some terrain. The light was fading fast and by the time they had gone another hundred meters it was so dark that the lead man almost stepped off the cliff. They stopped and formed a half-moon perimeter with the cliff at their backs, about twenty meters from edge to edge. Mac and Horton laid in the center looking up the slope, with Wes just to the left of them.

Wes cuts in at this point, telling me that it was freezing that night, so cold that he and Horton got the body bags out and climbed in them to stay warm.

Mac laughs and tells me, "I thought about it 'cause it was real cold and wet, but Cuman took one look at those two fools and told me 'Ooush! Numbah *Ten*! *Trung Sí*! Body bag for dead peebles!' So I stayed out in the cold." They spent the cold night alternating sleeping and waiting for the dawn.

> Just before true dawn, Horton woke Mac up and whispered to him that they were about to get hit. Mac got ready; he could hear the NVA setting up maybe a hundred fifty meters out, and from the sounds they were making it was at least a company. The bad guys got on line and started coming down real slow in the Ranger high carry, looking and searching, staying on line, in a classic sweep formation.
>
> About a half an hour had elapsed from the first sounds of their deployment, when a B40 rocket exploded twenty meters in front of them and up in the trees. The NVA had fired it over the heads of their own troops from the trail above. Then came the concussion of several grenades that landed right in front of and amongst the team. A grenade fell right between Mac and Horton, and then went off. Mac felt the hard slap of something against his leg, and his calf felt like it was on fire; he looked down and the complete half of a Chicom Pineapple grenade was stuck to his calf muscle and his jungle boot top was melted on that side.
>
> Horton was screaming that his leg was blown off; it seemed to Mac that Jimmy had lost some of his right foot and part of his calf. Everyone else was gone from the cliff top, evidently blown off by the concussion. Mac turned to Horton and told him, "We got to jump for it," but Horton couldn't move. Mac could see shapes moving not twenty-five meters away, so he sprayed the area with his CAR-15. He then grabbed Horton and announced he was going to throw him out to a tree about twenty feet from the cliff they are standing on. 'Just grab it and shinny down." Then he tossed him.

I ask, did he make it. Mac kind of laughs a little, then he and Wes both say at the same time, "No way!" Jimmy didn't get halfway to the tree, and went straight down thirty feet screaming the whole way. Mac threw a grenade at the approaching NVA as he turned, stepped back a couple of steps, chucked another straight behind him, then took a couple of running steps and jumped for the same tree.

They don't grow gazelles in Southern Alabama. His short little stumps got him about the same distance out in space as Horton, and he plummeted to the ground, landing right on top of Horton, adding insult to injury. All this happened in the space of probably two minutes from the time the first rocket went off.

Mac pauses and Wes gets up to stretch and snag a beer out of the pail with the ice in it.

"You need to remember that the Mini Mac ain't no football star. Ole Jimmy had a better chance a getting to that tree if he would have drug himself over and flopped out into space." Mac looks at him and sardonically quips back with:

"Wes says he got blown off the cliff, but what really happened was, he abandoned us like a flea leaving a blue tick in a rainstorm. He just quick hopped over the edge. He was gone so fast he dissipated."

Wes settles back down and looks at me.

"We all landed down there, jumping or getting blown off doesn't matter shit. Daart landed down there with the radio handset still in his hand, it was chewed up where shrapnel had hit it, only thing missing was the radio, because it was still in his rucksack at the top of the cliff. He looked like he had tangled with a boar hog, his clothes and gear were all cut up." He chuckles.

"Yeah, he had the handset and the wire but there wasn't a radio attached," Mac adds. "Anyways I was outside the perimeter, I do a quick once over on Jimmy's wounds long enough to see his foot was all tore up. I put a tourniquet on it and was looking for the team." His story continues.

> He got up and moved slightly to the left, to see better, when rounds started hitting all around him and Jimmy, ricocheting off the rocks and thunking into any tree trunks near them. Mac grabbed Jimmy and dragged him over to where two fallen trees had crossed each other, and they both got down behind the twisted mass. A gap of about ten inches gave Mac a view up a natural cut coming down the cliff to the left and funneling from the top of the ridge.
>
> Then the grenades started coming over the top of the cliff they had just evacuated and landing all around them. Again it was the broken nature of the terrain that saved them: most would explode but other than a few shrapnel wounds no one was getting seriously wounded. Cliff had gotten the team into a defensive perimeter, with Wes helping him. He was on the radio and talking to Covey, trying to get some air in on them. Wes had been busy moving from man to man getting everyone tied in.

I knew that responsibility, which is how Mac and I would operate: his job was to lead and be on the "phone" and mine was to take care of tying up the loose ends.

> Woody, the medic, was doing what all chase medics do: patching up the wounded.
>
> Mac was still about ten meters outside the perimeter, and the NVA were still hammering around him with automatic fire from up the hill, at the top of the funnel. He could see up the opening, and what he saw wasn't good. There were NVA in pith helmets, green khakis, wearing AK vests and Bata boots, coming down the split. They were jumping from boulder to boulder, working their way to the bottom. They were firing in the direction of the team, then a quick dash to the next boulder, or hop across a gap to the next cover. Every Infantry cuss in the world knows that one, it's called "fire and maneuver," and it means trouble.

Mac could see them, but they couldn't locate the team yet. One squad was trailing, covering the guys in front that were doing the maneuvering. Jimmy was screaming and Mac couldn't even shoot him up with the morphine that teams always carry, because Jimmy is allergic to it, so he was in terrible pain. Mac got settled in low behind the log and put his CAR-15 on semi-automatic, flipping the leaf sight to the low range.

An NVA emerged at the bottom of the cut; Mac took aim and popped him. The NVA dropped like a sack of wheat. Another NVA attempted to follow and again Mac dropped him with a shot in the left side as he emerged. He fell next to the first body. Then Mac dropped two together: the first one just past the two bodies, and the second one on top of the two first casualties. He knew he was killing them because they weren't moving afterwards.

He transferred up the slope and quickly dropped another one too slow on his hop. He could hear them yelling at each other.

Sergeants on all sides do the same thing, getting the troops and the guns to find where the fire is coming from and put some suppressive fire on it.

Mac and Jimmy, though, were perfectly situated. The NVA couldn't shoot effectively on them or rush them until they got to the mouth of the cut. Only if they could mass and rush out of that opening would they be a real serious threat to the team.

This went on for some time: Mac slow and methodical, just like hunting, you don't shoot unless you have a target and when you shoot, kill it. After a while there were five bodies stacked up at the mouth of the cut and probably near that number that he had tagged up higher. He saw them scurrying back up the cut from below. The troops at the top were pouring fire into the area, but most of it too high and in the trees. Woody came rushing up to look Jimmy over. He reassured Jimmy that his leg wasn't blown off, because his boot was still attached.

This is called bedside manner.

Woody grabbed him up after dressing the wound, and as Mac full auto-ed the cleft and area above, he dragged Horton inside the team's perimeter. Then the team provided covering fire for Mac as he rushed back to their position in a crouch.

He may not be any good at One-Zero Tossing or the broad jump, but the Mini Mac was built for broken field running in brush.

Then he moved down to check on the rest of his team. Nearly everyone had been wounded by the shrapnel but they were still fit to fight. All except Daart: he was in shock and had squeezed himself into a fissure in the cliff face with the handset welded to his ear. Still no radio attached. He had lost it.

No shame there, you have that much ordnance cook off near you, it would make most anyone a bit nuts.

Cliff was on the radio talking to Covey, who was overhead, ordering up some air. He wanted to have the fast movers come in and rocket the cliff top to get the NVA off the top of them. The team was vulnerable if the NVA could get a toehold above them and bring in direct fire on them.

Wes cuts in, which gives the Mac a chance at the bucket with the beer and ice stash.

"Yeah, they were arguing with Cliff that if they tried to drop on the cliff ridge that we were going to get showered with shrapnel. Cliff told them basically, 'Shoot down among us then cause one of us needs to have some relief.' The air package came in and worked that top of the hill all along it like a meat grinder. It made the NVA on top get to finding another playground."

> But the NVA didn't break and disperse right away, they stayed and slugged it out, would wait for a bomb pass then try and get back on top of the team.

Hardcore little heathens, you have to give them that. They had been fighting since near first light and it was getting on around two in the afternoon when the team were finally told they could expect to get picked up.

> They were using up their blood bags on Horton and the other seriously wounded to keep them from bleeding out and going into shock The air package from the Phu Bai site tried first and their gunships were working overtime. In fact, the four gunships were working in pairs and had been there for a couple of hours, two at a time, working with the fast movers; they would use up their ammo by the time the second pair arrived back from the arming and refuel. When the day was over they had used up 5 sets of fast movers with their entire ordnance. That's 10 aircraft. Plus they had A1Es and the gunships providing additional coverage and they were still getting fire.
>
> The slicks came in and tried to get to them by dropping a ladder for exfiltration, but they drew heavy fire and eventually pulled out. The guns and the Spads would work the area over and they would try again. Finally SOG decided that they would send a Jolly Green from Da Nang. It came in and they started extracting using the jungle penetrator to ferry people from the ground to the bird. The Jolly has a minigun with lots of ammo to provide suppressive fire and the gunner was burning the barrels up keeping the NVA down, but the bird was still taking hits. Horton and the worst wounded of the little people went first, until it was just Mac and Newman and a couple of Yards left. Mac was going to go last, when Newman told him to get his ass on it when it came back. Mac started to argue that it was his team so he should stay until everybody was out. Newman told him get on, and he would be along shortly.

Wes looks at me and says that the ride up the cable was the longest of his life. He said that he fired up the cliff lip the whole way. When Mac was finally winched aboard, Wes told him to grab the M60 and fire out the tailgate because they were getting chewed at from that direction. Mac grabbed the 60 and started firing up the area to the chopper's rear and uphill. They would discover later that Mac had also managed to shoot the strut that keeps the big bird's tail from hitting when it lands. That's alright, just about the time he gets ready to retire I'm sure the paperwork will catch up and Mac will have to pay for it. The Air Force is funny about that sort of thing.

"I sent him back there instead of the Yards because I was afraid the Yards would shoot the bird up," comments Wes. Smart move Wes, I am thinking. The team got all aboard and the big aircraft lumbered up and powered away from the site. It was late afternoon and they had been fighting for close to twelve hours.

They took the team right into Da Nang and offloaded at the airbase. CCN was there waiting for them. Horton was taken over to the evacuation hospital as soon as he was stabilized. It had been a disaster in one sense, but they had pulled a miracle out of their asses.

* * *

This whole discussion has been for my edification. We are talking tactics and bull penning; that's how we pass knowledge and combat lore to each other. We go over the mistakes and the good things, log it away in the old brain-housing group.

We finish up the beers, and for good measure watch the sun gliding over the deep blue sea. It actually is very beautiful. I can only wonder if Mac and I get in the same kind of jam, will I be able to rise to the occasion? Nah. That's too deep for me, better to let it be a surprise to me as much as everybody else.

I am getting spooky about the upcoming new program We have been war gaming every chance we get. Mac and I are sure that we can use the same trick again to slip in from the west wall of the A Shau. We have been looking at all the old target folders, and had the Cookie up there at the TOC going over some of the real old ones. The old folders from the Stone Age, like 1968, when Budrow and Manes, were young One-Zeros.

I remember the Watson and Lloyd mission; it was when I first got here. Jesus it seems like it was so long ago. I remember Daart, he was here one day, then puff, and he was gone. No shame there; when you lose it, it is best to go. True courage in realizing that one cannot work this environment. If you try to stay and you are shaky, you will only get the rest of us killed. I have seen two others do the same since I have been here. This job isn't for everybody.

"You thinking what I'm thinking?" Mac drawls.

"Club?" I ask.

"Nah, too sedate," he replies. "Pink House then the China Night."

We dig out the last beers from the pail. We are finishing them up when Wes looks at me, and then kind of cocks his head over to one side. He looks like Efrem Zimbalist Jr. You know, the guy who plays the FBI weenie on the TV.

He looks at me and says quite simply: "It gets hairy out there sometimes." No shit Sherlock. It gets downright suicidal out there.

As we wander back toward the company area, I am thinking about the team, and what we have been discussing. No matter how proficient you are, eventually bad things happen that are beyond your control. The helicopter that tried to pull those guys out either lost power or had taken a hit. Either way, the bodies at the end of the strings had dragged the bird down when they caught in the trees, just plain bad luck. No way to see it coming or avoid it. I hope that if I get it, it will at least be quick. I don't want to spend a lot of time thinking things like, "Oh shit, that looks bad."

CHAPTER 7

Windows into the Past

It's just before dawn and I am sitting with my back to a tree. My own sour sweat is starting to annoy me and I am beginning to wonder if the scent carries too far. This is the second night we have spent on the ground and we haven't come across any sign that the enemy is here. It feels like the old days when we were able to insert on the fly. No LZ prep, not a lot of traffic upstairs, just like old times. We had taken no ground fire and moved off the LZ: no trackers, no signal shots, nada. The bush went back to its normal rhythm, and we dropped into the steady pace that would allow us to put some distance between the LZ and ourselves. We planned on getting to the center north quadrant of our target box and then work the boxes in a zigzag to the southern end. By dusk we had made it to that point and had RONed on a shelf that jutted out from an almost vertical ridge near the top.

We had been super careful after we moved in and settled for the night. But still no enemy contact. Yesterday we heard rifle shots to our south but we thought they were hunters, not signal shots. Now, in the few minutes on the bush time clock when night leaves and the day begins, we are all standing to. The nocturnal hunters and feeders are on their way back to their burrows and warrens, and we will soon emerge and begin our stealthy casing of the joint.

We will begin the day clinging to the high ground as much as possible to make sure we aren't being suckered. The terrain is good here; we can move on this leg for over a kilometer and never have to leave neutral ground. Working our way down we will be on the plateau by tonight and will have crossed the area where, if there was going to be any sort of encampment or complex, we will have stumbled onto the fringes before too long. We are casting back and forth trying to observe what we can from the high ground and may just spend the day watching the open areas below to see if we spot any activity. This is almost as good as it gets.

The night was chilly to the point that my fingers are still numb. I am trying to slowly blow some circulation into them without making any noise. I look over to my left and Bang is looking at me, making a face like I am committing some heinous crime in trying to thaw myself out. He looks just like a miniature version of Chico Marx. He has these big, bug-like eyes and has clipped his boony hat so that it has a stingy brim. I can only make out his head and part of his shoulder in the vegetation around him.

We wait, and gradually the bush comes awake and begins to chatter. This half-light is the time when they will hit you: in those close hours where you let your guard drop or exhaustion takes over and your senses dull. Most troops would be just starting to wake up or would be scratching their nuts and shaking out the kinks. I am rubbing my legs quietly yet vigorously in case I have to get up and run. My left foot has gone to sleep and I can imagine myself having to try and make a break for it with one foot dragging behind me like Igor. That's just marvelous. Just bloody marvelous. I can feel the circulation coming back with that electric shock feeling in the muscles. That's almost as bad as the numbness, especially if I have to run on the thing. Bang makes a small sound and I look up from my ministrations and he has his hand out and in the palm are several large larvae, all white and swollen with a darker head area. He is indicating I should try some of this *haute cuisine.* This is probably leftovers from our walk yesterday, or he had charmed them out of the rotting floor of the forest during the night. I decline his offer, remembering the last tasty tidbit he had offered me which tasted like rotting fish.

The light begins to get better. I can see definitions in the shadows now and start scanning out three meters at a time, shifting from right to left without moving my head. That is what gives you away in the bush, movement. We are situated so each man has a set field of fire and observation. Once you go still, you don't make sudden movements, you make everything slow like a sloth.

I can see out some fifteen meters now and I am listening to the bush at the same time. If they are out there, now will be the time they make their move. There is nothing that ruins your day like waking up to the sound of hand grenades. I have been there before, getting hit just before dawn in the RON. They had us ringed in when someone got nervous and cooked off a rocket, but we had managed to fight our way out of it before they had any depth to their ambush. We had cleared the ring by punching through the base. We left a tangle of theirs, down and mauled, and had run for the next four hours, between stopping and fighting. Ever since then, these are my worst times, moving into the RON and getting ready to leave.

I take out my canteen real slow, raise it to my mouth and take a long cool sip. The water is as chilled as I am. Mac makes a small sound and the Yards start to get in all the claymores except two: one will be pulled by the tail gunners and one by the point when we move out. Mac signals again, and he and Cuman and Thua begin to move off to the north.

We fall in behind them, each man taking up his position in the file, checking any high or low sign left by the ones ahead of him, and securing the left or right flank. Everyone has a number and that number signifies which flank you watch. Evens get right, odds get left. Anyone gets killed or wounded, everyone adds one to his number—that way we never have a hole. I am with the tail gunners and we are disguising our track and providing rear security. Ti Ti and Xam Pat are good at this. Right behind me is Bang with the M203, so if I need the launcher, we can blow a hole in anything that comes up on us.

Now that we are moving I am beginning to warm up despite the slow pace. The bush closes down if we move too fast, so we are staying right on the edge. We have learned to move like the Yards do, disturbing as little as possible. The bush always knows when there is a disturbance. It always has eyes on you. Why not? Everything down here is divided between the eaters and the eaten. It's a nerve-wrenching exercise in trying to keep from crapping yourself over any sound, or lack thereof.

I am getting loose now and the kinks are working out. After nearly an hour we stop again for a longer break than the periodic listen-and-wait sessions. Mac has chosen a good place for our stop. There is a slight depression with open country to our front right and the left also opens up some 200 meters out, so we have a good line of sight from our hide to see most of the area around us. We break for chow with half the team eating and the other half on watch. I let the little people go ahead and eat while I pull watch. As soon as they are done they give me a hand signal and I concentrate on getting out a PIR, or patrol indigenous ration. The rice and dried fish are delicious. After I finish it I make sure I haven't left any scraps or trash and put the empty plastic container in the inside flap of my rucksack. We have food for three days, but we can stretch it another two, or in a pinch we can forage.

As I am finishing up the *cuisine de bush,* Mac comes over and squats beside me with his map.

"We are here." He points with a twig to the approximate location on the map. "I figure that we can hug this terrain feature until we get to this area *here*." He points to a position on the map some five hundred meters to our southeast. We look off in that direction. The whole area is splotched with what appears to be old slash-and-burn plots, evidence of subsistence farming over the decades. The area is deserted now; new growth on the older plots is nearly two meters tall. The forest wraps around and hugs these little semi-clearings. I look at Mac and wipe my face and neck with my cravat in an attempt to clean at least one spot on my body.

"This place is as deserted as I've ever seen, Mac. That is almost as spooky as finding the place crawling with NVA. You have any idea why?" I can see that he is as tense as I am. We don't get a lot of dry holes in our targets. And the Yards have been jumpy ever since we got off the birds, more so than just waiting for the other side to bust a cap on us.

Mac sits back against the rock that I had been using as a table and lets out a sigh.

"I don't know either, it just is. Cuman says that there are no VC here because of the Snake people. As near as I can get out of him, these are Yards, but a different kind of Yards."

"Different in what way?" I am starting to get a queasy feeling about this. I had noticed that the Yards were extra vigilant when we had been in RON. And they are moving with a cautious air, with little of their usual foraging whenever chance permits it. Snake people? What the hell are they? It could be their name for some spirit or some lore from the past, or it could be a clan name. I am hoping that they mean Pentecostal fundamentalists that speak in tongues and handle rattlers to affirm their faith. My mojo wire has been nagging at the back of my consciousness for the last two days. Something isn't right. Granted, this area is not ideal for hiding a division or two, but still it is eerily quiet.

Mac is chewing on a blade of grass, and continues. "Cuman and Bong say that they are 'peeble like Tahans, but different.'" He imitates Cuman's accented English. "From what I gather they are a very shy and backward tribe." He thinks for a moment and lets out a subdued belch, holding his gloved hand over his mouth. "Near as I can figure they are related to the Bru and the Sedang, but they aren't either one. They are different and if I read their meaning, they are fierce warriors."

Fierce enough to keep the NVA out of here, I am thinking. Now that is not a pleasant thought. If they scare the crap out of the NVA, there is something truly frightening about them. They aren't fighting with us, they scare the NVA, the Yards know about them but apparently don't trade or intermarry with them; there has to be a reason for that. I am not sure I want to find out what it is.

Cookie comes over and squats with us. His face is pinched up and he looks as tired as I feel. The day is warm and with the meal I am feeling the desire to sleep for a bit. I look around and the Yards are all at their positions, with Cuman and Thua making the rounds and checking on them. Cookie looks at both of us and speaks in the same low voice that we have been conversing in.

"The Yards are spooked about something. You guys got any idea what it is? I asked Bong and all he says is that we no stay too long, Snake people come." Mac brings him up to speed on what Cuman had said earlier. The gnawing thought that has been creeping up on me finds the words that I don't want to say, but it comes out anyway.

"You think they might be head hunters don't you?" I look at Mac and he looks at us and he makes a sweep of the Yards before answering.

"Could be, and could be double, they might be cannibals." I look at Cook and he has the same shocked look that I am sure is on my face at this little jewel of information. "Best not to get all heeby-jeeby about it. Let's keep our eyes open. Regardless of what or who they are, they bleed just like the NVA."

There have been whispers of wild people that inhabit small enclaves in the highlands, people so primitive that even the Jesuits had not been able to reach them when the Frogs were here. Like all things that are perplexing or disturbing, the Yards would talk around it but never give it or them a name. Snake people? It must be their generic name for these reclusive cousins; to say their real name must invoke some kind of bad ju-ju.

Well, the little people weren't in a panic, so that was one good sign. Whether they weren't afraid of running into them, or were just hiding their fear, didn't make any difference as long as we could finish our target box. Cannibals? Shit! Nah, my mind doesn't want to accept that. Some of the Sedang and the Bru were head hunters not all that long ago, but cannibals? That's too long of a leap into the Stone Age for me to want to believe it.

Mac gets up and signals Cuman and we start to move again. I am too busy hiding the track and involved in the mechanics to be concerned about our conversation, but I am taking note that Ti Ti and Xam Pat are being real careful covering our track. The bush feels the same but there is a tension permeating our team that wasn't there before.

We move for about two hours, taking short security breaks to listen. Eventually we come to an area where the terrain starts to rise up and the bush gets thicker. We stop, long before it's time for a security break. I wait with the tail section. Cook comes back and whispers to me.

"We found a trail up ahead. Not much, not heavily traveled but still a trail and it is headed up through the gaps in this line of ridges." He points to our front where the ground heads uphill. "Mac wants to parallel it. They found tracks but they are old and they are barefoot tracks. The little people are all spooky again."

He slithers off forward and a few minutes later we are moving again. We step over the trail and cross to the other side where there is room to move and make our way up what appears to be a ramp, created in the distant past by a rock fall. As I step across the path, I notice that it is old but not that old, and Cook was right: there are distinct footprints in the earth where bare feet have pushed down the ground vegetation. The prints are small, and whoever had made them wasn't carrying a lot of gear. The tracks look like they are several days old.

We are real careful covering the crossing point to make sure that we leave little or no sign. We move at a steady slow pace and the jungle begins to thin out; it is still a jumble but you can see maybe fifteen meters. We are following the edge of the rock fall, picking our way around large boulders and automatically covering each other from one to the other. As we climb higher, we are getting up to the plateau again.

Just before we get to the top we stop again and Cook waves me up. I move the twenty or so meters to the front. Mac and Cuman are there, and in front of them and to the left is a cave. It's not all that deep but it is about twenty feet wide and maybe half that high. I see rotting poles of cut branches, and strung totems consisting of small animal skulls and what appear to be human finger and rib bones. There is a pile of other bones at the base and all of it is covered with a green fungus. Resting on a shelf in the back is what looks like a bear skull.

It's old; even with the rate the jungle takes over, this has been here a long time. Mac is squatting next to Cuman when I come up. I squat next to him and whisper, "What is it?" He looks at me and he is all business.

"Cuman says it is some sort of warning."

"You mean like a 'get out' warning, or a 'don't come in here' warning? What kind of warning?"

Cuman has this look like someone stepped on his grave. He just says, "Bad place, we need go now," and continues to look up towards where the plateau begins. I look back at the cave. There aren't any obvious signs that it was visited recently. The way Cuman is acting you would think there was someone standing inside and yelling "Go away!" at us. More than half of the poles that stand like guard posts in the doorway have rotted and fallen down, and the jungle is quickly reducing them to humus.

I am about ten feet from the opening. The cave is only about six or eight feet deep and the skull stares at me from the back. I notice what appear to be some metallic objects hanging on the pole furthest back and am trying to figure out what they are. They appear to be what is left of goggles or glasses. Whatever it is, no one is going forward to take a look.

"What the hell are those?" I point them out to Mac. "Do you want to take a look at what is inside?" I start to get up but I am stopped by Cuman hissing, "Ooush, numbah ten!" and Mac grabbing my arm.

"We are going to move out now, keep everyone closed up," he says. I turn and move back but I don't have to worry about closing everyone up. The Yards are all right there, so closed up they can touch each other. As we start moving again they all get a good look at the cave, and after that it is all I can do to get them to spread out a little bit.

Moving on, we come across more track, but the signs are old again. No shod feet either. Whoever is running around out here isn't NVA. We are about half a mile from the cave and up on the plateau when we come across what appears to be the wreckage of an aircraft: the remains of a piston engine, and part of a wing with foliage growing up through it. The area is getting more open. We are finding more parts of an aircraft but can't tell what it is until we find the remains of the fuselage, broken off in front where the engine had been and just short of the tail assembly. It appears to be a single-engine fighter, circa 1940s. You can still make out some of the paint which is a dark green.

Mac is standing on top, looking down into the cockpit. The dials and gauges are relatively intact and the seat is still inside. I pry open the compartment under the seat. A lot of our aircraft have survival equipment stowed in the seat pack. This would include gold chains or gold coins for use to buy your way out if necessary. The door squeaks in protest until I use my knife to pry it open. There is what appears to be a glutinous mass of decaying paper and bits of leather in the box. I scrape it all out onto the floor of the cockpit. There is nada, nothing of import, more importantly no gold coins, pistol, compass or souvenirs. Cookie finds what appears to be a boot and parts of a parachute harness at the base of a tree near the fuselage. We don't dig to see if there is a body to go with it. This thing is circa WWII or from the Indochina conflict. It isn't ours and it has been here a long time.

We are trying to figure it all out when Covey comes up on the air. Mac gives him a situation report and tells him what we have found. Covey comes back with instructions that we are to move to an LZ for extraction as soon as they can get the assets in place. I keep rummaging around inside the cockpit and scraping out the built-up debris. I notice a pocket knife wedged between the seat and the wall. After a few judicious taps I break it free. It's rusty but not so corroded that you can't see what it is. I try to open the blade but that's a no-go. As I am scraping away some of the dirt and rust I see some sort of stylized mark on the haft. I realize what it is: a Laguiole, or "Bee." That would make this a French aircraft since Laguiole has been the official knife maker for the French Army ever since Napoleon. The only reason I know that is my uncle has a folder made by the same company. It is a beautiful and well-made knife. Whoever was flying this tomb when it went down was either French or had good taste in blades. I put the knife in my pocket.

We are moving again. This time we are moving west, to an LZ that Covey has spotted. The Yards are still spooky and we are covering ground at a good pace, fast but not careless. It takes us about two hours to make the LZ. We move up and Recon around it. No sign, no disturbances, just us and the bush. We get the team ready and Covey comes over. The air package is on the way. We settle in and wait.

This is another dangerous time: you are getting extracted, you let your guard down, and you go slack. That's when Chuck kicks your ass. I am sitting with my back against the rucksack watching my sector when Covey comes over us again. I can hear the choppers off in the distance. They come in from the south, first a set of Spads that flash by off to the east a bit, then the slicks. The first one comes in and two of the Yards and Cook get onboard in a scramble. It lifts and I jump aboard the second one with Ti Ti, Xam Pat, and Bong. We are lifting off as Mac's bird comes in. He and the last three Yards scramble onboard and are lifting. I look back at his bird when Bong grabs my arm and points back at the LZ.

Standing at the edge and yet still in the cover of the bush are two Yards. They are definitely wild, not clothed in any modern clothing. One of them has what appears to be an old French MAT 49 submachine gun; the other is carrying a crossbow. We are gone before I get a good look at them. They just stare at the departing aircraft. Bong looks at me and he shakes his head, as if the sight of the two wild Yards confirms something.

We rise up into the chill of the higher altitude and soon are beating our way back towards the launch site. It has been a dry hole. I've never had one like this. We have been on the ground for three days and we haven't had anyone shooting at us. My mind drifts back to the wreck and the cave; they seem to be connected, but how is beyond me. Did the pilot go down with the bird, survive and manage to pull himself free of the wreckage? We hadn't found a body, but whose rib bones were in the cave? Too much coincidence there. Maybe he parachuted free and later walked out or made it as far as the wreck. In the back of my mind is the suspicion that the Snake people, as Cuman called them, had found him. If they were head hunters or even cannibals, his end would have been a messy one.

At the launch site, we give a brief back on what we saw. We file the coordinates for the French fighter, and relate what we saw in the cave and the tracks on the ground. Afterwards I grab Mac by the arm and relate what I saw as we pulled out. He smiles and says that Cuman had seen people shadowing us after we left the aircraft. So had Bong. They hadn't made any hostile moves so we had left them alone.

The next few days are a rush of getting ready to go back and doing housekeeping tasks like filling sandbags and improving the bunkers at the launch site in Quang Tri. Later in the afternoon we are getting on a Caribou for the trip back to Da Nang.

The Yards are subdued, as if they had come into contact with the spirit world and didn't like it. They do some sort of cleansing rite down in the huts the day we get back. That's when we find out how close these wild Yards had been to us. Ti Ti had looked up from when he was covering the track and one had been within arm's reach of him. He had never made eye contact, but looked down as if not seeing him. I guess if one of the Snake people looks into your eyes he steals your soul, or maybe your pecker falls off, or some other primitive taboo.

They cleansed Ti Ti and isolated him and Bong for two days. I had to go with them and sit through a couple of hours of sweet grass smoke and some other ministrations, because I had seen them also. Bong kept looking at me, explaining that he wanted to see if I was missing my spirit or something. I decided then and there I wouldn't tell them about the knife. Probably wake up with warts all over my dick or something horrid for removing it. I still have it to this day. Every time I start feeling sorry for circumstances, like bad women or bad luck, I console myself with the thought it is all because of the knife. It's easier than admitting that I have character flaws.

Mac took all the ju-ju stuff in stride. He and Cook gave me a hard time about it until I threatened to tell Bong that I saw the two of them actually talking to the Snake people and giving them the names of all the Yards. Weird place, weird time, it all confuses me. All I know is that there are still some places even Nguyen won't go, and there are things out there that are beyond the grasp of reality. I do know that the wild ones I saw had tattooed swirls on their faces. I can still see them to this day, standing at the edge of that little clearing as if they were gatekeepers to another time.

CHAPTER 8

Drums along the Mohawk

The rain is coming down like a solid sheet of water. This is supposed to be the dry season, but for some reason, there has been a weather event. I love the Air Force meteorologists. They can't just say it's a storm; it has to be a weather event. Whatever it is, it has screwed us royally if we get caught out here.

We have come in through back door of the A Shau. Another little trick we have come up with. The North knows we are not allowed inside Laos, so they use it as a staging area, without fear that that some US Army Division will come choppering in to mess up their nuc mam party hour. Since rule-breaking is our forte, we accidentally, through anomalies in the Earth's magnetic field which degaussed our hooterfritz compass, strayed over the border and landed in Laos to confirm terrain features. Since our landing was at a high altitude, the chopper had to lighten its load so it could take off again. We graciously volunteered to walk back, thus freeing the gallant aviators to safely return to base with their multi-thousand-dollars' worth of flying scrap metal. At least that is the story that we will tell. Who cares; for once I have inserted into a target without some gaggle of pissed-off pith helmets immediately opening up on us with everything including rocks. I am a happy camper.

We have spent the last two days working our way down from the lip of the highlands to get in position to be the surprise punch for another of the Saigon Brain Trust's tricks. Actually it is the unholy troika of Manes, Waugh and the TOC, plus whoever appears to be whacked out enough to add special insanity to the sauce that make up the brains of these "strikes." We be lean and mean, my man. We are the shadow men who make them shiver in their fart sacks with fear at night. Never know when or where we are going to strike. Shit, I had better stop. I'm scaring myself.

A flash of lightning illuminates the other nine figures hunched against the cliff, snuggled up to the roots of trees, under little overhangs, anywhere for a break from the rain. Shades of *Götterdämmerung*, this is the opera of the twisted and bizarre. When the lightning flashes, it illuminates everything all in grays and greens. This scene reminds me of the film *The Man in the Gray Flannel Suit* with Gregory Peck, specifically the scene when he shoves the bayonet into the German sentry. Uh oh, got to watch that: all that ethereal thinking will probably send out some kind of karma and the Cookie will pick it up. We can't have that. His Ranger mode might click in and he will start crawling up the cliff face with a bowie knife clenched in his teeth, looking for the starring role in someone else's nightmare.

I am tripping. We have been on Green Hornets, our generic name for the amphetamine tablets that we carry, for the last ten hours. We were at the last of our energy but we could move under cover of the storm: if we got contact it would muffle out the noise of the guns. We wanted to be in position so when the rest of the lads come smoking into the adjacent target box at first light tomorrow, we could be there to help direct the anvil.

Despite the weather, we have made good time and are in the perfect spot over the trail complex that is tomorrow's target. We have decided to hug this cliff until the storm abates then move down to be in position because at first light the sky is going to be full of aircraft hitting targets on the forward edge of our target box and the adjacent box as well. There are several regiments tucked into these folds in the terrain and their troop complexes are protected by layers of anti-aircraft guns to keep the Air Force at bay. Saigon has opted for using the data collected so far to plan the air strikes and, hopefully, drive the NVA out of their prepared positions…and more importantly to make them come up on the radios and RDF their locations for more accurate follow-up.

That's where we come in, along with the team inserting in the adjacent target box who will be conducting a modified Bomb Damage Assessment. The hope is that they can position themselves to act as bait to draw the NVA out in an attempt to dislodge them. They don't know we are there above the juncture of two major trails that are part of the network that makes up the Ho Chi Minh trail. We had found plenty of signs as we moved closer to our position planned for the morrow's activities. We glimpsed a two-ton truck moving on one of the trails that snake down from the plateau and Covey had kept us informed of what was moving in the area. He had flown an offset so as not to draw attention to where we were. He got fired up twice over the western edge of the A Shau and had been mapping the gun positions when he could. As far as we knew they didn't suspect that we were on the ground.

Lightning flashes again and I see the light reflected off the hoods, illuminating the Yards closest to me. They look like Meso-Americans in the strobe of light, adding to the surreal scene. It is strange, in fact, how much they look like the Indians of South America. Maybe I will stay here and write some anthropological masterpiece about hill people all coming from the same great Earth Mother. Another flash of lightning and I can see Mac now. He is up under a rock overhang like I am. We have the two best places. Mine has the roots of a giant hardwood tree, like supporting pillars, shrouding the opening. His has a slab of the rock face against it, giving him about three feet of overhead cover.

Cook is down from him against the roots of another forest giant. He is looking intently into the driving rain that still manages to get through the canopy cover of the forest. I look back at Mac who is crouched down and talking into the radio. I am surprised we are able to get anything on the horn. Storms virtually close out radio communications when they are like this. One of the Yards comes up and settles in my little dry area with me. He pulls his hood back as I have. It turns out to be Bong. I had just been thinking how surreal the scene was, almost monochrome and thoroughly electrified by the storm.

Oh great, I am in the middle of Indian Country in a howling storm, with the voodoo man. He looks up and gives me that shaman shrug. There are volumes in that shrug. Bong never says much, he just scares the crap out of me with his prescience. He always seems to know what I am thinking.

"*Trung Si*, do not think so fierce, you will attract the spirits." He looks at me in all seriousness. Then turns and looks off into the rain as if expecting something that has forty eyes, very sharp teeth and a bad attitude to come slinking out of the forest and start devouring Americans and Yards for brunch.

I don't reply, I just try to be as mellow as I can. That's the trouble with the Green Hornets, they make you jagged and flitty. It was worth the effort to use them because initially they also heighten your awareness, but now we are stopped here and want to let them drain out before we take any more. We have been here for about five hours. Enough time for some of the team to get some rest and lose the effect of the drugs. Kind of let the body catch up before you supercharge it. If you use too many too long you get completely whacked out. Then you are no good to anyone.

Mac makes a motion and I put the hood on over my boony hat, slip out of the dry hole and slide, scramble and claw my way over to him. We use the soft indigenous ponchos because they don't make as much noise. They are about fifty percent as effective under prolonged soaking but they act as a sauna so you at least stay warm. Once I am in Mac's little cave, I pull the hood back and wipe my face with my cravat. Shit, I want a cigarette. No go on that one Buckwheat. Cigarette smoke carries all the way to Hanoi out here. It would probably wake up Uncle Ho himself, and he would telephone down here to have the lads hunt down my skinny little ass for breaking the Commandment, "Thou Shalt Not Smoke in the Bush." I slide in and get comfortable as Mac looks up from the radio.

"I got Covey up, they are about 25 klicks east of us riding the face of this storm."

"That's comforting, did they say anything about if it's going to clear?"

"He says it looks like it will be a go in about an hour. The southern end of this thing is already fracturing." Fracturing? Now I wonder where he got that. Maybe he is reading old medical journals when we aren't looking.

"Okay, so we are a go then?"

"Yes, he is going to give us a green light when they are about twenty minutes out. It should give us time to get in above those gun banks, and be able to help direct Covey to hit them just as the rain breaks." He spits a looger at the end for emphasis. I look around, checking out the area, then turn back to him.

"Okay, same plan, you still want me to take the ass end as we move down, then spread off to the right when we get to the deadfall we looked at earlier?"

He looks at me and nods affirmative. The rain has started to slacken as the first hints of dawn begin to seep light down into our enclave. We are about a hundred meters from the spot we had picked to tuck the team into, where we can see off and below us into the valley complex and still be able to defend if we get jumped by too many people.

Our job will be to observe the trail junctures and watch as Chuck brings up reinforcements. Then we relay that to Covey so they can direct air strikes to stir up their concentrations. We had been the bait initially, but we had managed to work our way to this location without being discovered. The other team will be the meat in the sandwich. Their infiltration will be obvious and it is hoped that they will entice the NVA to mass on them. We will be at their back door and, hopefully, increase the accuracy of the strikes. After they have stirred everything up, the second layer with an Arc Light will come in and turn the area into a new time zone, right after both teams get clear. At least that's what they hope to do. What will actually happen will again be on the toss of the dice of circumstance. We might get lucky and destroy a couple of regiments and their infrastructure. And if it's successful we might be able to recreate it and cripple their effectiveness in this sector at least.

* * *

We are moving now, as swiftly yet cautiously as we can. Any time you are in motion your senses are on swivel. You use all of them in the bush. The senses of hearing and smell are as important as vision.

One of the reasons that we eat the indigenous rations is because then our smell is the same as the enemy's. I didn't believe it at first but I noticed after a while that I could smell Americans because of their diet; it affects even the smell of a person's urine. As careful as we are not to piss unless it is into a hole then covered up, a good tracker will key on the sign as quick as Jumping Jack Flash. Most of the guys take the "no crap" pills that stuff them up during the mission. I personally dislike taking anything that the Army describes as not harmful. Their track record with Agent Orange is a good milestone for that caution; besides I haven't had the need to defecate out in the bush and don't plan on it unless we get lucky and stay for more than three days on one of these, which is a rarity these days.

We move under some deadfall about twenty meters from our hide position and as the light becomes stronger I make out a beautiful violet fungus prospering in the remains of a dead and rotting tree. It flashes by as I move up to where Mac has positioned the team and start to tuck the Yards in where we want them. Cuman is with Mac and looks up as I crawl up beside them to our vantage point. From where we are, we can see where the trail breaks out from the west then reenters the old growth about four hundred meters to our southeast. We can also see about seventy meters of the main trail that crosses it from the north. We can't see the exact intersection but we have eyes on two of the major trails that feed Nguyen's locations to the east.

We are settled in and waiting for the bush to go back to normal as Covey comes down and flits across our short axis to our front. He is being careful, but to no avail, as a line of green tracers track his movement from the area that they want to insert the other team. He grabs some altitude and almost immediately the first set of fast movers come in and start the LZ prep for the other team. They are followed by two other fast movers that start to work over the area to our front and then to the north. The bombers are getting secondary explosions, indicating they hit something other than a nuc mam stand down in the triple canopy. Cookie snaps his fingers to get our attention and points down to the south; we can make out troops moving into the area from the west and call it in to Covey.

The birds are plastering the hilltop where the team will insert and the other targets. As he uses up the aircraft and their ordnance, Covey is replacing and stacking more for the crescendo, layering it out from where the team will come in. Mac stage whispers to me that he can see more troops and what looks like some sort of armored vehicle off to the north, just before it wheels off into the trees. The area below is getting hammered now as the overhead is pulled back and we can see the slicks with their accompanying gunships insert the team. All that activity will certainly draw the NVA. As they are getting offloaded, a set of A1Es shows up and starts looking for targets of opportunity. Suddenly dirty little tufts of smoke start tracking them across the sky. Mac tells Covey that it is coming from the area he had seen the vehicle disappear into.

Covey flips over and unloads a white phosphorus rocket as a marker. The A1Es drop ordnance on that area and there are a number of secondary explosions. Dirty black smoke rises up through the canopy. We are seeing more movement, not just on the trails but through breaks in the canopy: it looks like they are getting organized on the ground. The second team starts calling in air strikes as the bombers stir up the anthill. More and more flak is being thrown up and, just as quick, Covey is vectoring strikes on suspected gun positions.

The other team reports that they are starting to get probed about the same time our luck runs out. I have to move back down where I had left the B40 and our rear security overlooking our bug-out route to the first LZ. As I get there the Yards fire a couple of M79 rounds and I can hear people moving about a hundred yards out. They are more to the south of our route but will give us problems if we have to move through them. Mac gets Covey to look us over and he comes up with bad news: we have troops moving toward the other team's area, and they are spread out in the bush in such a way they will uncover us soon. The NVA react quickly to the 40 mm and start firing up the area in the hope we will start returning fire. So far we haven't gotten any real pressure.

Mac is talking with Covey about our situation. The battle has been going on now for a half hour, with the air strikes continuing to provide a protective cover and pound the enemy formations. The NVA are starting to crank up their artillery.

I watch as two rounds impact around the hill the second team is on. These are artillery shells coming from somewhere to our west. They bracket the hill, but then the next set is three rounds and they land right on the hilltop. That's not good. The NVA had obviously registered the hilltop as part of their planning. They are going to leave the guns in Laos where they are assured the air can't reach them. I heard the second set leave the tubes and they are at least two klicks on that side of the border. They might be heavy mortars, but I couldn't hear the guns clear enough to get anything other than an estimate.

Mac waves me over and I slide down to where he and Cuman are facing off to the east. He looks at me and tells me:

"Start gearing up for getting out of here. That last barrage left the other team with casualties and they are going to pull them out. Stay loose, we are going to move up to the primary LZ as soon as Covey has air packages on the way. Hopefully they won't need to Bright Light the other team."

No shit, I am thinking, Bright Light means that there won't be enough birds to get us out, especially if they get jammed on the extraction. Let's hope no one thinks we can slip away and hide in the target box. They know we are somewhere along this ridge and as soon as the first team leaves they will send a cleanup group to locate us and kill us.

As the choppers are leaving the orbit point, we start packing it in and moving to our LZ. Covey has the birds drop ordnance ahead of us and around the extraction LZ.

This makes the going easier as we don't have to stealth it. I am bringing up the rear, keeping everyone tight, ready to be the pivot point if we get hit from the side or front. The vegetation is splintered and churned up but so far we haven't had any contact. We break the edge of the LZ and set up, waiting for the air package.

Covey is busy pulling the other team: they have four wounded, three real bad, but manage to make it to the birds on their own. It's our turn now. Mac tells me they are five minutes out. We set up a perimeter around an old deadfall and some rocks that mark the edge of an old bomb crater. I get everybody tied in and we wait for the birds. I am congratulating myself on surviving, when we start to get some ground fire from the ridge to our north. Mac has Covey mark it, then the first set of gunships flashes over with their rockets and chin turrets chewing up that area and one back the way we have come. Jesus they got on to us quick, we had just covered that ground, which meant that they were already moving on our location when we vacated it. One of the Cobras almost hovers and spins in three quarters of a circle above us with his chin turret blowing 40 mm and the 7.62 minigun, then pulls pitch and slides off just as the first slick starts to settle in.

Cookie and his Yards get on and then they are away. I am next; as the second bird settles in, we run and climb up a mound, then throw ourselves into the chopper. I feel something crunch under my left boot when I clear the last few meters. I look down and spot the partially buried remains of someone who hadn't been so lucky in the past. As we lift off I notice that there are scattered remains all through the LZ. This had been someone's killing ground in the not too distant past.

I see Mac load on and leave the LZ as we gain altitude. The Cobras stay on station with the slicks until the last moment. Mac's bird stutters, slides to the side as if it got swatted, then climbs up with us. The entire air package then moves off towards home.

* * *

As we pile off the birds we get the team together, take a head count, then move off to the huts and the debriefing. I have a chance to compare notes with Cook and Mac. We had managed to stay in for three days, got to see some of the bad guys and helped smash their little base in the trees. The air strikes are continuing and rumor is that they will carpet bomb the area as well. I don't care as long as they can finish this without us having to be on the ground.

Cookie is all pissed off because he has lost his big P38 can opener, which he had gotten from some Aussie. It's three times as big as ours and you can open an ammo crate with it if need be. He had it from some distant past when he was on an A camp and it was his talisman. I am wondering what the hell he had it out for; I was too busy to be eating. Is it possible he and Mini Mac were sharing a can of peaches while I was sweating away two lifetimes, expecting to die by design or accident?

CHAPTER 9

Death to Cheetah

RT Kansas is dying. Their suffering and drama is being played out on the radios and being relayed to those not close enough to hear. It is hot outside, and muggy, and we are all gathered around the commo van that is acting as a temporary TOC near the front gate.

All of us who are back in Da Nang are gathered up, drawn by the urgent message that came down to the company and was shortly followed by the mad rush of Manes, with all the company hierarchy, to the Alamo. By the time Cook and I get there with Mac there are several other teams standing outside. We are listening to the piteous battle on the speakers, trying to piece together the scene on the ground.

Kansas, with Tony, Festes, Klaus, Orrin, Berg, Willie Queen, and Jesse had gone in on an old firebase in an attempt to do a prisoner snatch. The plan had been a fairly good one but held marginal survival possibilities if they got hit or heavy weather closed in. They had done an insertion right on the heels of another team that was being extracted, hoping the NVA would send a party up to see what was about. Their insertion had been on a hilltop, the old firebase. They had reinforced the old bunkers during the night and were waiting in ambush for the watcher team to come up and scour the area.

The NVA always went and looked at any area that we had been observed in. This whole area abounds in their troop concentrations, and there are miles of commo-wire from a multitude of operations dating back to the Frenchies. They know we do a number of wiretaps into the nets as a methodology. So they send wire chasers and scouts to see where we have been. They also look for things we may have planted; not a good job for whoever is sent out, since we booby-trap and leave special munitions for the hapless to pick up, or stumble into. It is just the sort of job you give to an experienced anti-recon unit, with a couple of expendable privates for the detection crew tagging along.

These guys will report directly to the higher headquarters, so consequently they know more and have seen more than some former flower-picker from Hanoi. Kansas had spent the night reinforcing and building fighting revetments and tightening the firebase perimeter to accommodate the small team.

They have fourteen people up there with two machine guns and a mortar. With that kind of firepower and a hilltop, you can kick some major ass. But if the rice-powered crowd get the first punch in and mass on you, sooner or later you are going to pay for it. Early in the morning Brother Ho and his buddies did just that. The early morning fog had not yet lifted when Tony and the others heard movement, lots of it, at the base of the hill. Add to that, off in the distance they heard trucks moving up. To us, that means lots of troops—mean, pissed-off troops, who are not looking for dancing partners.

They had stood to, just as an RPG rocket came out of the fog and hit the bunker that Berg was in, impacting at the revetment and collapsing it. Shortly after that, four more impacted around their perimeter. All the rest had missed bunkers, but the rockets initiated the assault.

The team didn't know it but they had approximately an entire battalion in an inverted "V" moving up the hill firing in the assault. Tony and Festes quickly realized there was little adjustment for the team, since they were being attacked on three sides at once. The entire hilltop was kicking as if alive by the number of rounds impacting in and around their position. But they fought back, and forced the first assault to wither short of the sandbags. The NVA had fallen back, regrouped, and then quickly reorganized and tried again.

In the first assault Berg had died, or at least it was presumed so, since his bunker was collapsed and he was in it. The B40 had gone in the aperture and exploded. If he was in there he was dead, dead, dead. Three of the Yards had been wounded and one killed. Festes had been on the horn and Covey was soon over their position. Heavy ground fog was making it impossible for him to direct the aircraft that were arriving on station, but they dropped on the road junction where they had heard the trucks stopping, and got a secondary.

The fog was beginning to lift when the second assault came. Festes told Tony he was going to check on Berg, then to tighten the perimeter. Accompanied by one Yard, he headed off over the small rise that comprised the crest cutting across the perimeter.

He found Klaus kneeling, with his face in the dirt, shot through with two mortal wounds and dead. Orrin is dead laying near the mortar pit. The area around his body was chewed up from the number of rounds that had impacted since he had died. The mortar was temporarily out of operation, but Willie and two Yards were trying to get some rounds in the air. Before Festes could make it to Berg's bunker he was hit. He went down, shot through the body, got back up, and continued moving around telling the rest of the team to get fighting. Cool, calm, though mortally wounded, he was trying to direct their defense.

He never made it back to Tony, but collapsed, dying after being hit again, this time in the head. The Yard who had gone with him came back and relayed it all to Tony. In the space of less than twenty minutes, they had sustained the deaths of three Americans and one Yard; two more Yards were seriously wounded.

The second assault rolled up the hill with all the intensity that a full NVA battalion can bring to bear, with B40s and hand grenades, the explosions adding to the mounting roar of three hundred automatic weapons. All this directed at the small team's perimeter. Still they held, beating back the second assault, dropping some of the NVA at the lip of the sandbags and bludgeoning some with rifles and entrenching tools, in and amongst their own positions. The dead and dying NVA littered the slope in front of their position.

Standing, listening, we hear Covey's alarm as the fog begins to lift and reveals hundreds of NVA around the hilltop. He begins to work the air assets on station. There is a short lag after Tony's strained voice telling them where he thinks they are massing; Covey is relaying the information to the bombers on another frequency. We hear him tell the team to get down and then the loud reverberations of the explosions in the background, with Tony's muffled voice saying that they are coming up again. This is the last one they can meet as an organized group.

The NVA will sweep over them like a tide of wildebeast. The lucky few of the team that may survive will either die trying to get off that beaten piece of real estate, or be taken prisoners. Not likely you will have long in captivity when you punish the NVA like that. The consequence is a short 7.62 mm to the head on the spot, or getting beaten to death with a rifle butt.

The gunships arrive and what they find isn't pretty. In fact it is the stuff that haunts our nightmares: a Recon team in its death throes. The top of the hill is such that the team is all together, crouched in and around the mortar pit. They are unable to raise their heads above the rim. Grenades are being chucked at them and they are throwing them out. Putting their weapons over the rim, they spray thirty rounds in a fan, hoping to catch and chop off the lead elements.

Castillo and Gast are the Bright Light. They are right on the heels of the last NVA assault. We can hear the Cuban talking to Covey, describing what he sees as they are coming in. The gunships are right beside the package and you can hear the miniguns' steady staccato burp. Tony's voice comes on, telling them, "Shoot right on us, they are in here with us." Castro and his crew are on the ground. They move across to the team and their added firepower, combined with the air support, breaks the back of the NVA assault. The green-clad figures flee downhill, dragging what wounded they can. They have paid a terrible price for trying to take the team.

Castro is all business, talking the air in. We sit and listen. The crowd is so quiet that you could hear a mouse pissing on a cotton ball. Everyone is silent, listening intently, with your inner thoughts on being in their predicament. Castro gets to Tony and the rest of the survivors. They are patching what they can, while he is talking to the chase medic, telling him that the worst cases will be on his bird going out. Virtually the entire team is wounded.

They load the worst cases on the chase bird, and then the remainder on the second. They manage to get Klaus and Orrin and the three dead Yards on board the next bird. The NVA are laying it on still, so the decision is made to evacuate the hill. They are unable to get Berg, but locate Festes' body lying there in mute testimony to the viciousness of the assault. The last bird lifts and clears, and Castro calls the air and tells them to dump it on the hilltop.

The Bright Light and the survivors make it out and manage to get airborne, although all the ships have holes in them. Once they are off and headed back to the launch site, Covey lets the Air Force drop everything they have on and around the lonely hilltop. Once the armada gets back and regroups, the decision is made to go back and retrieve the bodies. The air support has been steadily working the hilltop over since they left, as well as the surrounding area. Another armada of ships lifts off and joins the fighters coming up on station. This is going to be a hard strike: bomb the hills around the crest into the Ice Age, and insert the recovery team. Tony has gotten some medical attention and, despite the harrowing hours of the battle, forces himself on the Bright Light. None object. It is his right; his team is lying out there.

We listen as they come back on station. There is little ground fire, and the bombers are working the area over very heavily. The second Bright Light is on the ground. They move out through the fighting positions, looking for Berg who is missing. The NVA dead on top of the hill are gone, except the portions of bodies like arms and legs. They find Lieutenant Hagen's body. He is buried up to his neck and they can't figure out if this is the result of a bomb strike or if the NVA did a hasty burial. The bunker that Berg had been in is partially excavated. They search but find no discernible sign of Berg's body. They gather up the remains of the lieutenant. The whole operation is over inside an hour. There are still dozens of NVA lying around the approaches to the hill. Later we would hear that before the NVA cleaned the battle area up, an Air Force FAC counted more than 300 bodies lying around the team's position.

They are coming back to Quang Tri; it is over. The action winds down as we all start to drift back to the Recon area. Solemn, Each of us is full of thoughts about the guys who were our friends and comrades. Both the living and the dead are in our thoughts. This is the event you fear most, when your time runs out and you die.

Half of the team never made it off the hill and the survivors are not much better off. They are shot, fragged, and shocky, but they made it. I know that feeling. The next day is the most glorious of your life because you are alive. You have danced in the dragon's jaws and escaped. Everything is more brilliant and vibrant; even the smells you dismiss normally come flooding back in a tidal wave of odors.

The remnants of RT Kansas will be on a bird heading back to Da Nang tomorrow. Castro's team will go along and they will bring the dead back with them.

* * *

I am sitting alone in the hootch; the others have gone over to the club. We go into isolation two days from now so it is normally a raucous time. But a somber cloud has settled over the camp. That makes two teams, in less than two weeks, that have been mauled to the point of extinction. I remember Festes from the raids and other operations. He was from North Dakota. A tall, good-looking man with a quiet competence, he was the epitome of a combat leader. He and Tony were made to run together; what he lacked, Tony made up in sheer audacity and courage, coupled with the keen hunter's instinct of a pool shark.

Bruce Berg and I had gone through the Recon team leaders course in Long Than. Our grader had been Moose Monroe. The One-Zero course was an amalgam of lessons learned by past Recon teams, designed to prepare you to lead a team. You couldn't take over a team until you got through it.

The last phase is an actual operation in War Zone D. Plenty of bad guys running around doing mischief, but nowhere near the concentrations found up north. We had inserted without incident, and on the second day had picked up sign. We followed it to where we found wood cutters working. We watched them, photographed them, and continued on. We heard shots later that afternoon and Moose figured it was someone bagging some game rather than signal shots. Our route took us up the side of a slight elevation rise. Here we decided to pick a RON position.

Late that night it was raining so hard it hurt. I was huddled under a lightweight poncho, when I noticed that Berg was under the hood of his, and he had a red lens light on. I thought to myself, he is writing down a patrol report. This was going too far, the little apple polisher. He nudged me with his boot. I looked down and he had a note stuck in the laces. I felt my way down to his laces and removed it. I ducked under my poncho and turned on a pen light with a red lens, figuring it must be a message of great import. Something like "They are so close we can't even whisper." I read: "He thrust his rock-hard member against the soft willing flesh of her womanhood…" Just the right edge to insanity: he is out here writing porn. This is one sick boy.

I looked up and he was grinning like he just pulled in a fish. By the time we got out the next day, we had become fast friends. I liked him mucho, and now in the searing seconds of a detonation, he was gone. Vanished forever.

* * *

I get up and stretch. Time is a-wasting; might as well go over and join the wake at the Club. Tonight we will regale their memory. In fact, our wakes make an Irish wake look like a Baptist sing-in by comparison.

I can hear the noise as soon as I get outside. As I enter the club, I can see that their spirits are being heralded on a sea of alcohol. That's the bad part; you remember you aren't going to live forever. I see Mac and the Cookie; the little rascals have ordered me a drink for every one they had, so there are now five or so cognacs waiting for me as I pull up a chair.

"Drink up. You're behind." Cook glowers at me, as if I haven't been holding up my end of some sacred oath. Oh this is cool, southern temperance at its peak.

"The team is coming in at 1100 tomorrow, they are picking them up at Da Nang and ferrying them over by slicks," Cookie slurs between belches. Marvelous, I'm thinking; best thing to do is try to roll with the wave of grief and alcohol that will soak this place before too long. I take the plunge and a half an hour later I am as sloshed as they are. No one goes downtown tonight, except maybe the hardcore sex junkies that try to lose themselves in sensations. Not for me. I wander back to the Yard hootch and sleep it off.

The morning comes and we all assemble down at the chopper pad as the birds come in and the remnants of RT Kansas and Castro's team begin to unload. We all move in and help them. They are beat to crap. The hollowness in the eyes is still there.

Later in the afternoon we are sitting in the club with Tony and the others. They have taken care of the details and tomorrow Tony will be escorting the Montagnards' bodies back to Mai Loc. It is a sad task, but a thing we do out of honor to the Yards. They are a tribal people and to not do it is an insult; besides, these little guys are as close as family to us. When you lose them it's the same as when you lose one of your brothers.

Tony is giving a blow-by-blow of their actions, starting at the point of insertion. He details the intelligence that they had from the AST.

The visual reconnaissance had shown no massive presence near the old firebase, nor had they any indication that the enemy would react with so strong a force. From his recollection, it seems that the NVA may have wanted to wipe the team out and maybe take a prisoner. More likely, they wanted to kill them as a warning to stay out of the area. Well, they had made their point, but they had paid a terrible price for it. Tony says that he is sure that the team had been observed on the false extraction, and as a result, that the enemy commander had spent the night preparing for the assault.

Being familiar with the area, the commander would know how long the fog would cover the area so that the team could not use air support effectively. This is how we pick apart a mission. We find out how the other side is operating. Willie chimes in on the tactics and the ferocity of the first attack. The NVA had every intention of overrunning the team on the first assault. They all agree that the troops that came on in the first wave were seasoned troops. Sometimes the NVA will use a green outfit in an assault like this to toughen them up before they get into a slugfest with a conventional unit. They are beginning to learn, though, that we have a bite bigger than our size.

Kansas broke the back of the first assault as they became visible through the mist and fog. Tony believes that the NVA had tried to get a lock on where he and Festes had placed the machine guns, but as it had been too foggy, he thinks they only counted one. It was in Berg's bunker, which explains why they took his bunker out first, thinking they had removed the gun from action. They had, but there was another M60 there with the team.

We get through the account of how Festes died, and Klaus. They had died doing what it takes to stay alive as a team. You have to get up and move around even in a firestorm like that. You can't see and direct from one position.

There were two Binghams, on the team, Klaus and Orrin, both were dead, both died trying to keep the team intact. Orrin had died trying to get the mortar up and lay in close protective fires.

The second and third assaults were the same as the first, very quickly timed so that the team couldn't reorganize much in between. The fact that they came back each time shows that at least a senior commander was directing the attack. From the body count seen on and around the hilltop, they had been hit by at least a regiment not a battalion.

Tony is describing the last assault and how the NVA tried to keep so much fire on the hill that sticking your head up was a fatal mistake. He says at the last, they were shooting them as they came up on the lip of the position. The incoming fire was so intense that some of the NVA were getting hit by their own supporting fire.

"I saw a North Vietnamese soldier come up to the lip. He was wearing green kakis, carrying a type 56 Chinese AK, and wearing an AK vest with one grenade in the side pouch. He was also wearing a green pith helmet and Bata boots, and then I shot him."

Simple, a straight forward account. None of this, "I am a hero here," just the facts and admissions to your peers that you were so scared you couldn't shove a needle up your ass with a sledgehammer.

Willie and the others are saying about the same. They all agree that they thought they were goners. They also agree that Festes and Tony's actions were the reason that anyone had survived. That's the highest accolade you can get. When your peers say you have it all together in the worst situation, that's better than a Congressional Medal of Honor.

In the end Lieutenant Hagen would receive the Medal of Honor and both Queen and Tony Anderson would get the Distinguished Service Cross. The other Americans received silver stars for heroism.

* * *

Castro comes and joins in, giving his account of the Bright Light. I look over at him when he is done, and tell him that Mac and I are thinking of going into DM-10 again, and wonder if he and Trantenella would be willing to act as Bright Light for us. He looks at me, makes that little head nod of his, and looks back up and says,

"Fuck you. You guys are worse than these guys. Of course if you and Mac and the Cookie leave all your gold chains with us, I will see if we can work out a contract." Then he cackles.

"No way, you Cuban Shylock, if we have the gold on us, then you will have to come in and get it," I answer him, figuring I have him there.

"Nope, I don't want the gold that bad, I'll just rifle your locker before they ship your carcass back. I am sure I can find enough cash and trinkets in there to satisfy. Besides that, I can buy that gold in Bangkok for thirty-five an ounce and not get shot at." Then he grins for effect.

"You shifty little Spaniard, I bet Castro kicked your family off the island along with your black little capitalist heart, just so you wouldn't soil the glorious revolution with your greed. You'd actually charge us for a rescue? Us? Your only friends in the world?"

"In a word? Yes. In fact for you, it's double just in case I have to admit to saving you later." He cackles at his own sick humor.

"What? You have a scale for rescues?" I fake indignation.

"Yep that's us, the official rescue squad. In fact it will be two hundred more if I have to actually carry you and you bleed on me or any of the equipment. Hmmm, this is such a good idea I might organize the chase medics. If you don't have a credit card we can work out a prepayment plan. You can leave gold, cash, your girlfriend… any gold or silver fillings in your teeth need to be documented just in case you are short."

The Beaner is off and running with the idea of organizing paid-in-advance Bright Lights. We spend the next thirty minutes honing the concept. It's a great idea; at least it is something to focus on instead of the serious shit like dying. We are in full swing now. Cook looks at us with distaste—this is bad Ranger ju-ju—but we reassure him it is just what we are fighting for: Capitalism, the only true ideology, is rearing its ugly head. It is such a good idea, in fact, that maybe we can get Saigon to pay us by the mission to even go out there. Then we can double dip by having to go save ourselves.

Tony and the others drift out. They are trashed; it will take a few days before they get their legs back. The rest of us are working out the intricacies of a paid-for operation. Let's see now, we can charge by the pound for people like Manes. Butler can match what society will pay for us not to go in and save him, and for Bolton, we cannot only charge by the pound, but maybe auction him off to some psychiatric school as a training aid. Bloody hell, we are sitting on a gold mine here. I don't like the way the Cuban is eying me though….

Eldon comes by and we run it past him. He suggests that we should read *Catch-22*, and maybe think real hard about getting some professional help. Well, I have read the book, so maybe we could work out a deal with the NVA. You know, like in the book: we can come in, blow a bridge, shoot up the area, they can chase us around, and then we all get together under the shade, have a barbecue, and wait for the cash to arrive.

Nah, won't work. They probably have their own version of Manes and Butler. Hey, maybe we can swap them: even up. We give them Butler and Manes to settle the chop in their gene pool. Throw in Billy as a kicker, wait a couple of months and they would sue for peace. We take their version of the terrible trio and train them to fight pit bulls and make a fortune in Mexico. Eldon saunters off, shaking his head at us.

Now most people would find this distasteful but that's the way it goes; we get past the heavy stuff by looking at the bizarre. I remember something Berg told me in One-Zero school after the note in the boot incident. I asked him what the hell he was doing in Vietnam.

He looked at me with that little smirk he always affected, smiled and said, "I'm trying to develop a sense of humor."

* * *

The wake continues and we head for the town around eight. All of us pile on the deuce and a half and in a couple of jeeps. We are going to the Pink House, then to the China Night. I am sober by the time we get downtown. The Beaner is too. What probably helped is that Frank Pulley is driving, and you force yourself to remain cognizant so you can actually see your life flash in front of your mind on impact. Frank has the theory that there is no obstruction to a deuce and a half. The frightened faces of people on little Hondas register, as they swerve to get out of the way. Frank is more insane than Tony, when it comes to driving. He thinks every trip should be a rendition of "Moonshine Run." The worst is Jesse Thompson, who thinks that it should be an Olympic sport.

Soon we are motoring into the parking area next to the Pink House.We pile off and head up the stairs to get a refreshing steam bath. We have a change of fresh clothes and two more days before we have to get another target. The Mama San sees us coming and launches into the house rules: "no shooting, no fighting, good place here, you no be numbah ten." Yeah right Mama San, we can't possibly be bad guys, you must be thinking of someone else. She just looks at us, cackles in disgust, and reminds us she knows us. Castro and Cookie and I peel off up the stairs. Actually the Pink House is officially listed as an R&R center for the Korean officers. As we are walking up the stairs, a gaggle of Marines are coming down.

In their case it is bad timing. The Cookie is leading and refuses to give ground. Naturally, the Corps takes offense at this lack of manners. They are all young officers. One reaches out to gesture the Ranger Monster out of the way, and gets tossed ass over teakettle down the stairs. A short rush with fists and kicks, and we are past. We get to the top and peel off to the steam rooms, strip down, and get in the box. The heat feels good. A girl comes in with a tray of Ba Mi Ba beer and glasses of ice. Perfect. Cook looks up from his box; he looks like a talking head, one with a swollen eye anyway.

"I'm going to miss those guys."

"So are we all, buddy. That's the way it goes though, some days you get the bear, some days you are bear food."

"You ever think about dying?" he asks.

"He's too stupid to think of dying," Castro chips in from across the hall.

"I used to but it's really just a reflection now, too busy living at the moment," I reply, letting the steam relax my muscles.

"Yeah, I guess that's so with me too." This is getting too serious. I spit and tell him,

"Now the Beaner there, he thinks about dying all the time because he is such an obnoxious little shit."

"That's not what your sister said," comes from across the hall.

"The only sisters you know were smacking your genitalia with a ruler, who are you bullshitting?" I shoot back.

"That's why they put me across the hall alone with my own little beer fetcher and you two are in the peasant suite."

Cook slips out of his steam box and is gone for a few minutes, then comes back in.

"Where did you go?" I ask him as he is climbing back in. He hands me a refill on the beer and some more ice for the glass.

"I turned up the steam on the Cuban's steam box; we should hear him in a few." We both giggle in anticipation of par-boiled Cuban. I look at Cook and ask him in jest, "Do you suppose Cubans taste like pork?"

"I'm sure going to miss those guys," he muses to himself.

Yes, we all will, and still do to this very day.

CHAPTER 10

Dancing in the Dragon's Jaws

It's hotter than hell, and for some reason the air conditioner has broken down. I look over and see that it appears to have MGW. That would stand for multiple gunshot wounds. Oh great, I wonder which of us did that last night. We are recuperating at Marble Mountain in Da Nang. The wounded AC will facilitate a panic operation to secure a new one before the day is out.

I'm dressed in a towel, my gold chain and 24-carat dog tags. I am proud of them. J. Graves, a seriously demented alumnus of Delta project, had given them to me. On one side is all the usual data except on the line for religious preference it says: Close Air Support. The flip side has an inscription in English, Vietnamese and Chinese: "If I am dead and you are pilfering my body, fuck you." I open the door and step out into the glaring morning sun. It hurts your eyes with a normal head, and right now I have a head the size of Milwaukee.

Adjacent to us is the RT Moccasin hooch. Dave Daugherty is sitting on a lawn chair, dressed in some kind of swim trunks, with a garden hose ending about three feet from him in a lawn sprinkler. The sprinkler is rotating in a swizzle of water being thrown everywhere. Lying face up, obviously unconscious, is Wagy, and next to him is a figure in what appears to be a hula skirt and a fireman's helmet that I think is Laurent.

"Dave! What are you doing?" He shakes himself up from what must be the bad night of record. He leans up in some kind of Komodo Dragon stance and says to me:

"We're practicing for the monsoon." Clear, simple, perfectly logical. I need a beer.

I wander back inside. The Cookie is curled up in an indigenous sleeping bag. Mac is sprawled naked on his bunk, with a grenade clutched in his hand. I peek, and sure enough the pin is still in it. He must have taken it to bed in some deranged idea of it being an insurance policy against being trifled with. With the light on, that would have been hard to miss. We always sleep with the lights on because if you turn them off, thousands of cockroaches come out and crawl around. I actually woke up one night and had a blanket of moving roaches on the poncho liner I was lying under.

I swizzle a cold beer from the cooler and spit it outside just as Captain Butler, an officer who leads RT Anaconda, and Lieutenant Festes Hagen, the other half of a running team with Tony Anderson on Indigo, come up the walk. I need a shower. I grab my shaving kit and start out the door. Bad news in this place always comes in pairs.

"Where are you going?' Captain Butler inquires solicitously.

'I need to paint my toenails, Sir." I reply.

"Is Mac awake?" Festes queries.

"No, he went home to Alabama and took Cook with him to help train his dogs." I reply. What the fuck do these two want this early in the day? Whatever it is, we want no part of it.

"There is a meeting of all Recon personnel at eleven hundred hours this morning," Butler says in his best Army lingo-ese. "We just wanted to make sure you guys are up." Sure, I am thinking, like the two of you are the welcome wagon for the neighborhood. Something is up and it smells bad. I don't know what Butler is doing here anyway. He is supposed to go become something at our Thai launch site, like supreme gorilla or bouncer at the orangutan orphanage. I don't know, I don't care, and I have a bad head. This is too much cranial activity this early in the day.

I head over to the showers, vaguely noting a red spot on the ground at the base of Mac's monkey pole. God it is bright out here. Is all this sunlight necessary? We know where we are. I fetch a metal folding chair, and sit under one of the showerheads with the hot water on. It is hot and it hurts. I am not the only one that feels this way: I see Frank Pulley in a chair and his eyes look like they are made out of lasers.

"Frank, are you able to understand English?" I ask him, but it appears Frank isn't home yet. His head lolls to the side and a groan escapes his lips.

"Okay Frank, but do you know what happened to Mac's monkey?" I ask him. This perks him up. He slides up in the chair, spits, looks at me, and smiles.

"Well, son," he starts in a slow drawl, real wicked and nasal. "You must have been real messed up if you don't remember that."

"Remember what?"

"Does *Mac* know what you and Cook did with the monkey?" he inquires, with a snide look. This is not good, and he is starting to eye me like I am soon to be the goat on the altar of some crude get-even joke fest. On top of that, there is the insinuation that the Cookie is involved. Well that's disturbing news because one doesn't make the Cookie part of a practical joke unless one wants to be leaking from multiple holes. It is double bad because Cook hates the bloody monkey.

"The monkey? I don't know, Frank; does Mac know what about the monkey? Is there something wrong with the monkey?" He looks up at me and snickers; an evil cunning look passes over his face.

"You mean the Mini Mac doesn't know that you killed his monkey yet?" The best defense here is offense, I decide.

"I don't know what you are talking about, Frank, besides I am sure that there are witnesses that will testify that Cook and I were with the chaplain when this sordid affair happened." This only elicits a snort of derision from him. My mind is starting to wind up, I am thinking of plausible excuses for the memory that I can't retrieve. How do I extricate Cookie and myself from the scene of the crime? Frank is still babbling, following me out into the sunlight as I walk back up the sidewalk.

I decide to take his tale of woe into RT Moccasin's hut, now occupied by Dave and Wagy. Dave has a bemused look on his face as I dig through their team box. Frank is going on and on about the monkey. I am intent on finding some sort of defense mechanism before Mac gets stirring and finds the red spot at the bottom of the pole. I haven't much time. I will need something that has some range, but won't kill my little Swamp Creature hunting buddy; something that will only knock him out. CS gas grenade? No, it will take too long and he can still shoot, besides we have thrown so much of it in the club, we are all immune to its effects. Aha! Dave has a Taser in his locker. I remember that the acronym stands for Tom Mix's Amazing Secret Electric Rifle. It is just what the doctor ordered. I check it, making sure that it is charged and ready.

I am only half listening, but I get the whole story from Frank, who is now gleefully pushing me into the deep kemchi pit. Evidently Cook and I had come back from the club and discovered that the monkey had broken into our hut with his usual insidious craft. We chased the screaming little shit back out, after discovering not only had he eaten the beef jerky I received in a care package from home, but also he had shit on everything. Then we mutually decided to end his terror campaign once and for all.

I evidently came up with the bright idea to feed the monkey screwdrivers laced with Darvon in the hope of overdosing him. The fur bucket loved screwdrivers. The monkey was all whacked out on the drugs and alcohol when Lamar came sauntering by. We threw the half-shitfaced monkey on Lamar from the dark and shrieked with glee when Lamar came completely unglued. He pulled out a 357 revolver and tried to shoot the screaming little banshee but had only driven it back up the pole. By this time, all the dogs in camp came over to see if the time had come for canine payback on their hated antagonist. Lamar was reloading at the base of the pole. Herr Monkey was wobbling at the top. All of a sudden the monkey spread his arms, as if beseeching some great simian deity for salvation, and keeled over backwards.

The monkey did a back flip, landing at poor Lamar's feet. Lamar stared at the monkey for a second, but before he could react, about six of the camp dogs rushed in, and in a snarling, snapping, frenzy, rendered the unconscious monkey into a few tufts of fur and a memory.

Cook and I threw some gasoline on the monkey's remains and set it on fire in some sort of primitive cleansing ceremony, patched up the totally freaked-out Lamar and then went to bed. Mac must have come home so pie-eyed he didn't see the red spot and charred pole.

Taser in hand, I slip over to our hooch; I can hear Cook and Mac stirring inside. I hide the Taser behind my back as I step up to the door. I close my eyes for a few seconds to restore my night vision, then step through the door. Mac has his back to me and is hopping around on one foot trying to put his pants on. I don't hesitate: I fire the Taser and it hits Mac square in the left cheek of his ass and 150,000 volts at one thousandth of a milliamp race down the monofilament and zap his nervous system into orbit. He yelps, and then hits the floor in a twitching heap. I sling the Taser over on my bunk and jerk the wire and dart out, then yell at Cook to help me get Mac undressed and into the bed. As we are doing that, I bring him up to date on the monkey nightmare. He looks at me when I am finished and asks:

"Why did you shoot Mac with the Taser? He is going to be really pissed when he wakes up now." And he looks at me with a scowl.

"Not if he doesn't know what hit him, moron, and I'm sure not going to tell."

If you have ever been hit with a Taser a number of things happen, not the least of which is that you are befuddled and have severe memory loss for about half a day. I quickly explain that our cover story will be that he was hit last night by lightning when he was standing outside by the monkey pole. Luckily the monkey took the brunt of the charge. It was entirely the monkey's fault, perched out there in the howling rain, like some sort of simian lightning rod.

This is why I am the One-One on this goat rodeo; I am supposed to be the one that comes up with Plan B for emergency situations. We are getting our collective story together as Mac begins to come around. By this time, more of the ghouls have showed up. They are crowding the doorway with Frank in their lead. When they see what we have done, there is a collective snickering, and bets being placed as to our surviving this.

Cook is glaring a warning to all and sundry as we solicitously help Mac get up and dressed. All the while we are both cooing about how we were concerned he would never come around, and rushing him so we can get to the meeting.

He is pretty mushy but we get to the club and sit him squeezed between us. If we can make it through the morning, this will all blow over. Maybe we will buy him a bamboo bear, let him have a pet if he wants one. Anything is better than a monkey.

The rest of Recon comes stumbling in and takes their seats as well. Everyone looks at us and makes their little jibes about us being so solicitous towards our One-Zero, followed by laughter. Mac is starting to shoot us sidewinder glances as Manes strides up to the front. Well, actually striding is something he physically cannot do. He *stomps* up to the front of the room. If you close your eyes it sounds just like a runaway Clydesdale.

"Gentlemen, the party is over," he begins. "As of last night we are going to have to deploy more and more teams on a fast turnaround in order to meet requirements from Saigon. That means that teams in training and teams that are being reconstituted will be getting on line faster and you will all be seeing a lot more of the launch sites." This goes on for about an hour and a half. In the end, we are all appalled to find out that our missions are not only going to get more frequent, but also that stand-down time is going to get shorter. We are supposed to get one day stand-down for every day on the ground. We had managed to get two days out of our last suicide run. Now it was going to get worse? Christ, aren't they killing us off fast enough?

The monkey episode is forgotten, as we all have knots where our guts used to be. This is catastrophic; we are bleeding to death as a unit. We are having dark thoughts, on top of the spine tingling sensation of impending doom. Don't those assholes in Saigon realize that we are dying out there? I know they put up with a lot of indiscretions, bordering on multiple court-martial quality, from us. We know it and push our leeway to the limit because we know we are vital, but it seems as if they just finally decided to put a stop to that. Shit, they are just going to run us until we all are dead.

The general feeling is that Saigon doesn't care, since in many cases we are just bait anyway. Get in, stir them up, and make them come up on the radio. At least with some sort of modified raids we can do just that. But, our area is going to be the A Shau and there isn't anyone there except bad guys. The A Shau is the perfect place to hide divisions and support them from over the border. Besides, with the new plan it saves Saigon the trouble of mislabeling these as Recon missions. We are going to shoot our way in, then shoot our way out, which would fit the term "raid" to a tee. The only other thing we have in our bag of tricks is the static road watch. That is where you grab a hilltop; fortify it until it looks like one of the robber baron's castles, and hold on while you direct the air force to bomb everything around you into mulch and afterthoughts.

As we are leaving the mess hall, Mac stops and turns to look at us. His face looks like a hound dog that just found out he wasn't going to the coon hunts.

"I know you two killed my monkey, I know it as sure as I know my name. Don't bother to deny it because neither one of you can lie your way out of a paper bag." I look at Cook, who just shrugs and makes some sort of mumbling noises. I look at the Mini Mac, and then say to him with what little contriteness I can muster for the simian nightmare:

"Look, we are sorry Mac, we can't undo what happened. If you want a monkey, we will go buy you a new one, we might even force ourselves to like the little cretin if it makes you happy."

He looks at us, then chuckles as we walk along.

"Screw the monkey, I have you two, that's enough pets for anyone." He grins and snickers. "Lamar came over last night real late, and told me what happened. I was going to make you two sweat it out this morning."

"Does that mean we are even?" I am just grateful he took it so well.

"No."

"Uh, and why not?"

"T. A. S. E. R." He spells it out, and then laughs as he starts to walk away. Cook looks at me, shrugs, and then says to me:

"You want to tell me again why you are the One-One, Stretch?"

This is great. Not only do I have to worry about thousands of pissed-off NVA gunning for me, I will have to watch my back for the pay-back if and when we ever get a stand-down again. My mind is reeling with counterstrokes, and in the process, I forget my fear of the turn in events in Saigon's tactical plan for us.

CHAPTER 11

No Rest for the Wicked

"How are you doing?" It's Mac, and God he looks terrible. I'm even further gone than he is: my lungs are on fire, and my whole body is exhausted. I lay where I have fallen, taking big gasping breaths, trying to get back to where I don't have tunnel vision.

"I'm dying, that's how I am!" I gasp again, and when I inhale my throat and lungs rasp with dryness. I pause and dig for my canteen. I need water. I need oxygen.

We are lying on the side of an old rockslide, now overgrown with scrub and grass, with a canopy of pine trees that shield us from overhead observation. Above us is the summit of this damn hill and a ridge loping up across a narrow spine to the top of the plateau. We are sprawled where we stopped, in a spread formation to compensate for the open terrain. We are all exhausted. I can see the agony that is plainly marking everyone's face; but we need to get to higher ground, somewhere we can defend and give them no access slope. We are on the run, we are almost out of options, and we are in Laos.

Mac is moving around, checking everyone in front of me. I struggle to my knees, then get up in a crouch and start moving down the formation in the other direction. I get to the first Yard; he is staring down slope attentively, but still taking in raking breaths. Just walking around is murderous. I tap him on the shoulder; he turns and gives me a strained look. He nods his head and then turns to look down slope again. We can see about two hundred meters, and we are spread out, low against a rock outcropping. I check two more Yards; when I get to Cookie, he is up and checking the two Yards behind him. Good old Cookie, always the Ranger, probably has some Ranger technique that keeps him focused. He probably put a couple of rocks in his boots and sprinkled lit gunpowder on his tongue because he wasn't miserable enough. He comes stalking back, gets real close to my ear and speaks softly. This is incongruous because I am sure they can hear us wheezing in Hanoi.

"I checked the tail gunner and the rest of the Yards. They are alright, but they are getting ragged." I look at him blearily, and between gasping and wanting to throw up from the nausea, manage to get out a short acknowledgment. Cookie looks at me, then asks me softly:

"How far behind us do you think they are?"

"I don't know, Cookie. That last change of direction may put them off for a while but they are bound to bring up more tracker teams. They still have a lot of daylight left. We got maybe a half hour if we are lucky, and if we can get up there where we will be able to fight, we have an hour before the shit hits the fan." He looks at me and mutters "It will" before moving up towards Mac.

I am getting a little better. We have been stopped for about ten minutes. I am starting to get my wind back and my vision is back to normal. There is a breeze but we are soaked in sweat and it is chilling us, despite it being relatively mild temperature wise. Much better than on the valley floor, hundreds of feet below us. I feel like I have lost twenty pounds, most of it on the grueling switchback we have just thrown, trying to buy some time and room. We need room; we need to get somewhere we can fight and hold them. More importantly we need the weather to clear because without the air getting here we are going to get run to earth. Then they will come and kill us. Thank God the NVA don't have helicopter support or we would be dead already. As it is, these guys are good—way too good.

Bop is the only one in a really bad way. An AK had shattered his arm and we compression bandaged it and put a squeezer of blood expander in him. He is sitting on one edge of the bag, to force the stuff into his blood. He doesn't look good at all. He was on his feet when we stopped but he's going to go shocky soon; he has lost a fair amount of blood.

Mac is bending over him, checking his bandage, and Cuman is with him. Bop gives Mac a wan smile. We haven't given him morphine. We have been on amphetamines since late morning. If we give him morphine, he will overdose on a speedball for sure. The amphetamines will counteract with the morphine and your heart just stops. He knows it, but he is in bad pain: it's etched on his face. We need to get out of here.

* * *

We had infiltrated just after dawn yesterday and moved down from the plateau. It was meant to be an area Recon. No contact until this morning when we left the RON and started down the ridgeline from where we had spent the night, moving as fast as we dared down towards Vietnam. We had been moving and stopping for a listen periodically, as was our normal procedure. Just as we sat down for one of these halts, the tail gunner motioned me back. I looked in the direction he was pointing. We had stopped so that we could see back over our trail for some distance. Back where we had started down the escarpment, exactly on line with the trail we had created in our passing, was a three-man NVA element. Shit! Trackers.

I pulled back up to Mac and told him what was happening. We got back up and started to move again. We were traveling down through an old bomb strike. Worse, it was an old CBU, or cluster bomb, strike. These are nasty little affairs with metal winglets that help them slow down and spread out as the canister drops from the aircraft. Out of say five hundred in a canister, probably a dozen or more will not detonate, either because they hung up in a tree, or it was a bad day in Omaha when they built them. So they hang around until someday you come waltzing along and the little demon decides to finally explode.

Sure as spit the NVA know this area, and probably have it marked on their tour maps. Still we figured that we could shake the tracker team and buy some time by leading them through the bomb strike. Going as fast as we dared, we got through the strike and found a small clearing about twenty yards across. I had dragged Pandora's box along with me. This is a homemade anti-tracker device. It consists of a cigar box with the motor out of a toy powered by a nine-volt battery. The electrical leads to the motor which has a reduction gear that attaches to the pins of a mini CS grenade and a white phosphorous grenade. The switch is a plastic tube with a metal ball bearing in it. If the device is moved the ball bearing slides down and completes the circuit. The motor pulls the pins out of the clipped off spoons. The CS goes off first and then the WP.

I had added a bright red propeller on top, and a row of itty bitty Christmas tree lights that blinked on and off, which we had stolen from Capt. Butler after he got shot in the head. His mom had sent him a miniature Christmas tree with blinking lights on it. Perfect for my creation. It sounds ridiculous but it worked once before. The natural curiosity of the trackers would make it irresistible. After a hurried conference we decided to give it a try.

We made a concerted effort to obscure our trail, as it skirted the long axis of the clearing. Just as if we were trying to buy distance yet still being cautious. We had placed the device on the ground along with a PIR ration pack, as if they had fallen out of an open pouch on someone's rucksack. I removed the safety and we went up a bit further, then fish-hooked back on our trail.

We laid out in a position where we could see the device and took out the silenced weapons we had with us. We didn't have long to wait. After twenty minutes or so, the trackers broke cover, three of them. The first was crouching and looking for low sign. The second one was scanning the area with an AK ready, and the third had a radio. If they didn't fall for the device we were going to take them out with the silenced weapons and grenades. If we got lucky, everyone would figure that they ran into one of the old CBUs and it detonated. That was the plan anyway. The radio was a bad sign and changed everything because they were obviously in contact with someone. On the other hand, if they didn't have a radio it would mean they had backup right behind them.

The trackers moved over to the device. The one with the radio motioned the first one over and the other two stood back. The first one took out a wood stick and probed around the food packet, and then the device. He grinned and said something to the leader. He had obviously found the mousetrap detonator affixed to the bottom. He seemed perplexed that the safety was still in it…all like we had planned. We wanted them to think the thing was inert, that we had dropped it by mistake and had not placed it on purpose. The other two came over as the first one stood up. They had almost reached him when the circuit closed, the lights started flashing and the little propeller began to whirl. He stood there with a shocked *oh shit* look on his face just as the CS grenade went off.

The gas got all three perfectly. As they were hopping around, the white phosphorus went off. The one without the radio tried to get away but he had a great burning wound in his side. Mac shot him with the silenced weapon.

We then picked up and started back up the slope, trying to grab some terrain we could either hold or shake them in. These three were only the eyes and ears of the group that would be hunting us. It worked, in that we bought some time. It wasn't much but it was enough.

We ran into a squad-size element about an hour later. They were just suddenly there. Both sides looked at each other for a second, then we rolled over them. The survivors fled from our initial assault and scurried off to the east. We did a quick rummage through the dead as we passed, just a cursory grabbing at their pockets and equipment for any intel that will help fill out the picture for the analysts back in Saigon. Looking the weapons over, Cook found one of them with some sort of scope on his weapon. He was still carrying the weapon.

We had moved quickly back the way we came, then struck south, planning on letting them follow our back trail and hoping our pursuers wouldn't notice that we had stepped off where the trail climbed past a low cliff. Loi had done his magic in covering the trail. I thought these guys would have to be really good to pick that up.

They had been. Two hours later we ran into a larger force that seemed to be the flank of some sort of line formation. We rolled past their flank, then began to get shots, lots of them, from downhill. Breaking contact, we started moving southwest, then due west.

After that contact it dawned on us that this wasn't a normal NVA infantry unit. We had either been spotted, or we'd had real bad luck because an anti-recon team was pursuing us. Those guys hadn't been on line for nothing. They'd been on line because they were sweeping up to where a blocking force would be waiting for us. Once they closed the box we were dead: they would just shrink it down until we had nowhere to go.

They would wait until more troops came up, and come kill us. We had no choice: we had to move fast. We got Bop patched up on the run and everyone took a Hornet. It worked enough that we were able to get outside the box. We took the high ridge as a route. It would take time to get their guys down from the top and we could force the bastards behind us to climb like us. They wouldn't know where we were so they would come on slowly, but there would be a lot of them. Whoever the enemy commander was, he knew he could block us from the plateau. There were plenty of trails up there. They had trucks and their troops strategically placed so they could close off a grid.

Our little ruse would throw off the average run-of-the-mill regular, but these guys were working very coordinated and precise. Their trackers tended to be Montagnards just like ours but from other northern fringes of the Bru and Sedang. We called them Indian Bru. They could pick up sign from where a gnat peed. So far there had been no signal shots. That was bad. That meant they had radios at the maneuver level. All my nightmares were coming true. The sniper scope was the clincher: they didn't have snipers or shooters with the line units. These guys had all been fairly well seasoned too, not a bunch of kids. We got a good look at the three we killed. They looked like they'd been eating regularly and were in good shape. We had to hope the Hornets would give us a little bit of an edge. It wouldn't be much, but terrain and our ability to outrun them was all we had.

The last hour had been a grueling ordeal: it stretched us to the limit, even with the added boost the Hornets were giving us. I knew what Mac was looking for.

We needed a killing ground, some place where we could buy time and hold, praying that we could get some air on top of us. We finally made contact with Covey. He was reporting a solid socked-in fog situation above us, but the wind was blowing upslope so it might clear the edge of the plateau. I was fervently praying that the winds be strong today.

We get up and start moving again. A couple of the Yards are with Bop, helping him along, and we are moving fast. We top the small rise in front of us and see a finger ridge protruding off to the south. It is forested and about twenty meters wide in some cases. The far side is a sharp series of knifelike fingers, sloping up to the plateau. More importantly, there is a stand of trees at the top with thick trunks, and large boulders about fifty yards from their bases. We have to get in there and we have to get a position prepared before they overtake us. We will have to climb up the web to get there, but it means they will too, and *they* will be winded and ragged just like us, when they come under our guns.

The terrain we are climbing is almost vertical in places and slippery, leading up to the ridgetop. I am gasping for breath by the time we get there. We spread out. The boulders and the copse of trees are as perfect as it gets when you have to pull it out of your ass. We have high ground behind us but they can't come in any force.

The knifelike ridges and the ravines might give us trouble later, but we can guard our back door with three guys, leaving the front for the rest of us. That's a lot of firepower we can throw out front, at anyone who assaults across the open ground. We might get lucky. We had better get lucky; we might be able to hold them for awhile but weather and time will be on their side if it doesn't clear.

We can see the killing ground between us and where the ridge begins to slope up: it is downhill and narrow and the sides drop off. I go down one side while Cook takes the other. About twenty meters from the edge of our perimeter the ridge drops off to the north in a vertical cliff about fifty-foot high with few or no hand holds. There are a few roots near the top but none down below, and no tree crowns on line with the top. The massif behind us is no better. They could, over the course of time, get a couple of guys down here and maybe get at this side, but it would take awhile. I put a claymore in the area that will cover the most of the shelf below, then work my way up to my position. Cook gets back a few minutes later. He is sweat-stained like I am and out of breath. The Yards are digging with what they can, and pulling branches into position to give us protection from shrapnel.

The NVA will use B40s, and in these rocks, the rockets will create hell. They will try to put so much fire in here that it will make us keep our heads down. The trees will absorb a lot of the punishment; we will have to live with the B40 problem. Since an RPG is accurate in this terrain only for about a hundred meters, there aren't that many places they can fire from, at least not without our being able to kill them. Anyone that even looks like he is carrying one of those water pipes is going to be a prime target. I am worried about them bringing up mortars. That will be their killing stroke.

"How does it look?" Mac asks Cook and me. I am least ragged so I tell him:

"Pretty good on this side. We have dead ground to our rear though, and they may eventually get up that cliff." I explain the lay of the ground, and then he turns to Cook. It's about the same on his side. No cliffs until you get about fifty meters down, then it drops thirty or so feet to another shelf. All the times I played war as a kid, I would have loved to have this terrain.

We huddle, working out the plan and getting claymores out. We will let them come up to us. Let them get as close as we can. They won't come in a group; the terrain won't let them. If we wait until they are real close we can blow the claymores and get the first order. No shooting till they come on again. We will use the two claymores furthest out on that side to open up with. They might be fooled into thinking we booby-trapped our trail and trick them into coming at a run. If we can catch them grouped up, we can kill a bunch. They will back off and regroup, but they will come back. The first two ploys are going to buy us time, is all. If we are lucky, we may buy half an hour after we get the second group. This is a seasoned outfit that is hunting us, and they will be ready for some other tactic.

We have one more claymore. We will save that one for breaking the assaults when we can. Mac says he will take the two clackers for the first one and blow them. Make sure none of the team opens up until the second group comes. Mac has the radio; he is slightly behind and between Cook and where I have positioned myself.

We are in a horseshoe formation, with three of the little guys about twenty yards behind us. I have one of the Yards with a B40 to my right and Bop to the left of me with another as the flank. I take out grenades and start digging as best I can with my knife and hands. I need a shallow hole that gives me some cover. I pull over two logs, about five inches in diameter, to protect my side. The roots of a tree about forty-foot high protect my left side. I hope it's ironwood; I don't even know if that grows here, but I read that it's the hardest wood there is. Right now, I wish there was such a thing as a bulletproof steel tree, and this was it.

I finish digging out a depression. I can see Mac; he is crouched down and talking on the radio. The clouds are starting to thin out a little, then they close back up. I see a glimpse of blue through a thin one. Please let this weather clear, I'll be nice to old ladies, won't pick my nose, and won't do that other thing. Just please make a hole in these clouds.

Mac comes down to where I am, in a crouch, and tells me that Covey can see patches to our west, and then it is clear about ten kilometers out. The clouds are moving west but they seem to be crawling. He slithers off and tells Cook the same news, then goes back to his position. We will fight here, and try to hold out. We might as well because we haven't time to find another place that will give us the edge. If the weather closes in and we get pounded, we will try to hold out until nightfall and hope it rains and we don't have too many wounded. If not, we will attempt to slip out and make it to the river.

We had climbed up and back west so we may still be in Laos. They aren't supposed to be here and we aren't either. I doubt if we can call time out, and everyone will go off and find some new place to have this out.

They are going to come and finish this, and soon. I am checking all my equipment and putting out some drums where I can get to them. I have the RPD and six hundred rounds. Cookie comes over with another 300 rounds, all belted up that his half of the team had been carrying in their rucksacks. I will use them first, since my ammo is in the drums. I make sure the gun has plenty of LSA grease on the slide arm. It works the best. First it will melt and then it will sustain itself in the metal.

After about twenty minutes Covey is still reporting he has found no holes in the cloud big enough to get down under and see where we are. The top of the plateau we are on is the cloud base.

There is some furtive movement on the other side. I snap my fingers at Bop and the others, point in the direction I saw the movement, then at my eyes, and shrug. They all tune in. I see the first of the NVA about a hundred and fifty meters out, as he steps cautiously between a tree and a small boulder. Three more follow him. Shit, the third one has what looks like a PRC-25: must be the Chinese copy. He has an earphone on one ear. Bad news: it's a tracker team, and they have about ten others that we can see ranged out to the left and right of them.

Cook is snapping his fingers; I look over and he points to his right front, makes the walking motion with his hand then shows two hands full, ten fingers. That means ten more on his right flank. At least a platoon is close on their heels, probably a company behind them climbing up after us. I hope they all have heart attacks. That climb almost killed us.

The trackers come on, the two in front looking for high sign and then the team leader and two guys behind him. They are spread out and are looking right at us. They get about halfway to us when they go to ground. The leader rises up and fires a full magazine right at our position, and then another guy opens up. Everybody on our side holds their fire. They too saw this was a good defensive position and surmised if we were going to ground we would do it here. They are just trying to see if they can spook us into firing.

Their team leader gets back on his radio again. He makes a hand motion and two of them start zigzagging up to us. They are almost up on the far claymore when the rest of the tracker team comes up in a rush. Mac lets one of the claymores go and it sweeps the ridge, killing all of them. The leader is down in the middle; the others are blasted into limp dolls in front and to his side.

We hear shouts from the wood line on other side when an RPD starts to rake our position from left to right. You can hear the rounds ricocheting off the rocks. They are high. People tend to shoot high uphill. The gunner adjusts, and they come pinging in the cracks between the boulders and trunks. Everyone is down. There is a clamor on the other side and some shouting, then it goes quiet. We see a figure come up and look us over with binoculars; he is obviously an officer of some sort, and doing his leader's Recon. I see Cookie has the Draganov with the scope on it taking aim at him, but the figure crouches by some trees, then slides off to the right and disappears. We wait.

After about fifteen minutes there is a roar from the wood line to our front, and the tree above Cook blows itself into splinters. I get smacked in the side by something. I feel my way down and there is no serious leaking and nothing vital hanging out, so I am fine. I look over at the little people. Bop looks like warmed-over death; the others are scrunched down but still alive.

Another ten minutes go by. A little bit of sky opens up above us then moves by. The winds are really whipping the clouds over and past us. We get three more rockets thrown at us, then here they come, about ten of them moving in a crouch, and another group behind them about fifty meters. They are hugging the little bit of cover the right flank affords. There are about six close together on my left. The B40 is aimed right at them. There are four guys on a line about twenty meters in front of them. We wait until they are within twenty meters of our position when we open up on them. The lead figures dance and jerk, then fall. The B40 catches the six that were on the flank, and shreds them into pieces. One is blown right off the cliff on that side and I hear him scream as he goes over. We are working from the far left, then towards the middle, and back again. We have caught about thirty of them with their pants down, as quickly as that it's over. They know we are here now, and that the first claymore wasn't a booby trap. They will get organized now that they know we have gone to ground. Save your ammo, we are going to need it.

I push the claymore I have left between two boulders then move it to the left. The rock will protect me from the back blast. I promise myself I won't use it until there are a whole bunch of them.

The weather is trying to clear. The other side knows that and if they don't get right on us they are going to be in a bad spot when the cavalry comes. We are getting a spot of luck here, I am thinking to myself, and have begun to think we might actually survive this one when four B40 rockets crash into the trees above us and the concussion gives me a nose bleed. Right after that come four more. Too bad Clyde, you are going to have to get closer to get a low enough shot for that trick to work. At least they don't have a mortar, or our heinies would be cooked.

The only way they can use the B40 effectively is to get behind us on one of those spurs and shoot down on us. There is no way around us, at least not a quick way. I am being smug about maybe surviving this, when two of the little people open up from the rear. Not on auto, but single shots. I slither back and check what is coming up from that side.

Ti Ti points off toward the north, grins and tells me, "Two VC, I kockadau them." I can see a Bata boot sole sticking between two rocks out about seventy meters. They must have slipped off the ridge in front of my position and run along the base to try to climb up and behind us. I go back to my position. In about ten minutes, I see a bunch of them move real quickly and slide off the ridge to my left. I wait until I calculate they are below the claymore I put there earlier, then I torch it off. There is an immediate secondary explosion then another smaller one, and you can hear a couple of them screaming their hearts out down there. It must have caught someone carrying a rocket, and the hot pellets detonated it. The second explosion sounded like it was a grenade; probably the same thing happened again. I wait a few minutes and bounce a grenade over the edge. It goes off and the screams stop.

Cook's side opens up and I can hear him shouting directions at the little people. I hear two grenades go off, then another B40 smacks into the trees above him. Someone is whimpering over there but it sounds like it is outside our perimeter. Mac is talking on the radio, then Covey comes down through a hole and crosses to our front real quick and pulls back up through the soup to the north. An immense relief passes through me. At least we aren't alone.

Mac's face is furrowed in concentration and the radio is glued to his ear. Another B40 impacts high and to the right, then a sustained long burst of fire comes from our right. The rounds are hitting mostly above Mac's position, but some are getting down in the rocks with us. You can hear their angry, mean little screams as they ricochet around in the rocks. Mac rolls to one side, then curses and yells out that the radio is dead. We all go on to the emergency radios. I can hear Mac talking to Covey on the URC-10. He is calmly giving a status report and I hear Covey tell him that he has Spads up there, they will try to come down through the hole and thread the needle.

He no sooner finishes than I hear the Spads coming from the southeast. Mac yells "Get down, nape!" and they flash by. Seconds later the ridge to our right is engulfed in flame. The heat blasts us, but the carnage down there is unbelievable.

Two figures come stumbling out into the open and one of the Yards drops them. They are completely on fire. We hear a fifty open up to our northwest, along the top of the plateau, then both Sandys are gone up through the soup. Before I can get my breath back, Mac yells, "Here they come," and I look back at my front and see lots of folks moving. They need to get right on top of us, or die out there in the open where the aircraft can get at them.

I hear another set of Sandys coming, as the figures start to reach some of the open ground. The ridge is a dirty smudge now, with little wisps of smoke and open flames coming from the brush and scrub that is still cooking. There aren't any leaves left on any of the trees. It looks like one of those films about the Somme in WWI. I suddenly have a craving for a can of C-ration peaches. I can taste them, it's so strong. Fear must trigger your memory receptors.

I can see a bunch of them working through the trees: they are shooting and screaming, to keep up their courage. Cook is yelling back at them, pure commando comic's stuff. Me, I want to be on the beach, anywhere but here with all these angry people. I hear the second set of Spads roaring closer, then two more walls of flame wash over the hill, preceded by 20 mm shells that rake through their formations. About fifteen are up close when that happens and I trigger the claymore I promised I wouldn't use until there was a bunch. Well, fifteen is a bunch. That knocks the wind out of the assault and it drifts off over the ridge to our front. Another set of Sandys drops out to the northwest and dumps more nape on the reverse slope. I hear Mac yell that choppers are fifteen minutes out, and I see glorious sunshine lighting up the valley off to the southeast.

More help arrives in the form of two F4s that come roaring in and drop hard bombs on the hilltop to our front and on its reverse slopes. I look out at the crumpled bodies in front of me; I can see two of them real close. They are wearing a bluish green uniform and they look young. These are different uniforms from the tracker team that was following us and pushing us hard. This is probably a reaction force comprised of regulars, usually a semi-green unit. Makes sense: use the troops less trained once they have boxed us in. Save the bunch that ran us to ground for the finesse work.

Some of the other bodies that aren't burned so badly still have a few remnants of uniform left; all have the blue green except the ones we dropped earlier. Amazingly the team leader of the tracking team is still lying out there in a little patch of green, completely unburned…dead as you can get, but unburned. Go figure that one. I am sure that somewhere, wherever they made the napalm, it must have been Friday afternoon and someone in a hurry screwed something up so they weren't armed or filled right. Somebody in a hurry to get home to get laid left this poor bastard with a clean deathbed. Perfect: the circle of life, or some other great karmic mystery, I am sure. All I know is that I, and my friends, are going to live.

Mac yells out that we will use the ground to our front for an LZ. Cook and his group are to go first. He has two wounded there. I shift Bop over to him and Bong comes chugging past me to fill in his slot.

"*Sieg Heil*," he mutters at me as he goes past, and grins like a possum in a henhouse. He has spent far too many years with those krauts in the Legion when the French were here. They warped his young mind. Hell, he must be at least forty-five by now, but he isn't even breathing hard. Yep, Bong is harder than Chinese poetry. Twisted as you can get, but hard.

Two gunships come up from the south, then two more; they are working over the far side and off below our right front. Then I see a slick coming up and we are moving down to the LZ, about fifty meters into the killing ground. There is just enough room to get one slick in at a time. The guns and the rest of the air gods are working over what is beyond that and the ground behind us. The first slick comes in and settles, and Cook is on it with his part of the team. They lift off and start to pull off to the north. There is no ground fire. Too bad the bodies up here are all burned; we could maybe grab some documents off them.

Cuman comes running up. He has the tracker team's radio and some other stuff. He looks at me and points out at the body, and says *Dai Uy*. Ah, the leader was a captain. Not a good day for captains. The second bird comes in and smacks down hard and we are all scrambling to get onboard. It jumps into the air and we are pulling for altitude.

To say that the flight back is anticlimactic is an understatement. The sheer joy of being alive is almost intoxicating. Mac and I exchange a few quips about the mission but both of us are soon lost in our own thoughts. The steady vibration of the helicopter and the cool fresh breeze coming in the side have a sedating effect. The door gunner is a young kid, who keeps looking at us as if we were some sort of apparition.

As we settle into the landing pattern at the launch site, I spy Manes standing at the edge of the landing pad. What the hell is he doing here? Did he finally commit some act that was so terrible that he was banished to the launch site?

We land and begin to get off. I pick up my rucksack and with Mac walk over to where Larry is apparently waiting for us. He looks at us and pinches his face up into a grimace.

He starts off, "I heard from the neighbors that you were out there coon hunting and shooting up the real estate. That's got to stop, you degenerates, this is a quiet neighborhood." I look at him and lean forward like I have a big secret.

"We had a prisoner but we let him go. Yessir *Dai Uy*, he knew who is ripping out the last three pages in all the novels up here, before you get to read them. Yes sir, he told us the name."

There is some bastard that has been ripping out the last ten pages or so of all the books at the launch site. So you get into reading one and when you get to the end, it is missing. We hate whoever it is, and have vowed to find him. This doesn't bother Squatty though, since reading isn't on his entertainment list. Instead he quips back,

"Why did you let him go, was he ugly?"

"Nope. Cuter than you." Mac joins in. "In fact there was a strong resemblance to someone we know." And he inclines his head toward Budrow.

"Yes sir, when we found out who, we had to let him go. He was a mason you know, fellow brother and all that," I join in.

Manes looks at us and screws up that bulldog face.

"You two aren't masons, I am the exalted Grand Wizard and we wouldn't let trash like you in. We certainly don't have any morons in the Order."

Cookie looks up and drawls out:

"You sure you're not referring to the Klan, I know for a fact they make that Grand Wizard sheet in an extra stout squat size."

"Okay, you are alright. I was just giving you my superior officer test, to see that you aren't shell shocked or anything before I ask more important questions."

That's a good one if Larry has designed a test. He would have had to because if they actually taught such a thing in officer basic, I guarantee that he skipped that day and a bunch more days like that. Still, it said something that he had met our flight.

We have been talking as we walk over to the head shed. Manes opens the door and all of us pile in and take a seat where we can. The medics have taken Bop over to the Evac hospital with the chase medics. His arm will eventually heal but he can't run Recon anymore, so we will make him a guard at our safe house in Da Nang. We get down to the debriefing.

This has been a scary one. We thought that we could slip in from across the border. Well, it worked, but the valley environments were crawling with the other guys. Worse yet, they had what we'd been suspecting: anti-recon units. Our mission and the one before us were the same. We were run out by the same group with green khakis, trackers, and quick reaction forces, tied by a central command. No horsing around with this bunch. If they get on you, they will run you until you drop, then bring up hard units and kill you. The only hard intelligence we had was what we saw, and the few things from the rucksack and radio from the dead NVA captain. Captains don't command tracker teams; these guys were starting to smell like our counterparts. Not good. This is probably the same group that got Kansas.

Eldon had gotten run out of the AO north of us just a day before we launched. That means they are operating in a box about forty kilometers wide all over the northern end of the A Shau. What is in there that they don't want us to see? Whatever it was, it must be ugly, and I hope someone else draws it before we come up for rotation. We are clean and are going back to Danang tomorrow and then getting four days off.

We finish up and wander out to take a shower and then eat. I am sitting on the team hootch steps when Cuman walks up. He has an NVA canteen with him. It smells like plums. I take a sip. It's delicious. I take another; it is some kind of wine. Cuman says that it is a very special wine, comes only from an area up in the edge of Laos. Near where the Bru lived, at one time. File that for later. Meanwhile it's delicious. It must have been the officer's. Here's to you, Nguyen, I'm thinking. Mac and Cookie take a drink as well. We didn't get but a two-day turnaround after this last mission. So many teams are getting shot up that we were forced to take the mission, with little or no time for a breather in between. This time, I swear, they had better give us some time. We are worn thin, and when that happens you get ragged. That is when you make that final fatal mistake. I need to sleep for about a week. On top of everything else, I am not feeling too good, and it isn't the side effects of the Hornets. I think that I am getting malaria again.

CHAPTER 12

Water of Life

I am shaking like a leaf and chilled all the time; that is, when I'm not burning up with fever. My old nemesis, malaria, has come back to haunt me. So far I have been lucky: I was able to rip all references to it out of my medical files before I came over the last time, and have not had a relapse since I've been here.

But my luck had run out. We hadn't even left Quang Tri and the launch site before I was into a full-blown reoccurrence of the bloody disease. I have been put into the tender care of Doc Wang and his dispensary, which is at least better than being admitted to the field evacuation hospital. That would be the kiss of death, since they would send me back to the States.

For those of you who have never been cursed with malaria, it is the world's fastest weight-loss program. You shed water and body weight, between being chilled or fevered into a cramped and nauseous mess. Once you have it, malaria chooses when it wants to hit you again, usually when your immune system is low from poor diet, stress, etc. That pretty much describes life in Recon. I am wrung completely out, and now I have nothing left to throw up, so my body is slowly consuming itself.

As a bonus, all my ghosts have come back to haunt me. It's like the mind surrenders to the horrors, and you get snippets of demons that come in, torment you, then flit out of your delirium to wait on the sidelines.

In my delirium I am cautiously picking my way through the tall elephant grass, pushing the stalks aside as I move forward. It is hot and I am soaked through and through. Where is the team? I am lost, and I must find them. I keep hearing movement to my sides and front but I never catch a glimpse of who or what is making it. There is something out there and it is hunting me. Not people but some terrible monster. I hear movement to my rear and spin around, taking the safety off my weapon. Come on, you bastard. Come on up close. I feel overwhelming dread. I am so weak and thirsty. Where is the team?

I check my Stabo rig, find my bush axe, and pull it out. I start slashing the elephant grass, chopping it down and pushing it into the ground. I am working feverishly, trying to chop out a clearing in the vast sea that surrounds me. I stop and throw up from the exertion, my guts empty and my bowels void until I have soiled myself thoroughly. It starts to rain again and the cool waters wash the fatigue and the filth off me. I have a clear area now, at least two meters in a circle around me.

At least when whatever is hunting me comes, it will not be able to reach out of the grass and grab me. I am panting and feverish, and oh so weak. I check the gun again, making sure that I have a full belt in it. Come on, let's get it over with; I cannot live with this dread. But there is no more movement, and I hear birds trilling around me. Strange though, they are red wing blackbirds from home. I know they don't have them here in Vietnam. Why are there blackbirds here? Where is the team?

The bush seems totally real to me as it goes quiet as something moves through it. I start to move again. I push myself into the wall of grass at the edge of the clearing. I mark the sun and where the clearing is, in case I have to run back here if a helicopter comes. They won't see me down here in the grass; I might have to use the clearing as an extraction point. I can't think clearly, I am hot and feverish, my mind keeps drifting, and I am so tired. Where is the team? How did I get separated?

The air is muggy as the rain begins to slacken a bit. I break out of the elephant grass and get my first real view of the area that I am in. It is smoking and torn up, with hundreds of bomb-blasted trees. There are craters everywhere. I start to pick my way across the twisted landscape, as the rain continues to fall. The smoke and the mist are obscuring the view, until it becomes like a dense fog that winds and twists itself around the battlefield.

I crawl over the shattered trunk of a tree and come across the site of an air crash. The aircraft was a helicopter, but it now is a twisted mass of metal. There are four guys next to it, obviously the aircrew, broken and wounded. They all are looking around bewildered. They ignore me as if I don't exist. The mist clears and I see that there are hundreds of soldiers from both sides stumbling towards the horizon.

Everyone is stumbling forward, in silence; all ignore me as if I were a mute witness to their agony. Long lines are forming, with American, NVA, Vietnamese, and civilians all mixed in together. I see a Marine and a young girl helping carry an NVA who is trying to hold his intestines in with pale white hands. Neither speaks nor looks up as I pass them. Both are wounded but they are not bleeding.

I cannot stand this, these moving lines of corpses. I see men representing both sides, children, a woman carrying a baby clutched tightly to her chest. The light is fading but there is an orange glow over the horizon, as if a great city was being consumed by fire. I must get there. I must leave this horrible landscape behind.

So thirsty, I am so parched that my thirst drives me to look for water. I stumble over to a crater and apprehensively look over the lip. Please, I plead to the slate-gray skies, don't let there be corpses in it. As if to answer, the bottom of the crater is full of clean water. Beautiful, clean water, and I can see the gravel bottom, and there are small brilliant blue fish whisking by near the surface. I stumble and slide down to the edge of the water, then bend and cup some of it in my hand to draw it to my mouth. It is sweet, clean and my fever seems to melt as I drink it.

I look up and across the crater. Crouched down, and wearing the traditional garb of a Bru tribesman, is an old man. He has a brass pipe in his mouth and he is serenely observing me. It is Bong, our prescient Bru team member who unnerves me at times. He smiles at me and reaches out with his left hand, palm open. The Bru have always taken on the responsibility of watching over the Americans on our team. A warm, safe flush comes over me. I am full of questions, but I know that if he is here, the team is nearby. I want to be safe. I want to be with my team.

"*Trung Si*," he rasps in that gravel voice of his. "You must come out of this place. This place is not for you." He takes a pull on the pipe and exhales a wisp of blue smoke. "I have come for you; it has been a hard journey." He rises and walks around the crater, his feet making no marks in the soft ground. He touches my arm, and then his hand slides down to mine and he grips it tightly.

"Come, we must go now, you must look at me all the while, it is a bad place here," he says softly. Then he turns and we walk off toward the orange glow in the distance. I am no longer stumbling; I feel refreshed and stronger.

"Bong, the water…" I begin. He squeezes my hand before I can finish the question.

"I put the water there, *Trung Si*. I knew you would find it, and you would come to it," he explains. I do not understand how or why, but I know that he did.

We walk for a while longer and the mist begins to close in again. I can no longer see anyone else, and Bong is like a dim figure next to me. I look down at my feet and see that there is green grass in clumps growing in the soil, and the earth is beginning to become the familiar red. I feel Bong's grip loosen and I look up. He is gone, but I hear his voice in front of me.

"Come, *Trung Si*, you are strong enough now. It is not much further and we are waiting for you."

That is enough. I am tired but I know that the team, my team, is ahead. I can make it. It is only a little further…

I realize that my eyes are closed. I open them and I am surprised to find that I am lying on my back. There is a ceiling fan slowly turning above me. A face looms over me. It is one of the nurses from the dispensary, Cho, I think her name is, and then she is gone. I am in the recovery ward at CCN. Then Doc Wang enters, examines the chart, looks up at me, gives me a thin smile and says, "How are you feeling?"

"Like shit," I rasp out; my throat feels like it is lined with sandpaper. There is an IV running into my arm; he checks it and pats my shoulder.

"Don't talk. You need to rest."

"Doc, how long have I been here?"

"Six days," he answers. "You are going to be weak for a while, but the worst part is over. You should have told me that you had malaria before."

"They wouldn't have let me come back."

"Are you glad you did, all things considered?"

He goes out, and I hear voices in the hallway outside. The door opens and eight little smiling faces loom into view. It is the Yards. They are touching my face and patting my arms; all of them seem to be happy I am awake. They stay for a few moments, before the nurse comes in and shoos them out. I sleep for awhile, and then am shaken awake. I look up and see the Mini Mac and Cookie and about six of the other Americans standing around the bed.

"About time you are awake. You have been lying on your malingering ass for nearly a week." Mac grins and punches me on the arm. It hurts; in fact I hurt all over.

"Don't let them send me back to the States, Mac," I begin, but he silences me with a wave.

"Doc already fixed that. He even got Manes to sign off on it." He and Cookie are grinning like crazy, as he continues, "You are going to Taipei for a week's R&R, and the Cookie, Jimmy Johnson, and I are going to Okinawa."

"The team?"

"Oh they are happy as pigs in shit; they are going to Mai Loc for the time we are out." Cook hands me a bottle with a straw so I can take a sip. I look at the both of them, relieved that I am alive and also that I am not going back to the States.

"When do we leave?" I ask.

Mac looks at me with a wry grin and answers offhand, "*We* leave tomorrow, you go as soon as you are stronger, probably three days."

"Mac…" I pause; I need to tell him about where I have been. "Bong, is he here?"

"Don't talk about Bong, the Yards have been acting real weird since you got sick, and Bong has been acting the weirdest of all. They scared the shit out of everyone around here, with all that mumbo jumbo they've been doing down in their hootch."

They all laugh. There are a few more moments of small talk, and then Cho comes in and clucks them away like a mother hen. I'm not being sent home, I am going to Taipei? I drift off to sleep wondering what the catch will be. I will probably have to go there with Castro, that's it.

CHAPTER 13

Oh Brother Rat

Rest and recuperation is wonderful when the war leaves you alone and there isn't a bombing just across the street. I was accompanied to Taipei by friends who had down time, and used my allotted four days, to take in some sunshine as well as the absence of the war. Then, my leave got extended, thanks to Davidson.

On the last night, we had been preparing ourselves for the return to Vietnam when Davidson came back to the hotel with a cage made of bamboo. I didn't even want to ask him what it was all about. He was probably related to the evil-looking thing inside. It was by far the mangiest rat I had ever laid eyes on. It crouched in the bottom corner of the cage and made little hissing sounds.

Davidson whistled away under his breath as he took out what looked like a portion of a wiring harness about eight inches long. It was one of those strand cables with about fifty different-colored wires sticking out one end of it. He smeared the cable with cooking grease of some kind; it smelled of cooked meat and spices. Then he stuck it in the cage with Monsieur Rat, opened two Chinese beers, and handed me one. I started to let curiosity overcome caution, but he motioned me to be quiet. Best not to disturb Texans when they get like this, since thought is a ponderous enterprise for most of them.

After awhile the rat, overcome by hunger, skittered over and begins to worry the cable assembly in true rat fashion, gnawing and nibbling on the greased wires. Davy let him have it for about fifteen minutes, all the while sipping his beer and watching intently.

We sent for room service and ordered up more beer. The poor waiter nervously delivered the beer and Mongolian barbecue that we also ordered. The waiter took one look at the caged rat and the two of us, then hurriedly left the check and didn't even wait to see if there was a tip in it. Pretty smart boy: stay away from the gringos as they are up to no good.

Davidson removed the cable assembly and pulled another one out of his bag. This one was slightly different but about the same drill. He smeared it down with the meat juices, and slid it into the cage with Herr Rat. By now the rat was associating cable with food, so as soon as the rat saw the new cable, it pounced on it with delight.

There came a knock on the door and Davy was up like a shot. After a muffled conference outside the door and some haggling, he returned carrying another cage.

This contained four more of the rat tribe, who looked even mangier, if that was possible. He put the cage in the closet and returned to the bed, retrieving two more beers from the ice bucket. By now I could smell conspiracy with a capital "C."

"For the life of me, I can't figure what you're up to, you sawed-off misanthrope," I told him.

He looked me over like I was some carpet-bagging whiskey drummer that stepped off the stage, and snickered under his breath.

"These little critters are going to guarantee that we get another week here in the land of bliss." He fished out the gnawed chunk of cable, greased a new one and fed it into the cage. The rat obliged by starting to reduce the plastic insulation to shredded ruin. The cable assemblies all appeared to be from some sort of electronics equipment, military in origin. Davy smiled that feral little Wile E. Coyote smile, and continued.

"How many CCK flights come in here a month?"

"I dunno, maybe two?"

"Right, and what do they do when they are here?"

"Refit and repair I guess. I don't know, fill the tank, check the oil, do the windshield, whatever."

"Right. Those Blackbirds come here to do that because here is a secure area where they are able to do all the technical stuff on them. All those planes are full of computers and radios and all that top-secret, hush-hush, Air Force secret shit, right? And, we get to hitch a ride because we are top-secret Army pawns, right?" Both of these are true of course: we were the only ones traveling on the birds that were not members of the crew or the secret squirrels that operate the equipment. We hop a ride, the bird stays in Taipei for five days, and we hop a ride back. We have an R&R and it doesn't show up as one. And they know you can be back at a day's notice. Simple enough.

"Okay, Mallet Head, I am going to explain it. What connects all those computers and radios and ray guns and all that other secret shit? Wire cable, right? There are miles and miles of it."

The light came on. Davy had gone out to the airbase and had bribed or blackmailed someone to give him a whole mess of the discarded cable assemblies from the Blackbirds. Hell, he had probably simplified things and stolen it. Now I could see the mastery of his criminality. The cables that Herr Rat had been chewing on are from all different parts of the plane.

"Now, in about three hours, we are going to get on that plane. We will carry on the rodent cousins in this heavy canvas parachute bag, which we all carry anyway. The space cadets see rats running around, which they will, since we will make the first sightings and scream *rat*! The Air Force will do what, when that happens?"

"Ah, shut the plane down long enough to get rid of the rats?" I offer.

"No you nitwit, they will shut it down until they can check the whole plane out for damage. How long do you think it will take to check miles of wires and hoses?"

I finally saw the brilliance of the Varmint's plan. Shit, checking out the whole plane could take a week at least.

Davy began rigging up a new wire by taking the table lamp and unplugging it. He sliced off the cord at the lamp base, split the wire, stripped the insulation off and then attached it to the cable assembly. He smeared the cable with grease and inserted it in the cage.

He looks at the rat, and intoned solemnly:

"You, Nguyen Rat, have been found guilty, after an article 32 investigation, of willfully, with great maliciousness, trying to sabotage an air vessel of the United States Air Force. You have been found guilty by an appointed panel of your intended victims and are sentenced to death for your evil intents."

I could have sworn the rat was listening as it chewed on the cable. Davy leaned over and plugged the cord into the wall socket. Then, 220 volts at 62 cycles raced down the cord and slammed into the rat. He never had a chance: the electricity whipped him around the cage, and his hair started to smoke.

We spent the next two hours getting ready. We ditched the evidence such as the burnt cage, the cooking waste, etc., and managed to get the other rats in the canvas bag. By show time we were down in the lobby with the other miscreants, trying to look as dejected as they did about going back.

It was still dark as we rolled up to the Blackbird. As Dave and I boarded we were stashing chewed cable lengths under and around everything we could. The tour de force, though, was Dave's placing the electrocuted body of the rat with the short cable assembly under one of the electronic banks with just his ass and tail extruding.

I opened up the canvas bag under the seat. The rats were perfect: they scurried out, and one big mangy cuss made for the door, right in front of the loadmaster. The loadmaster spotted him and the rat made a beeline right up the stanchion pole at the rear. The loadmaster was talking a mile a minute on the boom mike, and we heard the engines shutting down.

Utter chaos inside the plane ensued. We all managed to get off and were standing around when we saw a member of the crew come out holding the dead rat by the tail. The rat still had the wires in its mouth. A senior Chief Zoomer examined the rat, then the cable, then went inside. He came back out a couple of minutes later and said something to the loadmaster and the pilot. There seemed to be an argument but the crew won out.

The pilot informed us that the plane would be grounded for a minimum of seventy-two hours. He looked over at us and asked if any of us were from CCN. Four of us, Davy and I included, raised our hands. The pilot was grinning like a Cheshire cat.

"I hope you boys don't know Wesley, or that this here rat incident was his idea, even though he isn't here. It seems that he did something similar about a year ago, and we never figured it out until we checked the aircraft and there was no damage. We could never prove it, but the base commander was fit to be tied."

He continued. "Air Force regulations clearly define that the aircraft and all its subsystems will be inspected regardless. That will take at least seventy-two hours, so you are free to go back to the hotel."

The Weasel. I should have known that Davidson wasn't clever enough to come up with this by himself. Then the loadmaster came by and as he passed, he winked at Davy. Ah, a fellow conspirator.

"The reason they caught Wesley," Davy tells me softly, "was that he never checked out of the hotel, in fact, he told the staff that he would be staying another four days before he came out to the airfield. We checked out, like we were going away forever, right?" Maybe Texans aren't that dippy after all. In the end we got an extra four days in Taipei, though we were searched like criminals when we finally got back on board four days later. I didn't mind since I was out of money anyway.

* * *

So here we are, back in Da Nang and in the club, with the usual beat going on around. Mac isn't back from Okie yet and who knows where the Cookie is. Everyone is talking at once, it seems, and the conversation again is about weapons. After all, that is how we make our living, with weapons.

"Because that's their close-in shock weapon, that's why they use it," a voice states clearly.

"They don't have a 40 mm grenade launcher, so the B40 is what they use in the assault," another voice adds to the information.

"They cover the landing zones we use, and blanket the 12.5 mm coverage down from the platforms, hoping that they can knock down the choppers before they get to a cleared area."

"Yeah, they blanket zones from altitude down to the ground level. They use the B40 like we use the 40 mm grenade launcher."

There is the usual melee going on at the club. A Philippine band has an American soul singer with them. We are waiting for the chance to send a message to the USO fun directors that we don't need floor shows. There is a cacophony of voices and several conversations going on at once.

Eldon has come back and the Americans are all sitting around bull penning his last mission while destroying some grey matter and drinking Mudhole's Old Rebel Yell. There are a number of the little people there and we are getting to feel like a group of doctors at a country club, dissecting the last foray of "Dr. Fingers" into the operating room.

Eldon has come out hot. He has been in that situation of "Almost Totally Fucked" and lived through it by the hair on his chinny chin chin. We are discussing the assault techniques used by our dance partners, the NVA. They use the highly effective 88 mm RPG-2 as an infantry assault weapon. So do we. It's a great big son of a bitch that makes a noise like a dragon shitting a fireball, then detonates with a loud clap that tightens everybody's sphincter. Eldon's team had counted twelve detonations of rockets during their extraction.

This was on top of every Nguyen within a mile firing his AK, with great glee, at the team. One of the rockets had passed right through the cargo compartment of the chopper they had just scrambled aboard as they lifted off the LZ.

Eldon was slightly bent over, checking the last of his team, when the rocket shot through one opening and out the other, never hitting anything. He had turned to his One-One, and asked, "What the hell was that?" His One-One turned to him with eyes as big as saucers, and his hair singed by the rocket.

"It was BIG, and ANGRY, and LOUD. I hope it was a rocket because whatever it was it missed and that would be good for us, right?" Eldon had surmised that the battle was over at that point, that it was time to get out of Uncle Charles' backyard.

"I've never been so scared so intensely in my life." he says. Now that has to be an understatement. We have all been on the receiving end of a B40 at one time or another, although this one, going through the open sides of the helicopter and not touching anything, defies the imagination. The boys were living on borrowed luck on that one. Had it detonated inside it would have shredded major components and the bird would have dropped right there. More likely it would have turned everyone into a red mist and bone dust, so the burning wreckage would have been a mere afterthought.

We talk and we drink. We are trying to figure how to get the edge on the other side. The targets that we are hitting are increasingly a gun battle from start to finish. We are running into small, highly mobile units that pack almost as heavy a punch as we do. We are eight to twelve people and they are using company-size units now, with mobile formations that can run us to ground. Their squads all have at least one light machine gun and at least one RPG2, sometimes two per squad. In simpler terms, we have to fight for ground. That means we can't just bloody them, move off, call for a false extraction and hope to stay on the ground.

"They hit us hard after we made the first contact. We think we mauled a platoon-size unit in the first firefight." Eldon starts in again. "Easily a platoon. Sang killed a three-man tracker team just as we got off the LZ. We hadn't moved more than maybe a hundred meters and these guys came hustling up and started sweeping for sign. As soon as they picked us up they were on the radio. The radio looked like a PRC-25."

"Yeah." Someone adds, "As soon as we killed them we planted toe poppers real fast around them and began moving. We heard the toe poppers go off and not five minutes later we hit about twenty guys coming at the run. They had a radio with them too."

"Sounds like an anti-recon detachment." Joins in another.

"No shit Sherlock. These guys are scary, they aren't ash and trash. They get on you, they run you, they keep you moving, and come at you as an envelope; sooner or later they are going to run you to ground. They are going to try and canalize you. Look on your map for the least defensible ground and that's where they will try to push you."

"They have PRC-25s?" I ask. That's not unlikely, since this country is awash in our military radios. I am sure that they have captured enough to have a parts' supply to service and repair. The scary thing is that they are using them at platoon level. That means someone is directing killer teams. They must not want us anywhere in the northern ring of targets.

"Yeah, I am sure these were PRC-25s. It's our equipment, not Chicom or Russian."

Some greenie asks from the outer edge of the crowd, "What's a B40 rocket?" Everyone cracks up. Eldon looks over the crowd in the direction of the voice and asks if someone brought their kid to work with them. The crowd is raucous, but it helps the fear and tension melt away as the jam session goes on.

"What is a B40?" the same voice asks again. The only answers he gets back are nicknames we have for it.

"MFBG! Mutha Fucking Big Grenade."

"Widow Maker."

"Death Ray."

Finally, someone explains to him it is a rocket-propelled grenade. This is true, technically, but to us poor unwashed cretins it looks like a rocket, flies like a rocket, goes boom like a rocket. It is positively *not* a duck. I look over to the new guy; he looks like he is right out of high school, or some junior college. You poor bastard, I think to myself, you have no idea what you are walking into here. You can tell someone who has never seen the awful face of war; they have certain softness about them. The rest of us appear young but we are dragging all these skeletons around. In fact, I have a whole graveyard full.

The talk turns back to the immediate problem, which is that they are going to keep sending us back in, small Recon teams against companies and platoons, and Chuck doesn't want us out there seeing what he has. We know that the NVA are getting ready for the big push someday. They are down south with armor and more rice-eating little killers than ever before. How do we get in and stay in long enough to see something of intelligence value that merits the sacrifice.

We could go in on the tail of a B52 strike, I suppose. You know: hide in the debris field then try to walk out into a surrounding area. It's workable. In fact, Mac and I had discussed it for a DM target. We could do a nine-ship Arc Light, which would give us about thirty square kilometers of running room in the debris field.

If we picked it just right and timed our entry, we would be masked from being observed during the infiltration. We could insert at the near edge and walk into an adjacent target box that way.

This would be feasible, since anyone at ground level would be hamburger, or so concussed they wouldn't recognize daylight. We would have a chance to get up under the debris and watch, let things cool for a day or so, then start moving. Keep all the air traffic off somewhere else, maybe Arc Light another area to see if it drives them above ground and out in the open. The downside was that it would take an hour or more to have enough air back in there to sustain anyone walking around, and for the ground to cool down and the dust to dissipate. That would make it a very tricky insert.

Some fiery wit two tables over suggests that we start digging a tunnel from here to the AO then just branch out. Someone else starts singing, "Hi Ho, Hi Ho," like in Snow White, when Larry the Midget comes sauntering in. Ah, the eighth dwarf, Homicide, has arrived. He stops long enough to yell at us.

"You degenerates may think you're funny, but you will be Hi-Ho-ing up the A Shau if you keep making fun of your brutally handsome and intellectually superior, glorious leader." He picks up his drink from the bar and pays for it with a chit.

A mini-smoke grenade the size of a camera film case streaks over his shoulder and wafts purple smoke up from behind the bar. They are good for gags, but not too effective in the bush, hence everyone has a bunch in the hootches. This act brings Larry to the apex of his thespian talents. He ignores the smoke, doesn't even flinch. He swizzles his drink and then sort of cocks his head. This is difficult since the little mutant has no neck. Well, not one that you would associate with the homo sapiens branch of the bipeds. Legs spread shoulder-width apart; he surveys the room with a jaundiced eye.

I hadn't noticed at first but with him is the inscrutable Dr. Wang, Chinese duck, Dr. Quack. No, it would be unwise to make fun of the good doctor because there is something feverish going on inside that melon. Chinese and New Mexican ancestry, whew; like some kind of weird Taos Shaman. He may be able to pass himself off as brilliant, but the idea of a doctor who will cut his own hemorrhoids using a surgical mirror and a Swiss army knife is disturbing. It is good that these two have found each other, that way they won't screw up any normal people. The Deuterium Dwarf and Dr. Strangelove are a team.

The good doctor has whisked some chits across the bar and has fished a snifter of what looks like cognac. This is disturbing because Jimmy Reeves keeps a few bottles, make that a case, of cognac behind the bar as my personal stash. I need to check the stock, and make sure I am not being surgically screwed out of the good stuff.

"There's only one way we haven't tried to get in." The speaker pauses, then he continues. "We could do a parachute insertion." There is a sump of silence following that suggestion.

Oh I don't like this idea at all. Every once in awhile someone resurrects the idea of parachuting into the AO. There are steerable parachutes that could put us into the type of openings in the bush that exist. The boon would be that the other side might hear a C130 passing overhead, but they wouldn't associate that activity with a team being inserted. But, there are a lot of drawbacks. We would have to train the Yards to parachute or go in as just Americans, which borders on insanity: the teams would be stripped of their best people. Plus, those that didn't go would be running more targets to take up the slack. And, another problem: the altitude for a static line insertion is pretty much between a thousand and three thousand feet in order to hit the small clearings. It is possible that you could jump at a marginal altitude, or mix in with the aircraft called Moonbeam, or someone out in orbit, then come in low and drop a team. The other alternative was going to come up in the conversation, but I was willing it not to happen.

"We could do a HALO insert." There it is, the other way. Someone has said the dirty word. HALO, as a concept, is perfectly designed to do what we want to do. The problem is that we only have so many HALO qualified people in the unit.

HALO stands for High Altitude Low Opening, or military freefall parachuting. There are a few guys here that have completed the course at Fort Bragg and had the experience, but a lot of them are One-Zeros. That would mean stripping two or three teams out of the lineup, to make one team of Americans. That is bad math. But, it is always being thought about.

Manes is watching the crowd and grinding his jaw. The Midget does that when he is pondering great strategic questions, like if he is going to have gravy with his fried chicken. Dr. Ming the Merciless is leaning on one of the stools. He has an even fuller snifter of amber liquid than before. I am positive that he is drinking from my hoard. I make a beeline for him but I never get there. A clamp-like grip closes on my arm, and I stop abruptly. It's the Midget.

"Where do you think you're going, my man?"

"I have a grenade, *Dai Uy*, and if you don't let go of me I am going to blow both of us up with it." This threat has no effect on him; obviously the alcohol has fogged his reasoning. I am beyond caring as I continue, "I know that fucking Chinese feather merchant you slithered in here with is drinking my cognac."

"*Your* cognac?" he queries, and cocks his head again. Aha! I can see where this is going. The two of them are in on this together. They are probably headed for some Occifer hangout downtown. One of those places where it's considered classy if you show up drinking cognac out of snifters. Heathens!

"Why it's only a figure of speech, *Dai Uy*. I had a bottle of good Courvoisier I brought back from Taipei with me. I thought we could use it for special occasions like toasting our fallen comrades, Christmas, the unlikely event of your promotion to major, you know: *special*." I look at him and try a long shot. "And you *know* that sawbones son of a bitch is drinking it." It is best to be a little aggressive here or Larry will think it is going to be easy. Mugged, that's the term for this. I have been mugged.

I thought I was safe to leave the good stuff behind the bar, since the idea of haute liqueur in the ape tribe is Crown Royal, and the officers generally swill some kind of scotch. My only competition for the cognac was Reeves and Wesley, both of whom were in on the supply and demand cabal with me. I had completely forgotten Wang in the equation. I see him over in the corner: he raises his glass, mockingly toasting me.

"Well you're in luck my man," Larry slurs, "because this is a special occasion tonight. The good doctor has informed me that you are fit for duty. You are completely recovered from the malarial incident which you illegally covered up from the United States Army, not to mention myself." He hisses a bit when he slides this last bit of information out, and smiles a jaundiced grimace to emphasize his point.

"Do you realize that I could have been charged with war crimes, my man, sending a pox-infected personage like yourself out there where you could have infected the entire North Vietnamese Army?"

Uh-oh, this isn't a mugging: this is extortion. There will be no telling this missing link that malaria is not infectious, unless of course mosquitoes are involved. It wouldn't matter anyway. It will be best to cut my losses and flee, if I can somehow break the grip, but I am not out of it yet as Squatty continues with obvious glee.

"Your running partners are coming back in the morning, and are in deeper hot water than you are, if that is possible." He makes that Manes grimace, which looks like an orangutan with a bad case of colitis, and continues.

"Mac and that flap-eared throwback, Johnson, have managed to not only screw up the program for HALO training in Okinawa, but they have also managed to overdraw the special account at Chase Manhattan, by writing bad checks." He shakes me for emphasis.

HALO training in Okie? What insanity is that? That concept is frightening enough, but to have Jimmy and Mac involved is absolutely terrifying. Who in their right mind would give Jimmy and the Mini Mac a checkbook? They have the spending habits of those hookers masquerading as a Congress back in the States.

"Do you know what they told the Sergeant Major, when he asked why in Blue Jaspers they were overdrawn a full four thousand and change?" I get another shake for punctuation. I don't answer since this is apparently a rhetorical question, so he continues. "They told the Sergeant Major that they couldn't be overdrawn since they still had checks." He delivers another shake for good measure.

"So your problem with your illegal stash of fine liquor is just icing on the cake." He grins and it looks like the Toad King looking at a fat juicy fly. Castro looms into view and jostles the Toad King, murmuring something about moving his fat ass out of the way. Larry releases me and turns on the Cuban, and I am free.

Manes starts a tirade but the Cuban is a born survivor; he fishes a smoke grenade out of nowhere and pops it, yells "Gas!", and darts away from the bar. I don't care. I am out the door by that time and over behind a jeep. Everyone comes streaming out in a rush, violet smoke wafting after them. Manes and Wang emerge in a violet mist and saunter over to another jeep. Wang has two bottles of my Cognac stuck in the cargo pockets of his fatigues and the Midget is talking to him and laughing. Castro shows up beside me and stands there for a moment. We both look at the crowd as it starts to drift back in to the club and laugh. Castro looks at me and shakes his head.

"Welcome back, dickweed. I guess you've heard that Mac and Jimmy are coming back tomorrow. Do me a favor will you? Don't hang around me for a couple of years, okay."

All in all, I thought that I handled it well. I will eagerly await the return of my teammates. Cook apparently never went to Okie with them; he is off doing some other chore. It doesn't matter; we will all be here tomorrow, and there is safety in numbers. I am going to make a gift of half of the remaining bottles of cognac to the officers' mess…after I spike it with some really powerful laxative, of course. It won't stop anything but it will at least allow me to make a statement. What is the worst that could happen? It is too bad Larry doesn't drink the stuff. That would be perfect.

CHAPTER 14

Door Number Three

It's hot and humid enough to be a sauna. I am hunched down in a dip in the terrain behind a bank of rotting sandbags and marginal vegetation, with an RPD tearing up the front side of the old bunker system that we improved to use as cover. The NVA gunner apparently has a belt of ammunition that runs all the way back to Uncle Ho's People's Collective ammunition factory. He has been whittling away at my position for about thirty minutes now. With the amount of lead that he is throwing at my location, he will eventually punch a hole through. He is getting to be more than aggravating.

I am digging, in an attempt to be below ground when he does. I have one of the collapsible entrenching tools; it looks real neat, and is adequate for the task, but right now I would rather have a backhoe. I am sweating like I'm in a steamer and trying to keep an eye on my sector occasionally to make sure that his peppering isn't a cover to move some more troops up where they can assault us.

After McDowell, Campbell and Larson managed to catch an NVA regiment in the open with their pants down, we drew a static road watch as a target to see if we couldn't catch another regiment in the open. It had become vogue. We weren't the only ones to get one. It was a concept that had merit.

The war had become large-scale offensives from the NVA and to do that they had to move men and material South. We were the first to maneuver elements that could direct the bombing campaign to stem the flow of both. We were the first to push back after they cleared their own southern border. The mighty air force was pounding them to mush as they came down the trail. We were the next thorn for them, to the point they would mass to dislodge us, which meant there were more targets for bombers in a defined area.

We weren't the first. Several teams had gotten very lucky doing the very same. Some had also gotten very dead when things went bad. It sounded just yummy in concept. Go out, establish a strong point where we couldn't be dislodged easily, get a long antenna up for good commo, and call in air strikes on anything moving on the road complex or in the neighborhood. Take a couple of machine guns, a mortar with plenty of high explosive and illumination, lots and lots of hand grenades and ammo and a whole shitload of claymore and toe popper mines, and generally become a carbuncle on the asses of the NVA operations and logistics chain.

We are using an old firebase on the top of a hill as a redoubt. After insertion, we spent the next eight hours tying everything in and starting to monitor the area. Soon we caught sight of a couple of trucks grinding away up the steep grade to our front, about 2,500 meters from the hilltop. They were accompanied by a couple of platoons of infantry and some real adventurous cats on a Russian motorcycle. Mac had gotten Covey up on the air and given him the details, but when he slipped over the area, the NVA had gone to ground, waiting for him to leave. It was almost too good to be true. We spotted for Covey and he laid in some marker rockets just as two Fast Movers dropped out of the skies and pickled their ordnance right on target. They hit both trucks on the first run and then cluster-bombed the patch of forest that the troops had dispersed into. The two on the motorcycle with the sidecar managed to escape, barely, but demonstrated a driving technique and expertise that would have made a Baja runner green with envy.

All sections of the trail have trail watchers, and apparently this section's security people were having a bad radio day, since the trucks and the troops had acted as if they didn't know we were there. After Covey worked two more sets over the area, evidently our little bit of luck dissipated. This group had unassed the trucks about two klicks from us and moved out towards us. They also brought mortars with them and managed to get about ten rounds off in our direction before one of the bomb runs obliterated that menace. We dug in and laid defensive mines; we caught another group coming up and the Air Force did another superlative job of turning trucks and troops into hamburger meat and scrap iron.

We had three rounds impact close enough for me to suspect that they had pre-registered the hill, so we started dragging over some of the old corrugated steel from the firebase and building some overhead cover. Mac's position was the old FDC (Fire Direction Control) bunker which over the years had become a mound of dirt rather than an identifiable bunker. The position that I picked was the most exposed, but covered the draw that came up the back slope. It wasn't going to be tenable for very long when the NVA got serious about pushing us off the hill, and they were going to get real serious fast.

Loi and Bang and I had cleaned out the old trench line, laid toe popper mines in the draw and used one of the rolls of concertina wire to string across the middle of the mouth. I laid in some trip flares for when nightfall arrived. Mac and Cookie got the 60 mm and its spare set up in an old bomb crater with enough depth to shield a gun crew, and we marked three other locations and deposited ammo in them so we could move it around when the push came. Our biggest asset was the bombers, if we could keep them on station. That's a big "if" in this country where the weather changes sometimes on an hourly basis.

Other than a few desultory shots on the insert, no one had been all that interested in us until we blew up the first set of trucks. Once the word got down the bamboo telegraph, they had gotten organized. We had a good location, and unless we were unlucky with indirect fire from mortars, we could even hold the hill for a short period of time if the weather got bad. They would eventually run us off, unless we got five days of sunshine. In that case, we could hunker down and call in air strikes until the cows came home. That was Plan A.

Katak, katak, katttatttat, followed by the sandbags spitting sand as the rounds hit them, interrupts my tactical reverie and I finish digging out the rest of my hole. I have Bang and Loi set up some ten meters to my right and a little higher. They have been busy camouflaging the gun position and staying out of sight. There is the shallow remnant of a communications trench that the RPD gunner can't see, leading from my position back up the hill to the main perimeter. When we get really pressed, I will slither up there after laying toe poppers in and around my position; if they gain the trench that will keep them out of it for fear of setting off more.

The gun will chop anything that comes out of the draw after the mines go off, and we should be able to make that a death trap until they just push so many folks up the hill that they overwhelm us. I have a supplementary position for the gun when that happens, which has better fields of fire, but it is the place the enemy would expect it and no doubt will mortar the hell out of it during any preparatory fires. At that point, I have what I call the fish shack. It is the collapsed remains of a bunker that looks like it is part of the hillside. I had Cookie extend a trench into the back of it and open it up. Even from down below when I was putting in the mines, I couldn't make it out. It's stout enough to take an RPG round unless they shoot through the aperture, and there are damn few places to get that kind of shot off with the guns firing down on you.

I hear scuffling in the commo trench and a moment later, the One-Two from Crusader joins me. He is straphanging with us since both Lamar and Kelly had gotten shot to ribbons. We have four of Crusader's little people with us as well. They are Bru so the two teams have clicked well. This guy is fairly new to the country and has that glow of adrenal excitement; the flush of someone about to shit his britches.

"Mac wants to know if that gun is still giving you a problem. He says he doesn't want to use the mortars until he has to." He pants as he is looking at me, as the NVA gun puts another long burst into the sandbags to my front.

"Tell him I'm alright for now. The little creep is behind that copse of rocks out about three hundred meters on the lower hilltop. He can't see us all that well, but I can't get a direct line on him either. Tell Mac we will wait until the next load of assets get here then we'll use them." I pause from my digging and sit back, take my canteen out and then light up a cigarette, making sure that I exhale into the bottom of the hole so the smoke won't plume and confirm that this hole is active. The gun chatters a long burst at the top of the hill, trying to knock out the big antenna.

"You see it?"

"Yeah, right down there by those gray rocks?"

"Yeah, that's it." I add, "When you go back up top, show Mac where it is, so that when Covey comes back with the cavalry they can light his ass up. Tell Mac that I have this place just about tied down so if we can't get Stinger or Spectre overhead at night, we can make it at least exciting for the first two assaults. Once they get organized, though, they are going to push us from all sides and use this draw to roll us up. We will need a passel of claymores up there, facing this way, when we have to abandon this position." I pause to let that soak in. He takes a drag off my cigarette, mimicking my exhale program. He readjusts his gear, getting ready for his return trip.

"Tell Mac that I don't need any more company down here. I will use the URC-10 to talk to him if I need to. Does he still have you guys tied in with Cook?"

"Yeah." He pauses as if searching for the right words and moment. I know what's going on in his head. This is the first time he has been out on a serious mission, and also the first time he has been around Cook. The Cookie is hard to take until you get to know him, since he is all business. He is like McDowell on steroids.

"Don't worry about the Cookie, he is all bark until you fuck up, but he will keep you alive."

The kid rolls his eyes.

"Do you know he puts names on his hand grenades?" He asks as if there was some secret inference, instead of what he suspects is a manifestation of insanity.

"Yeah, we know it, but it makes him happy. It's like nose art on a B17. He only has it on the ones on his harness anyway."

"No, he is up there chalking things on the ones we took out of the box." The kid reaches into the claymore bag strung over his shoulder and digs out four or five M67 baseball grenades. "He said to bring these down to you, and that you would know what to do with them." I look at them. Four have INERT chalked on them in yellow, and one has DOORWAY TO HEAVEN chalked on it. The kid says, "He said the last one is for when you have to leave down here." I look at the grenades and back at the kid.

"When you get back up top, tell Mac that the Cookie has too much time on his hands. Give him a shovel and he can try out his artistic talents by digging us a tunnel back to the launch site." The kid grins and starts to head up the hill again. There is a screech and two mortar rounds impact about fifty meters below our position and to the right. The kid takes off up the hill a bit faster than he came down and I duck under the overhead cover. I look out the peep I have that isn't chewed up by the RPD downslope, trying to spot the mortar. I hear three more rounds going out and concentrate in the direction from which they came. I have just spotted where I think the gun section is located. From the impact I think it's a section of 82 mm guns.

I am going to call up Mac with the location when Covey breaks out of the cloud cover; behind him are a set of A1Es. They bank and drop a couple of hard bombs on the mortar location, then come back and drop a 250-pounder on the position where the RPD has been giving us grief. The shock wave and concussion warp the moment and I look down to where the gun was. There is a big jumble of debris and smashed rocks, but for once the gun doesn't pepper the hill, so they must have gotten him.

The Spads come back out of the cloud cover after Covey marks two more locations for them. They stream in and drop what appear to be CBUs. The mini-bombs pepper a copse of forest that borders the road. I hear Mac talking to Covey and he is apparently outside the old FDC bunker. Covey brings in a set of fast movers and they napalm the slopes before us. The hot wind of the napalm flashes and the bush below my position is turned into a flaming graveyard for anyone who had been in the path of that destruction. I wave Loi over and he scrambles down the trench to my hole.

"Stay here, I am going up to talk with *Trung Si* Mac." He nods his head and turns to take over my position, as I scramble out of the hole and, bent over, make my way up the communications trench. On the way I notice that Cookie has had the Yards deepen it where it had fallen in and reestablish the zigzag, so someone gaining the far end couldn't control the trench all the way to the top.

When I get to the top I cut to the left to where I can see Mac talking on the radio. I can see down the valley from here and am surveying the road system and the surrounding area that we mean to control as long as possible. The two trucks destroyed on the initial bomb run still lick their souls into the air with black greasy smoke. The area just below my position looks like a charred California hillside after a wildfire. The only difference is that among the burning tree trunks and rocks are the unmistakable clumps of what had been a squad or more of NVA. They must have been careless and Covey spotted them before we did. At any rate, the reverse slope will be easier to defend now that we have burned off the cover.

I am working out the possibilities of slipping down and planting some more toe popper mines after it gets a bit closer to dark. Toe poppers will at least give us some early warning when the NVA come up after nightfall, and come they will. They cannot allow us to hold this position for long. We are blocking their transport route and there is no place to bypass the road to go around, except a possible route twenty kilometers north of our position.

Another team is getting set up south of us with a bit more stealth than we managed. When we get run off this hill, they will go active and close off that section of the trail. It is all part of an effort to shut down the pipeline of supplies. More importantly, we tie up their manpower. It will take at least a battalion to dislodge us from this hill. We will stay and hold as long as humanly possible, then come out in some sort of *Götterdämmerung*-inspired firefight of apocalyptic proportions. But, our presence here will bleed the pressure off somewhere else in the war effort. Bait. I feel like the worm on a hook drifting on a trout line over ambush reef.

If we can draw everything down onto removing us, the other static team can lie low and keep up the interdiction. The damage they do to the trail here will require the NVA to rebuild it under a blanket bombing later when we have pulled out. This is just the opening round. As soon as the NVA get tired of our aggravation, they will spend the lives and run us off.

Mac finishes up and stands to join me behind the rotting carcass of the revetment wall. We had brought several bales of sandbags and I can see that Mac and Cookie have used them to help reinforce those patches of the old revetments with judicious care. We have a strong redoubt where, when the attack comes, we can withdraw and drop ordnance and maybe survive, as a last measure. All depends on how long the launch site will wait before they pull the plug.

"Looks like that last group down there," he points to the still-smoldering clump of bodies, "were getting set to try to rush the side you were on. Cook saw them and Covey marked them so that the Spads could get at them."

It is afternoon and so far the weather hasn't gotten socked in. We should be able to keep the pressure on the trail and protect our position with air cover. But with late afternoon the rains will come, and with the rain and nightfall the NVA will mount an assault on the hill. By that time we should have Spectre over us. Unless it gets too nasty, they can mark our position and provide 360-degree coverage around us. The little infrared strobes won't work worth a damn to be our ground marker, so we have brought plenty of ground flares that we can chuck into a sizeable bomb crater almost in the middle of the perimeter. They burn with a bright incandescence, and Spectre can pick them up even through ground haze in their IR. At least we are hoping they can. I have no wish to be climbing up the 292, like Chapman had to when he and Butler invented this concept and actually flew the American flag; they even put a strobe light up there to mark their position.

Mac looks down the other side where I can see Cook with his shirt off excavating the trench. He is working slowly and methodically with two of the Yards helping him. The rest of the Yards are doing the same, with one man watching and standing to, while the other improves the position. The old firebase is perfect as the flat hilltop is about fifty meters in diameter with revetments for three guns, probably 105 mm. It had been built during the glory days of big divisional operations. They would helicopter lift the guns to a hilltop, along with ammo and a security platoon, and support the ground troops from these fortifications

The sandbags are white with age and we have managed to supplement the smaller perimeter by tearing down some of the walls and using the serviceable bags to build new walls and reinforce others. We have pulled some of the old concertina and re-laid it to cover blind spots and approaches, giving us some depth. It will slow things down, but in the end won't stop a determined mass assault. They know we were here, but if we can keep their big guns from getting in position, we can stay.

"I figure we have a day, maybe a day and a half, before this place gets too damn busy to hang around," I say to Mac.

"Maybe two," he replies. He looks over at Cook laboring away, and chuckles, "Cookie might be able to buy us another day if it turns into a rock fight," as Cook heaves a fair-sized stone out of his excavation and down the hill.

So far we haven't used the 60 mm mortars, which we will use if and when the weather socks in. I wish we had brought an 81 mm but we had nixed that as too heavy, and only the three of us know how to operate it. The 60 is a standard weapon for the entire team, so all the Yards could use it *sans* sights to hit targets. We have some ten cases of ammo for the 60 and we pulled the rounds and had them bunkered in the two positions as well as the primary. Unless they take a direct hit, they won't be a danger to us. After nightfall, I had a feeling the illumination rounds were going to be a big help if Spectre couldn't drop flares on us to help ID targets.

"This is the same thing Kansas did, you know," I remark, lighting up one of the small cheroots I brought along. Mac looks over at me and smiles, jerking his thumb down towards Cook.

"Yeah, but they didn't have Cookie."

"That won't help us for shit and you know it; this is a sucker operation. Why did we agree to do it again?" I ask him half in jest and half in a serious quest for the truth, but I already know the truth and he confirms it.

"Because we are almost as stupid as we look, that's why." He chuckles to himself again. We both know we have pretty good odds unless the weather socks in. If it does, and it will later, we have planned well enough that we can hang in here until daylight. We should be able to get a resupply in at first light to make up for what we will expend tonight. Whoever flies that will have the ride of his life. It will also mark what kind of AA we are going to have to contend with when we finally get pulled off the hill.

At this moment, Covey comes scooting out of the cloud base and makes a pass over our location. As he flies off to the south, wagging his wings, a stream of green tracers tracks behind him, followed by the unmistakable heavy chug of a 12.7 mm heavy machine gun. Covey banks, comes back lower and lets a marker rocket off from where the tracers came from. The Spads come in and work the position over with a rack of hard bombs—well-oiled teamwork; lots of practice.

"Well, Nguyen has brought some serious shit to this dance. I'd better get back down and finish up. Things are going to get interesting after dark." Mac smiles at me and points at a box with claymores in it. "Take that with you, so I don't have to hear you whining about needing them after dark." I grab the rope handle and drag the case with me back down the trench line. I have Loi put out three on both flanks and I save the rest for emergencies. Best of all, I now have a comfortable wooden box to sit on. I open a PIR and munch on it, using some of the scrap and some plastic explosive to heat up the water and make some coffee and the PIR ration.

By the time I am finished the sun is starting to slip over the mountains to the west. In about two hours it will start to get dark. They will start probing soon after that. Sometime later they will try to mount a ground assault. If that fails they will try again before first light.

The One-Two from Crusader comes sliding down the trench about an hour later. Like all of us, he looks exhausted from the digging.

"Mac says that I should help over here." I make room for him in the position and show him the fields of fire markers. It is nearly dark enough, so I grab a few trip flares and some toe poppers and tell him that I am going to put them downslope where the napalm caught the NVA. I grab Loi so he can go along and cover me. We crawl down slope until we are in among the bodies on the charred hillside. There is a declivity where it would be natural to group up before rushing the hill, and I string out the toe poppers in and around it with a few of the trip flares. I do the same to the left and place a few in among the corpses. It takes about half an hour and we are back up to the trench line. We both smell like a fireplace, but I am sure that no one saw us and that our little surprises will catch the unaware flat-footed.

The shadows are lengthening as the evening starts to dim. The valley, with the road cut through it along the eastern face of the escarpment, looks like an interrupted ribbon that sketches away at the face of the ridge. I can see a bit of movement near the burning wrecks of the trucks. I call Mac's attention to it and Covey directs a set of fast movers down to drop a rack of bombs on the area. There is no secondary explosion; they probably caught some clumsy NVA squad who figured they were too small a target for the air strikes.

Covey comes up on the air and informs us that they will be replaced by the Trail FAC and will have Spectre on station in about an hour. In the meantime Covey and Mac pick a couple of likely assembly areas and gun positions that the NVA will use if they are getting ready to move on us. The last two sets of F4s come in and work both positions over, with the added benefit of denuding the areas of vegetation as the napalm burns the underbrush clear. This done, they all move off and away, leaving us alone.

Out here, that feeling of just how alone you are is soon amplified by movement about 1,500 meters out, as we watch a squad plus of NVA break cover and move toward where the truck wrecks are. When they don't get their Bata boots blasted, they will confirm that we no longer have mother hen above us and the enemy commander will get bolder and move on us. They have a lot of ground to cover before that, but we will start getting mortared or shelled with bigger guns as soon as they can get them positioned.

Even with the hill being registered, we are still a small target to hit, especially since they will have to fire in defilade from us and we will be at a higher altitude. The difference in elevation will require some trick shooting on their part, but it only takes time to get the hang of it. The NVA are good at indirect fire. I will give them that.

Darkness will help us. The enemy will have to use flares after dark to help them adjust, so it will help us save our own flares. When they start dropping rounds on us without the flares, that's when they will have their ground forces ready for the assault.

Settling back in the hole I tell the kid to watch and wake me in two hours. There shouldn't be any real threat until after dark. In the meantime, I can catch a couple of hours and then relieve him. I check on Loi and Bang; they will do the same. I settle in under the overhead cover and am soon in slumber.

I am shaken awake exactly two hours later. It is dark; the moon will come up in the next two hours. The kid says that it has been pretty quiet except for some movement he saw, or thought he saw, at the mouth of the draw about thirty minutes ago. He wanted to throw a grenade but had thought better of it. At least the kid was sharp enough not to have shot and given away our position.

I switch places with him and check that I have an ample supply of grenades on the shelf dug into the front of the parapet. He snuggles in and is soon asleep. The next hour or so goes by with nothing disturbing the night. There are insect sounds and the scurrying of some small rodents out to the front, but nothing that would key my alarm mechanism.

With the night come the bloody mosquitoes. Annoying little bastards, they seem to arise out of the very ground itself. It starts to rain shortly after that, a drizzle at first but then the steady patter of rain masks the night. The rain stops and starts intermittently; each time it stops the night sounds pick up again. I stay alert, in spite of the reassurance of the bush being normal. A thousand thoughts, memories, and flickers of reason flit through your mind on a night like this. Most wander around the tactical necessity of what you are doing and where you are. The main thing is to keep your cool while having a responsible sense of paranoia in reserve…and still being attentive to the job at hand.

It starts to drizzle again, and I am occasionally using the Metascope, a primitive night-vision device. It is good for about twenty meters. The clarity isn't all that good, but I can at least see the draw and down into it with the concertina wire defining the far range in a green-white coil at the bottom. I put the scope down and close my eye to let it regain its normal night vision. I look at my watch. It has been three hours. I wake the kid up and whisper that we both will stay awake from this point on. I have let him sleep a bit longer but now is when we will get moved on. There is nothing worse to wake up to than the sound of hand grenades. I have had that experience, and it is most disorienting. The kid is pissed because he thinks I am babying him. I tell him to shut up, it was my call, and he settles down. We speak little, if at all, and it is always with a tap, then move closer for a whispered comment.

I have just put the Metascope to my eye and turned it on when I see an NVA down in the draw and just forward of the bodies caught in the air strike. He is moving stealthily, as if in slow motion, forward and then stopping. I touch the kid's arm and tap twice to let him know we have company. He stiffens but holds still, crouching a bit. I watch the NVA raise his arm and snap his fingers. He is signaling someone else off to his left. This will be their probe. They will try to get into the trenches with us, but failing that will try to get us to fire and mark where we have the automatic weapons set up.

They have to be right in among the flares and toe poppers. How the hell can they be missing them? I am almost convinced that they had watched us place them, when there is a clap and a bright explosion followed by screaming as one of them steps on a mine. One of the trip flares goes off and the night turns to day. There are four of them down there. The kid throws a grenade and so does Loi. The four figures are bracketed and crumple as the shrapnel shreds them. A couple of them are still alive because we can hear them moaning and crying piteously.

The rain is steady now and I hear the crump of grenades over on Cookie's side, along with a high-pitched scream that goes on for several minutes. From below us a dozen bright blossoms of flame erupt from the muzzles of many AKs. They are firing high, so they don't know exactly where we are. We both throw a couple of grenades as the fire peppers the hillside and finally the front of our position. The flare has gone out but in the bright flash of the last grenade I see two NVA pull one of the moaners and start to drag him downhill. They step on another toe popper, and all three go down.

So far none of us has opened up, so they have no fixed point on which to concentrate. They know by now, though, that the slope is mined. The rain slacks off and I hear the distant drone of an aircraft off to the east. Shortly after that there are explosions on the road as Spectre opens up on a target out about 1,500 meters. There are four quick crumps of the 105 mm followed by a red ribbon coming down from the sky and the unmistakable *buurrrrrp* of the bank of miniguns on board, then a series of secondary explosions. Somewhere over the next ridge a fifty opens up on the sky with its green tracers reaching up in a forlorn hope of pulling the bird down. Big mistake on the gun crew's part. The red ribbon arches down to the origin, followed by the crump of another 105 round, and the gun goes quiet.

We can hear scuffling and an occasional clink of metal on metal but it is getting further from us, so I think they are pulling back, taking what wounded they can with them. There are a couple of shrieks when someone gets moved too roughly, but we don't see any more movement. The kid leans over and whispers in my ear.

"Is that it?" He is hyperventilating a bit. Hell, so am I; night and uncertainty coupled with loud noises will do that to you. I take my canteen out, swallow, then spit some out before answering.

"They'll be back. That was just a probe. You did well. Don't shoot until we have to. Use the grenades. They still don't know exactly where we are."

"What's next?" he asks.

We hear a brief exchange of automatic fire from the other side of the hill, intermixed with grenades and a couple of RPG rockets. The noise peters out after one of the

RPG rounds overflies the top of the hill and impacts below us some hundred meters or so. It goes quiet and I answer him.

"They probably will try another probe or two, then they will start dropping big stuff on us to soften us up before they come up after us. They might try to send sappers in and try to get in among us when they shell us so we can't just hide in the overhead."

"Marvelous," is all he says. I am beginning to like this kid. He certainly has the droll wit one needs to add levity to situations when one is shitting one's britches.

We have two more probes that finally get to the point where he and I have to use our CAR-15s along with the grenades. The same thing happens, the NVA move back. I look at my watch in the lull and am flabbergasted that three hours have gone by. It is quiet again, but we have a problem: they know our position. When the attack comes, sure as shit we are going to eat RPG rounds like they were popcorn. The kid and I move off to the left where I have dug an enclave into the back wall of the commo trench as a supplementary position. We get set up. It isn't much, but a few meters might give us the edge.

About an hour later, I check my watch. It is two-thirty a.m. If the attack comes it will be now. Spectre has been over us all night, taking out targets out beyond the reach of our guns. They are waiting for the second ship to replace them when I see the flashes of big guns off to the northwest. I grab the kid and we both hug the back of the small enclave. I count the seconds and then we hear the whine of big shells descending on the hilltop.

We take about eight rounds and then the night erupts as two RPG rockets bracket the position we had abandoned, punctuating a growing crescendo of automatic fire from the hill below us. We can hear the NVA as they come up the hill, screaming to keep up their courage and dishearten us. It is a primal, spine-tingling sound, coming from the bowels of men as frightened and angry as we are.

The trench line is getting chewed up and they are getting closer. I hear a couple of the toe poppers go off, and we both throw grenades in the direction of the sounds. When they are getting too close I torch off one of the claymores on my side and Bang does the same on his side. The big shells just keep impacting all around the hill. One hits the top and one hits just to our left. As the air fills with dust, cordite and the coppery smell of blood mixed with viscera, we rise and open up on the slope below us.

The NVA charge has been decimated, leaving just a couple of them still a threat. As soon as we open up, we move back to our original position. An RPG whooshes down to our left and impacts in the trench we had vacated. Someone on top of the hill drops two M79 rounds on him. We can hear them as they stumble down the hill. The claymores have broken the back of their assault.

The second Spectre comes on scene, and they start pummeling the NVA below us with 20 mm and 7.62 miniguns. The NVA are driven further and further back.

As they retreat, the 105 mm opens up, impacting on what I suspect are groups of fleeing infantry. We check our ammo and I crawl out to replace the claymore that I fired. While I am there I crawl over to make sure the other two haven't been turned around or their wires snipped.

When I get back to the hole I tell the kid to go up top to get some more ammo for us and see if he can get some more grenades. We have plenty, but it is always better to have more. The moans and coughing of the NVA wounded finally subside just before light or false dawn. They make another try at us around the same time but Spectre breaks the back of that one before it even gets started.

As dawn starts to illuminate the landscape we can begin to see the carnage that the grenades and the claymores have wrought below us. There are shapes that represent the crumpled remains of the NVA who were chopped down before they got to our lines. We can make out about twenty or so as the light becomes more pronounced. There is still some light rain but I can see the clouds lifting. Spectre is working over a target about four kilometers from us. I hope it is the guns that have been firing at us.

I am about to open another PIR when Bang opens up on the M60. It scares the shit out of me and at the same time I am angry that he has exposed the position. The kid lets fly with about ten rounds at the same time. I look in the direction that he fired and see now that four of the bodies we had thought were dead, now most certainly are. They had feigned death and when it got light enough had popped up with an RPG. They were going to roast my nuts with it when Bang saw them. Another five that had been hiding below the dip off to our right had gotten up to follow their lead when the kid and Bang got them as well. At least no one got back with the information about where the guns were. I tell everyone to pot any bodies they can see to make sure we, and only we, are the living up here.

Covey comes back on station and the day begins anew. He starts to work targets as the morning slowly unwinds. We are fine until about nine when he reports that there are more and more people moving into our area. Around eleven, he is making a pass over to our north when dirty black puffs of smoke start to track him across his flight. He jinks and weaves and gets down on the deck, as at least three fifty-calibers open up on him. Shit, they have brought up anti-aircraft. They will start to layer it to keep the bombers and Spectre at bay. Covey flatlines across the valley with everything they have tracking his movement, then suddenly rockets for altitude. He gets up about eight thousand before the AA starts to slack off.

Two sets of fast movers come out of the east, real low, and try to work over the gun positions, dropping hard bombs and CBUs. One of them shits a dirty black exhaust and starts to smoke. He and his wingman limp off back to the east. Spectre will move off and let the bombers take over the heavy work. This goes on for about four hours with no slack. The more they bomb the shit out of the surrounding ridges, the more guns seem to be popping up.

Around three in the afternoon we have been at it all day without any artillery trying to turn us into ground beef. Now it starts up. We hear the distant booms of the artillery from at least three sides and all the while the AA is stiffening. I hear the rounds coming in and we all get under cover. The barrage lasts for about half an hour, with the guns starting to get more and more impacts on and around the top of the hill. I hate artillery, there is nothing more unnerving or frightening than having to lie there and take it. We have two rounds impact in the draw in front of us, as others do the same on top and on Cookie's side. We aren't getting any direct fire but the artillery is chewing up the draw and the slope. For sure, they have gotten all the mines by either sympathetic detonation or direct hits. Now they are throwing variable time-fused so that we are getting peppered with shrapnel from airbursts.

All the while the bombers are dodging AA and trying to knock out the guns. There are brief lulls in the artillery but each time it seems to come back even heavier. During one of the lulls, Mac comes slithering down the trench and flops into the hole with the kid and me. I am brewing some coffee and he nearly spills the canteen cup that I am cooking it in over some C4 explosive that burns with a blue incandescence. Another brace of rounds come in and plaster the east side of our perimeter.

"You guys alright down here?" he wheezes as he slides in past me. I whisk the cup out of the way of his boots. The C4 starts to melt his shoe lace. I throw some dirt on it to put it out.

"We were fine until you decided to come down. Haven't you got somewhere to be?" I ask him. He spits and reaches for the cup. I give it to him and he takes a sip burning his lip in the process. "Shit that's hot!" he exclaims.

"No shit? And here I thought it would be cool and refreshing. It is coffee, you dimwit. It's supposed to be hot." He looks at the kid and tells him to make it up the hill and join Cook on the other side. The kid waits until another brace of rounds come in and shoots out of our happy little hovel and up the trench to the other side. Mac takes out a cigarette and lights it up. He takes a few drags then leans back against the wall where the kid and I have been digging back into the hillside, between looking for the infantry assault and dodging the incoming all morning. Artillery is a great motivator for improving your digging skills and practicing control over your sphincter muscles.

"They are pulling us out of here in about an hour," he says through a stream of smoke. He is sweat stained and has a nick on his forehead, which trickles a bit of blood occasionally. "They think there is a weather front that is going to close in about five, and then even Spectre won't be able to help us." He passes the cigarette to me, but I take out one of my own and light it up. The artillery abates outside and we can hear the jets as they come in and drop rack after rack on positions on the other ridges. Covey flits in and out of the AA, marking targets for them.

"Who the hell is flying Covey?" I ask, but Mac just shrugs it off with no answer. "We are getting on the birds fast when they come in, so take only what you normally carry, everything else rig here and leave it. Do you still have those time pencils?" he asks.

"Yeah, let me guess, you want I should leave a couple of surprises?" He nods affirmation.

"They are going to bomb the shit out of the hill but it can't hurt. Right now Covey is stacking assets over an orbit point. Just before they pull us, they are going to work this valley and ridges over hard, then bring the choppers in and pull us out while they have the AA suppressed. Covey thinks they can pull us before the weather shits all over us. In about twenty minutes from now, rig everything and get your ass up the hill, you are going out on the second bird. Cook will take the kid with him with three of the Yards. Thermite the sixty ammo, it's too much weight, just take your personal weapons and ammo. If we get shot down at least we can fight and hold. Everything else, rig to blow or burn it."

"Is the weather that bad? I figured they would wait for night then pound the shit out of us and rush the top." I am watching through the gun port and still don't see any movement. The artillery is slackening but still going on; it has been supplemented by mortars which are starting to get the range.

"Twenty minutes then get up top. We have enough cover to get the whole team in up there. Get ready to see the cavalry come sweeping in." He adjusts his gear and raises to a crouch. He looks back at me and grins. "Oh by the way, it isn't just the weather, Covey thinks we have a division plus backed up and they are moving this way."

"That ought to make Cook feel better; otherwise he might think we went pussy on him." He laughs at that, then scurries up the trench to the top of the hill. I spend the next twenty minutes rigging everything we can't take with us so that the unsuspecting will have a kick start on their journey. I get Bang and Loi down with me. We have set a time pencil on a thermite grenade on the mortar rounds and with the excess machine-gun ammo as the bombers arrive. They are hitting targets all around us on the ridges and the AA fire is almost suppressed when we arrive breathless at the top of the hill.

There are still some incoming, but Mac is calling in where we think it is. Each time we mark a target, Covey responds and brings a set of bombers to work the position. Jesus there are a lot of birds up there. Two F4 Phantoms come streaking down the mouth of the valley, all green, black and deadly looking, their flight being tracked by twin streams of green tracers and black angry puffs of ack-ack, trailing them as the gunners try to adjust. The two Phantoms release their loads. Four tumbling silver pods spiral off and then the forest below erupts in a boiling inferno. Napalm. They must have gotten the guns because as they hook right and start to get altitude, nothing follows them back upstairs.

We are still receiving some indirect fire as the Cobras come into the valley. The gunships bank and come in to start to work the area around our hilltop. Automatic weapons fire starts to pepper the hill. The gunships fire their rockets and their chin turrets open up. I run over to the Cookie and we replace his guys in the trench as the first of the slicks come in, their blades slapping the thick air. I look down slope and there are bloody NVA trying to gain the top and get in amongst us. Not just a question of big balls, but also the safest place to be on this hill right now with all these wing jockeys and rotor heads blasting anything in sight. Cook gives me one of his single-eyebrow Ranger scowls and torches all of the claymores on his side of the hill. The NVA dissolve in a hurling wave of steel pellets. One moment they were coming up the hill and the next there isn't anything standing.

The first slick arrives and Cook is slinging people onboard. Once he is sure that he has all his people, he springs in the door; the chopper rockets up and away, bleeding off altitude for speed, then starts to lift away to the east. The next chopper, my ride, comes in. I get all my people up and we hog rush the bird. I do the same as Cook, throwing myself on last. As I get on I notice that the bird has a bit of art on the side. It says: "Door Number Three, Ticket to the land of the Big PX." Everyone seems to be a frustrated wit these days.

As we take the same roller coaster dip off the hill and dash off, finally gaining altitude, we spot one of the guns trailing smoke with his wingman riding herd on him. Jesus he is really smoking. I have the headsets on and there is chatter between Covey and the stricken bird. It looks like he might be able to clear the valley, but he won't go much further because there are already greedy red flickers of flame coming from the engine and transmission compartment. I look down as Mac clears the hilltop and starts up to join us. He hardly clears the hill when two Spads swoop in and drop their bombs right on the hill we just vacated. The whole hill erupts and the top jumps before collapsing back. If anything is left down there, and the NVA are able to salvage it, they will be lucky.

We are moving east as we see the gunship that had taken the hits make a hard landing about two miles from the hill we vacated. His wingman lands with him and they roll the ammunition drum out. The two pilots from the stricken bird load into the bay. The second bird is up before they get the door of the bay closed. It banks and turns back at the Cobra on the ground, which continues to burn. They rocket the wreck and it explodes in a shower of flaming wreckage. A Spad goes over after they are clear and dumps a bomb on it to ensure its destruction.

The breeze coming in from the open cargo doors is refreshing and as we gain altitude it gets cooler. I am listening as Covey starts to clear all the aircraft from over the target area. Everyone unasses the area, then I hear why. There is an Arc Light B52 strike moving in on our heels. They are going to carpet bomb the whole area. Evidently our little annoyance attracted a whole bunch of Nguyen. We were good bait.

The strike starts as we get almost out of sight. The skies are starting to darken behind us when the whole area seems to erupt in a rolling series of explosions. The concussion is so great that we can feel it onboard. It is beautiful and deadly at the same time. Men are dying down there, horribly. I try not to dwell on it. With that much ordinance down there, I am glad someone pulled the plug on us and got us off that hilltop. Off to the west I can actually see the storm wall. Had they waited, we would have been truly screwed, blued, and tattooed. With no air cover, they would have slammed us into dirt with artillery then assaulted up the hill and wiped our lily-white asses off the map.

I lean back against the pilot's seat and let the angst and pressure drain away as we fly into the night toward the launch site. I am exhausted and, at the same time, grateful that we have escaped our fate once again. The steady throb and vibration of the chopper lull me into dreamland. As I do, I realize how badly I smell. Fear and cordite. Eau de Trench.

CHAPTER 15

Bum Job

Greek mythology has poor Prometheus chained to a rock, with an eagle arriving each morning at dawn to eat his liver, and then leaving at dusk. He is condemned by the gods to suffer this torment for eternity in restitution and atonement for his giving mortals the gift of fire.

The Greek gods were at best a capricious lot, but no doubt, this bit of lore was generated to somehow impress on the masses the penalties for not following the rules, and the fact that irony exists with two sides. We poor mortals have a debt to pay with poor Prometheus but should temper our regret with the knowledge that we did take it a step further than heating up raw meat and driving game. From this gift of fire we forged metal, and learned how to harness its energy. After that, we unfortunately started acting like the Greek gods and fell to squabbling amongst ourselves, using those gifts to better slaughter each other. This gift from the divine has me in its clutches. All that fire and brimstone needs victims, and I am one of them at the moment.

Here in the cauldron of war that art is a practiced and piteous application. We have one saving grace, however. We have medical personnel that can do wondrous feats in the effort to save lives. These are our first responders to medical emergencies that would daunt the best-equipped trauma centers in the States. All would be the epitome of angels of mercy, and cloaked in the Hippocratic Oath, if it were not for a few distinct and disturbing tendencies. Our medical staff, though brilliant and dedicated, make the rest of us look like paragons of sanity by comparison. Usually, you will have a spattering of small cuts abrasions, gashes, and bruises. When you start calling in close air support, all that lead and shrapnel flying around shreds trees and ricochets off the rocks and ground. You are bound to get hit by some of it. Usually it's gravel and small pepper stuff from the 40 mm guns, grenades, and parts of helicopters if they get the range.

We normally dig it out in the shower or, if it requires a pluck and a stitch, have one of the medics do it. Unless it's serious it's not a real wound no matter how many pieces are involved. I'm not a ribbon junkie so no need to put in for a purple heart, or as we call them, VC Marksmanship badges.

I am ruminating over these ponderous issues because two such angels are busy removing bits of that same fire-forged metal from my ass and back. They are plucking away at my mortal remains and pulling the fragments out to deposit them in a pan next to the makeshift operating table, consisting of a table in the chow hall, at the launch site in Quang Tri. The whole affair is tinged with the somber reflection of their Hippocratic Oath, but deep in my heart I know that I am but another training aid to furthering their medical expertise. I have Woody working on me and, either by great luck or curse, Rowdy Yates is visiting from NKP and just happened to be available to assist.

I am on my stomach with my derriere exposed, numbed by lidocaine, but I'm aware of the incessant pressure and twinge of dulled pain as they meticulously probe and dissect, searching for the pepper shrapnel. Mudhole has donated a bottle of his Old Rebel Yell and it is being passed around members of the audience, consisting of my fellow chimps, and occasionally to myself and the two stalwarts from the medical community. It is like being in the hands of Dr. Frankenstein and Dr. Mengele, for all the bedside manner these two have.

I finally get a shot at the bourbon as it is being passed, and the whiskey burns almost as much as my ass will in the morning. I hand it back to Mac, and he looks at me with a bemused expression and inquires as to how I am feeling.

"I feel like I look, you dimwit, how does it look from where you are?"

"Pretty messy," he replies, then takes another swig and passes the bottle over to Pulley, who snorts in derision. Besides me, the patient, there are five others sharing the experience and listening to the drone of the two medics as they work on me.

"Ouch! Godammit! Give me some more lidocaine."

"Quit sniveling, and hold still. You're messing up our work," comes the retort, followed by the clink of another metal piece hitting the pan. I twist my head to see if I can spot what they're up to, but a rubber-gloved hand pushes my head back in place. I am beginning to suspect they are slicing me up, and merely picking up shrapnel from the pan and dropping it back in again. Most of the grenade had missed me and the rest embedded itself mainly in my lower back, and of course my ass. I only have myself to blame because I had thrown it. It had bounced off a tree and gone off way short of where I had wanted it to go. I felt the blast and a few sharp pains, but didn't think I was wounded. It had also peppered Loi and Xam Pat, though not as bad. They were plucked before I got my round on the table. They just smiled at me before they left. I could swear they snuck back in and had replaced the medics.

Mac giggles and bends down so that he is at eye level. He has just reminded me that this is probably the fourth time they have plucked pieces out of me. He should talk, we spend the first two days after a mission finding new and painful little pricks after the body begins to naturally reject whatever has been driven into it.

"Cookie went over to get the camera, so we can have positive proof that can accompany your recommendation for the Purple Heart. If I was you, I would be grateful that we don't press charges. After all that shrapnel is in your backside, not the proper location, being in the front, which would indicate that you were advancing on the enemy." He giggles again.

"Mac, you want to try your hand at this?" The comment comes from Yates, behind me. I am saved, if you can call it that, by Cook's arrival with the camera. He starts to take pictures, which just encourages the crowd to ham it up with me as the centerpiece of their little snap fest.

"How far are these two ham-fisted butchers from finishing?" I implore, but the crowd is apparently too involved in medical history and derision. Cook peers at me.

"Looks about halfway. Jesus, do you have to bleed so much? We have to eat in here you know." This of course elicits several comments about my uncouthness, and the possible infestations of cooties because of me. Cooties? I hope the whole damn crowd comes down with the clap. I wish I was infectious with some horrible affliction that would make their days full of swollen peckers and runny shorts.

We are here doing this because I didn't want to go over to the Evac hospital and have to sit all afternoon and have some pink-faced doctor doing the same with all the requisite paperwork involved. In that respect, like poor Prometheus, my pain is my own damn fault. My humiliation, on the other hand, is the result of the medics suggesting that they could use the occasion to do some dynamite training and get everyone involved.

Probe, gouge, tug, plink, it seems like it has gone on forever. I look up at Mac.

"Did these two meat merchants wash their hands before they started working on me? If not, make sure they use some of that bourbon to sterilize themselves, would you?"

"Don't worry about sterilizing, they are wearing gloves. Rowdy keeps picking his nose though. I'm not sure that is all that good of an idea."

"Ouch! What kind of gloves? Arctic mittens? Give me another pull on that bourbon, I feel like I am getting nauseous."

"No shit? If you're going to throw up let me get some color film," Cook interjects.

"Are you alright?" Someone bends over in front to peer at me. He and Rowdy have a whispered conversation about the effects of the local, and some other horseshit about the possibility of shock, but the docs never stop plucking metal out of my backside. Someone slides a bucket over so it is positioned in case I do hurl. Lovely. I feel like the rat plopped down in the eagles' nest as lunch for the chicks. I should have known better when I suggested that they do it instead of hauling over to the hospital. As soon as they started talking about debreeding the wound, I should have suspected that this was going to entail something more than tweezer-pulling the chunks that I could feel close to the surface.

I have seen chase medics do some amazing feats that defy medical logic, or practice. They save lives, but it is the butcher's shop of medical treatment onboard the helicopter. This is where the skill and focus pay the highest dividends. It ain't pretty, but they save lives. This little discomfort of mine is but a side bar for them.

All in all I would trust a Special Forces medic before I would most doctors, especially this crowd. There are a lot of us that entrust our lives to them; a whole bunch more that are no longer here, but back in the States, owe their lives to their expertise.

I don't know what Rowdy is doing here; he was over in NKP as the medic there. I suppose he came over to do a little hobnobbing with his contemporaries. Now as a group, we have a job that borders on insanity and we all have our, shall we say, eccentric behaviors; but the medics are by far the most colorful of any of us. Rowdy, for example, is a near legend amongst us; legendary not just for his ability, but because of his sometimes odd behavior.

Rowdy had a string of bad luck a while back. Every time he went in on a Bright Light, the aircraft got shot to ribbons, often resulting in the bird going down and the crew being on the ground with Herr Doktor. This, of course, does not endear you to the aviation crowd. Aviators are a superstitious group as a whole. Normally you can shake down any crew and find a proliferation of rabbits' feet, four-leaf clovers, Virgin Marys, ju-ju beads and whatever else passes for a talisman. This is just their way of ignoring the odds that permeate the act of flying in a lead hailstorm. Rotor heads are your basic wrench fanatics with techno vocabularies, and their brains are much the same as a Huey transmission: lots of stuff whirring around in opposite directions, in some kind of superheated oil.

Never-the-less, Rowdy was getting the reputation of being a bit of a jinx to airmen. After several downed airman incidents, Rowdy was inserted on a Bright Light. The air asset then immediately whisked off to high orbit as a precautionary measure. Of course, Rowdy took umbrage at this lack of etiquette. The next time he went in, he had to rappel in on a 120-foot rope. Not wishing to be left without a quick exit available via his superstitious ride, he deftly tied off the trailing end to the nearest tree stump. The helo crowd applied power to no avail, since they were firmly anchored to the bonds of the surly earth with a tugboat bowline with a half hitch. Herr Yates performed his act of medical history and deftly attached himself and the casualty to the rope, giving the helo the heads up and they slingshot him through the void above the Landing Zone.

There were recriminations and ass-chewings from the pilots to the crew chief about forgetting to have the bush axe that is installed on the inner cargo compartment for cutting away snagged ropes and like encumbrances. It wasn't the crew chief's fault since Rowdy had the foresight to take the axe with him when he exited the aircraft at 60 feet above the jungle.

This, of course, made him a pariah with the aircraft set: not only was he jinxed, but he was devious to a degree that makes that crowd uncomfortable about your intentions. He was a brilliant medic but had the aircrews in a snit over what they saw as a blatant disregard for safety regulations and concern for their carcasses. This was when they sent him over to NKP. At NKP we used the big CH53s owned by the Air Force as our rotary lift asset on the targets. You could tie one of those babies to a concrete pillar and all it would do is rev up the rpms before it jerked it loose and flew off with it.

Besides, the Air Force has its own rendition of chase medics, called para-rescue. It reminds me of that ditty, "The wind blew, and the shit flew, and there stood Para Rescue." No doubt Rowdy and his zoomy counterparts have dampened his past history to keep the Air Force pilots from getting a case of the jitters. Ouch! Then again, it could be the reason that he is back in Quang Tri, our northern launch site. The aircrews here had been nervous as a whore in church ever since he returned. The ill wind of bad karma was back with all his little Southern homily-laden quirks. This all would be funny except at the moment I was under the knife with him and the rest of the yak-yak crowd, clucking their way through what I suspect is the taxidermy manual.

"We're almost done," comes the news from my hinter zone, along with another clink of deposited metal. "We are going to sew up a couple of these, so it might hurt a bit. We want to save the lidocaine for something serious." Great. I have to be the victim of cost savings and some bizarre idea that they need to save anything other than my discomfort. They ought to save that lidocaine for mystery meat night, to deaden our palates.

No one has drifted off, since apparently my surgery is haute entertainment for the evening. At least Budrow and Slatten are off doing something over at the TOC.

* * *

I had come by this extra ornamentation during a last-minute Bright Light. Of course all of them are last-minute, but in this case we had been snatched from the airfield on our way back to Da Nang because they lost a number of birds on a particularly hot insert. Getting the team out was now compounded by the fact that they had two birds down and needed brawn and armed beef to go get the crews out.

We had drawn the easiest package. No wounded among the crew, just some broken bones and bruises, and the bird hadn't turned into a barbecue after it got done thrashing away at the vegetation. At least, that's what we thought at the beginning. As it turned out, most of the crew had survived, but the right door gunner was still in the aircraft, with the other gunner dead as a Christmas goose along beside him.

The pilot and the co-pilot had made a quick assessment of the door gunner and surmised that he was toast, so they had taken his gun and started to escape and evade. All this we did not know until we got on the ground.

We had inserted slightly above the bird and worked our way down with Covey flying a watch over us. He got the word on the emergency frequency that all surviving members were some two hundred meters from the bird and squawking for someone to come pick them up. We started moving toward the aircraft and Mac noticed that someone was moving around the inside of it. Cookie is our best hand grenade thrower, so he chucked a mini grenade at the chopper, thinking that it was NVA on the wreck. The grenade went off and cooked off something else just as I had thrown another and stood up to motion Thua and Bang to watch to the rear. I ended up with pepper shrapnel from the secondary. Mac said that whoever it was, the grenade didn't get them and Cookie wound up another.

That's when we all heard this small voice yell out feebly, "Please don't throw another grenade down here, there is fuel all over the place," followed by a sob. That's when we realized that someone from the crew was still inside. We moved in quickly and Mac and Cookie got busy pulling the kid out and tending to his wounds. We got him and the body and moved to an extraction point. The kid was in pain but still was game. More importantly, his will to live was bolstered by his desire for revenge. He was cussing a blue streak about the pilots leaving him for dead and adding insult to injury by taking the gun with them. Hey, shit happens. Who knows if he was even conscious when they hightailed it? What mattered was that he thought they abandoned him, so he was full of piss and vinegar, making our job easier in getting him to the LZ.

We had come out right after that, and the area filled up with NVA looking to dish out a little whup-ass. They eventually recovered the co-pilot and made the mistake of putting him in the same recovery ward as the door gunner. This resulted in another attempt at medical history as the wounded door gunner tried to haul his ass out of his bed over to where the co-pilot was recovering, and wrap his hands around his commissioned neck for a bit of asphyxia with dialogue.

I, in the meantime, was in pain because my carcass had been riddled with all sorts of pepper shrapnel front and back, and I had trouble sitting without bolts of pain accompanying any movement. It wasn't debilitating, but painful enough that I didn't want to continue as the steel finally set in and established itself. On top of that I heard that I might have to change my name to Magnet Ass.

It was Mac's idea that I get this rendition of Dr. Strangelove to remove it so that we can be on the bird back to Da Nang in the morning. If I went over to the Evac hospital I would be there three or four days in post-op. No thank you.

* * *

"Tell me again why we are using the mess hall instead of our dispensary?" I inquire as I tear up from the pain from what appears to be a badly placed suture. Mac sees that I am tearing and deftly dabs my face with his cravat, along with the admonishment not to be a cry baby. He takes another pull on the bourbon and hands me the bottle. This, of course, doesn't slow down the chop shop. Rowdy is busy detailing the statistics of Civil War surgery and the horrendous wounds produced by the .58 caliber minnie ball, along with the litany of symptoms of gangrene, including the cheese smell. There is an argument as to whether it smells like Provolone or blue cheese; all the while I feel like the subject of a saddle shop repair.

"We aren't chancing a streptococcus infection, you dimwit. The dispensary was flooded last week and we are sterilizing it," comes from behind me. From the way they say it one would assume that the dispensary was knee deep in mud from an overflowing latrine on the Tigris, and there was a crew of white-garbed technicians cleaning the place up. In truth they had soaked the place in chlorine and iodine and opened the windows to air it out. The water had never gotten above six inches, but to hear them describe it the place was a death trap for anyone with an open wound. I suspect that they are hiding some choice booze inside the pharmacy, or have chucked all the medication that needs to be refrigerated because they are hiding several T-bone steaks in the refrigeration unit until we all leave.

* * *

I have seen the true face of these meat merchants before. Once I had been on the peripheral of one of our rockets and had been perforated by many small splinters from the "blown" tree next to me. In that case the Woodham brothers surmised that I needed to be trundled over to the evacuation hospital, clucking about sterile fields and crystallization of wounds, along with cauterization or some other medical bullshit.

Normally we are odd enough as patient profiles to attract undue attention from everyone not directly involved in emergency lifesaving. Since it is a rule that someone from the unit be there when we are under anesthesia, lest we give away some horrid secret under the gas, our presence is attended by whoever is qualified... and the curious.

In this case they hauled me in, looking like the target at a pygmy blowgun tournament. I had probably a hundred odd splinters, ranging from a foot long to a few inches, sticking out of me. They took one look at me and insisted that I go to the hospital. On top of that, they painfully drove me over in the only vehicle we had at the launch site with full canvas covers on it. I could smell a rat at this point.

This first time, when I was taken to the Evac hospital, I was being plucked by the hospital staff while I had an unobstructed view through a window in the OR of the three-quarter-ton truck we came in. As the staff merrily plucked me clean of lumber, I noticed the twins and one of the commo guys shuttling back and forth and loading all sorts of equipment and supplies into the back of the truck; boxes upon boxes of stuff. The coup de grace was when they were finishing me up: I saw the two of them removing an air conditioner from an outside bracket and slinging it into the back of the truck as well. They popped out of sight and reappeared in the OR to join the first one who had come in just ahead of them, as they were finishing me up. They quickly hustled me out with the whispered admonishment to the staff that anything they might have heard me mumble was to be considered classified, etc. and whisked me out to the truck. I had come over face down on the stretcher in the back. This time I was shoved in the front and the commo guy squeezed in the back with the two of them on either side, grinning like baboons.

We had roared off in a shower of mud and careened out the gate of the medical compound. That is the nature of medicine with this crowd. I wasn't just a hallmark injury that needed the attention of a physician and surgical staff, I was a handy diversion to facilitate some pilfering. Of course, I had questioned their motivation as we careened down the track back to the compound. The only answer I got was that they had merely been re-supplying the medical section with tools and supplies to better assist them in patching us up. All the loot in the back was purely so that they could better serve their fellow chimps. In that case, I am still wondering what use the medical field has for a gross of: Panties, Small, Government Issue. I didn't want to ask since they probably would lie their way through some half-baked explanation of how in their off hours they unravel them to recover the silk thread so they can use it for suturing.

* * *

From the tugs and pulls on my rear bumper, the current mess hall surgery is almost finished. I hear Rowdy tell the audience that it looks like they have got most of it and to wrap things up before chow time. I feel the last tug and they bandage me, then I am hauled to a position on my side and helped to stand up. There is the sound of beer cans being opened and then a can is shoved into my hand, with the instruction to go ahead and drink it so I can rehydrate myself. I stand up and it feels like I am lifting an extra ten pounds in my ass because of the lidocaine. Mac and Cookie help me over to the team hootch as the meat merchants clean up the table and surrounding area, wrapping everything of waste category in the sheet they had used as a bed cover on the table.

Budrow comes over about an hour later and tells us that we are going back to Da Nang as soon as he can get us a plane, so that we won't be eating up his dwindling supply of rations at the launch site. He looks at me and says that the medics had informed him that the Evac hospital had given me a clean bill of health. Right. I will save this little escapade as blackmail material, in case I need it for later. It won't do any good to rat them out to Doc Wang, since his only response would be to bitch about not being there to evaluate and advise. At that point I don't care since the pain is coming back. Rowdy comes over about a half hour after that, looks me over and gives me painkillers.

The ride back to Da Nang on the Caribou is pleasant enough since I take two of the painkillers and spend the flight cushioned in a fog of Demerol. Four would have been too many, since being unconscious would have assuredly led to some sort of mischief with me as the centerpiece. All of this medical entertainment for others, and I didn't bother to put in for a slow movers badge, Purple Heart.

CHAPTER 16

Heaven Has Claws

Back in Da Nang, we are notified that we have a few more ancillary duties to perform. I have to go down to Nha Trang for a promotion board and also I have been selected for an interview for entry into the officer program, if I choose. The Army isn't handing out commissions like it did in the heady days after Tet of 1968. It is getting ready to wind down the war and is looking to fill its ranks by encouraging NCOs to take the opportunity to attend Officer Candidate School. I want to attend Officer School like I want to have a bad case of jungle rot. But by going to Nha Trang, I can get a few more days of slack time for the team, before we have to get serious again.

I also was informed that I likely will be transferred to Crusader because Lamar and Kelly will be leaving. Crusader needs to be built back up to get it back on the mission calendar. Peewee is also transferring in and possibly a third American. The team is experienced with the exception of three new Yards. It's a good team; they are Bru like on Habu. That means at least four more days tacked onto our normal stand-down. Peewee and I will have to do the transition after they leave. He is with them now and can share the One-Zero responsibilities on Crusader. While I am gone, he can organize the training for the new Yards so that when I get transferred we can start the training cycle. He can join me in Nha Trang after two days and we can kick back for a little Intoxication and Intercourse, or as the Army calls it, Rest and Recuperation.

I head over to the orderly room where Captain Manes is interviewing those selected for the august prestige of officer training. Frenchy, the company clerk, motions me to a seat and tells me that Laughing Larry has someone else in his office. We chat for a few minutes; he is solicitous over my having such a short time to get in the slot, and he says that we will probably not draw a target until we feel that the team is ready, so I should plan my timing around that. Now there are a few teams that take advantage of that latitude. In fact, there are a couple of assholes who do nothing but train a team up, then find some reason to fire half of them just before they think they will get a target. Or they only take the targets that are in the soft areas, under the guise of breaking in a new team: then they fire them and start all over again. They know who they are, we know who they are, and the reason for their lassitude is really that they're looking for a spine transplant. Jones is giving me free rein because he knows that in a timely manner I will have the team ready and we will go back on the ready list. It's a short list, brother, because of our casualty rate, plus the half-steppers who are too shaky to run and too proud to quit.

The door opens and Manes comes out with Lamar. He is being unusually patronizing.

"Well, just go on down to Nha Trang and, when you get there, go in front of the selection board and give them all the reasons you don't want to be an officer. But you are going because that's what the dad-blamed Command wants, and what they want is what they are getting, understood?" Lamar turns, grins at me, gives me a thumbs-up signal, then silently mouths, "Four...days...in...Nha Trang." He grins. Jesus, that boy has more teeth than an alligator, I am thinking, as he goes out the door.

Manes looks at Frenchy and asks him who is next. He points at me and Larry makes a grimace, followed by a hand signal to follow him into the office. He settles his chunkiness into the chair behind the desk and pulls out my 201 file. He looks it over for a few minutes. His jaw is working like he is trying to calculate some weighty question, which is good, because it is probably the prospect of how much trouble Lamar and I can get into with four days in Nha Trang on our hands. We do have a certain reputation for misbehavior, which is fine with Larry as long as he doesn't have to write any lengthy reports, and when we come back, we do our job. In fact, Larry is something of a genius at burying indiscretions. On at least one occasion, it is rumored that he actually reported the Mini Mac and myself killed in action, to quash further inquiries.

"You have been selected for the promotion board and an interview for Officer Candidate School. If you are actually selected for this privilege, you will be leaving here and robbing the war effort of one more body, and probably depriving a village somewhere of a perfectly good idiot. How in the hell anyone up at the Department of the Army even considered you and the other miscreants on this list for this opportunity is beyond me. They might want to give whoever did this a urinalysis and see what kind of drugs they are taking." I start to give him some flippant reply about how he received his commission, but he stops me with a wave of his hand and continues. "I don't want to hear any objections, or even if you are actually considering this as a possibility. I am simply following AR something-something-dash-something in conducting this pre-selection interview, prior to sending you and those other bandits down to Nha Trang for four days. Which is exactly three days, 23 hours, and 50 minutes too long, since any baboon that meets you brigands at the airport would immediately assume that you are a prison detail, not there for promotion, much less being considered for a commission."

"You can consider this the end of the pre-selection interview, promotion board and the beginning of the warning." He pauses and takes a breath. "You will be packed and ready to leave at 0630 tomorrow morning, and will be transported to the airport, where you will take a government plane to Nha Trang." I am thinking, no shit *Dai Uy*, I didn't think they would give us tickets on Air Nuc Mam. He continues, "While you are there you will try not to embarrass this command with any of your usual little hilarities, which in case you are vague on, I will list. One, you will NOT take your German uniform with you, and you will NOT wear it. Two, you will NOT attempt to commit acts that would bring discredit on this unit, or the army in general. That is just about everything running through that minuscule brain of yours at this time. Three, you all will stay away from the streamer bar. Four, if you do commit any acts that require me to cover for you, I won't. Five, speak French so no one knows you belong to me." He looks up at me again, then back at my file, which he closes, then tosses over onto a pile of others on the field table. He folds his hands over his gut and leans back in his chair. The chair squeaks in protest.

"I am sure I will think of more and will have the Sergeant Major reiterate them in the morning if he has time. Just go by the Golden Rule while you are there." I get a chance here as he is between breaths, so I hop in real quick.

"What would that be, *Dai Uy*?"

He scowls at me and works his jaws like he is trying to chew a steel bolt, then answers.

"I am watching. I not only see everything, I hear all. Now get out of my office and maybe I can get some work done." I get up and start for the door when he says to me, "Nick," and I turn to face him.

"Yeah, *Dai Uy*?"

"I am sorry about bringing this up but we need more teams running and you are qualified to take over your own team. You should have been in that slot months ago but managed to avoid it dexterously, through deceit. We can't have all that talent on one team. That goes for Cook as well. We need to fill up teams and get them active so that the rest of you get a break in the roster." I look at him and give it my best abused hound look "Thanks but I don't agree with you Dai Uy. Habu does well because we click together." I answer him.

"I know, I just wanted you to know your team has done an excellent job out there. Crusader is a possible and it has good people and will need someone to lead it and you will make it your own eventually. Go and do well on the promotion board in Nha Trang. They don't know you like we do, so you might slip by. For what it's worth, you ought to get through the promotion board simple enough, listen to what they have to say about taking OCS and getting a commission." Then he goes back to pulling another file out of the stack in front of him.

I go out the door and there are two more of us sitting in the chairs: Larson and Hendrick. They both look up, with quizzical expressions on their faces.

"The selection board has been canceled; we are getting new targets north of the DMZ," I tell them in passing. Larson looks shocked. Hendrick only knits his brows "This is the selection interview, you two; I am dealing with Article the door and views his next two interviewees. I hear him speak before the door closes behind me,

"This is the selection interview, you two; I am dealing with Article 15s and court-martials after lunch." I am happily on my way back to the hootch, mulling the prospects of the promotion and the OCS interview. Those heady days when they were handing out direct commissions are long gone. In fact with the war winding down, a lot of those who received them would get rifted back to enlisted ranks or forced into retirement before they upset the actuary tables for the ring knockers and cadet mills. OCS has always produced the majority of officers, so the army is falling back on its old norm.

* * *

Ah, Nha Trang, the jewel of the Orient. Of all the cities in this cesspool they call a country, it is my current favorite. I would love to buy one of the French restaurants here and settle down, that's how much I like this place. It is cooled by sea breezes and has a history that goes back to the Mandarin conquests. It has all the ambience of the East with none of the sprawling decadence that comes with Saigon.

By mid-morning, we are finished with assigning barracks and getting instructions. I take my TWs over to the laundry and pay the girl extra to hand-press them with military creases, and give my brass and such to the hootch maids, with some added cash to ensure they spin polish them. I have no intention of going to OCS, but I am going to look my best in front of the promotion board anyway. Pride, you know, is a terrible vice.

I run into several guys I know. We are all going to meet in the afternoon then make a night run on the bars in Nha Trang. The Special Forces are in town, pinheads, so lock up your girlfriends and lie low until we leave. We get at least four warning briefings. It all boils down to don'ts: don't do anything, it seems, especially anything that might draw embarrassment to the command. Well, what are they going to do? Send us to Vietnam? I have been busted before. I expect I will again. No big deal; rank is easy in a war zone. So we all make the suicide pact: if one goes down, we all go down. No witnesses. Huzzah! I love these guys. This is my family.

So we go downtown and have some fun. There are a whole bunch of guys here I haven't seen in an age. Some I have served on the ground with before, most I have been in trouble with at least once. There is a new sergeant major, and he seems to be a decent sort. He's given us the inside on the situation in Nha Trang. Basically, this is a period of downsizing all over Vietnam with every mother's son pulling out except the MPs. That means there are more MPs and fewer troops to look over. The Provost hates us, the MPs certainly do, and the Command isn't as inclined to turn a blind eye toward our frivolities as in the past. *Don't go looking for trouble* is the message…trouble is real easy to come by.

We are all having a few beers in the NCO mess before we go out for the day. Hendrick wants to go down to Cholon and see some of the Nungs, and that sounds fine with me. In the process we are going to stop by François and have some delicious French Vietnamese cuisine. We have enlisted Lamar as the official interpreter. He denies his Franco heritage, and knowing Lamar he is probably some sort of Creole, which means we might as well take a Martian as a go-between for all the good his linguistics will do us. Not a problem, since I have yet to land in a foreign country where sign language couldn't get your belly filled, something alcoholic to drink, and something that smelled better than yourself for company.

We go down to the gate as twilight is approaching, muster out through the portals and grab a cyclo-cab for the ride down to the Streamer Bar. The Streamer is a strange place, with almost a decade of history of being the Special Forces hangout. It has all kinds of SF paraphernalia on the walls and is done in early Team House decor. It does have a bevy of willing and friendly bar girls, one of whom is a tall half-French, half-Cambodian nymph named Chai. She is unofficially a certain *Dai Uy*'s escort when he is in town. She is convinced that her love for him will overcome all obstacles, and possesses some other obscure and insane conviction that he qualifies as eligible and cute. Tonight, however, it is open poaching, since the sterling gentleman is away and there is plenty of distance to keep immediate retribution at bay.

Rick and I are trying to out-position each other to get into her loving embrace. We launch immediately into a stream of condolences about how sad we are about what happened. This elicits from her a raised and haughty eyebrow response, along with the question of what happened.

"Oh gee, we are sorry, we thought you knew," comes our ready response. She looks at us with that sloe-eyed cat look of suspicion and distrust that we as a group seem to solicit from the fairer sex.

"We are sorry about how sad and angry you must be that *Dai Uy* up and got married like that. It must be real hard on you," Rick starts in.

"Yeah, especially since the woman was a Donut Dolly and all," I add. It is a well-known fact that Chai can't stand Donut Dollies since she believes they are official Army prostitutes, and they get a uniform and all, and she, despite being so beautiful, can't join because she is a Cambod. Go figure. I wonder where she got that idea?

I can see she is starting to get the ghost of vindictive revenge flashing through her eyes, so I press the issue, before Hendrick gets a first shot at climbing the mountain ahead of me.

"Oh yes he fall *beaucoup* in love with her, and she has all this money saved so the *Dai Uy*, he get half when he marry her because that is the law. They get married last week and go to Hollywood for honeymoon," I lie with glee, since there are two things that Chai wants: one is her amor, and the other is to live in Hollywood. Hendrick orders some cognac; in fact, the bastard orders a bottle of their best.

We both like it but he knows that if you feed Chai cognac it turns her hormones on full tilt. The sneak, he is going right for chemical warfare. She downs a whole snifter then heads for the girls' ready room. We clink glasses.

"Look, you might as well bow out now; you're too scrawny to survive this one," Rick says, pouring us both another one. I need to piss like crazy and so does Hendrick, but neither wants to leave the other behind. So, as if by some psychic mutual consent, we leave Lamar at the table with instructions to keep Chai there if she comes back. We go in the men's room, which is basically a glorified trough with a hole in the cement in the corner.

Ah, relief. We both finish about the same time, but Rick gets out about five paces ahead of me, bulling his way through the crowd. I am hurrying along and trying to get my zipper up. My bush ESP is working overtime: I am getting warning prickles on the back of my neck. I lag behind a couple of steps, then a few more. Something isn't right. My survival genes are working overtime, and for good reason.

I am obscured by a pillar when I spy Lamar, sitting in the booth we abandoned and drawling a mile a minute to someone across from him. The other person is hunched over, listening intently. Broad shoulders, square head, no neck. SHIT! It's her paramour. What is he doing here?

My mind is whirring at light speed. No cover story will help in this case. I need running room, and I can make the door if I slip out now. I cover up and start sleuthing for the door. Hah, I hope Hendrick doesn't see him until he gets to the booth.

Just then I get slammed aside by a rushing body. It is Hendrick. He hisses at me in passing.

"It's him, and he is sitting with Lamar. We have to go."

Well, no matter, we need to find another drinking place. Hopefully we can get a diversion going. Just at that moment we hear a shriek and our diversion arrives, all five foot nine of her. Chai lets out a stream of epitaphs at her love and heaves a beer bottle at his head before she launches herself across the room towards her paramor. He is smart enough to get to his feet to meet the rush. He has his hands out in front of him and he is shouting about it all being a lie, and what he is going to do to us when he catches us. Lamar sits there grinning and enjoying the show. I bet scenes like this are probably just like family reunions down in that drainage swamp he calls home. This is high entertainment of the finest kind.

It doesn't matter to us. We are out the door. We at least won't have to deal with our faux pas until tomorrow; he will have his hands full tonight. What we will have to worry about is staying out of his way for a couple of days. That will be tricky, since he knows we have to come back for the boards and the interview. Or do we? I don't really want to be an officer; it interferes with the thinking process. Then I see Lamar edging for the door and I tap Rick on the shoulder. Time to take a prisoner and interrogate the little lizard. He steps out the door and we close in on both sides of him.

"Hi fellers," he smirks out. "Gollee, you boys sure know how to stir things up, don't y'all."

I want to throw him in front of a passing bus but Rick stops me; instead, we frog march him along with us. Lamar doesn't mind, as being kidnapped is a form of social intercourse and the first phase of foreplay where he hails from. We are totally screwed, without even getting near the prize. This will require some serious booze and some Recon planning, possibly some explosives. It is decided that we will seek refuge at another of our hangouts on the waterfront, one of our less known hangouts and more importantly one that the behemoth doesn't know about. We aren't really safe even there, since virtually all of our friends will rat us out, just to see the fist fight.

Best to keep this Cajun Quisling with us, if nothing else we can shove him in front of the revenge train if we see it in time. Worse, Chai will spread the word about what lying rotten chiselers we are, so we won't get laid after tomorrow. Best thing to do is go for the ring tonight before the sisterhood turns on us. We had better give it our swashbuckling best, and cram all the pleasure into tonight.

We spend the night getting drunk as two Russian sailors on shore leave. Sometime during the night we lose Lamar. We don't mind, since with all those teeth, he had started to resemble some weird experiment from a bio lab...not a good thing to drag around when you are trying to round up some of the fairer sex. Of course, by that time we aren't exactly the pick of the litter either. We tag a ride with some troops who drop us at the front gate way after curfew.

* * *

Promotion boards are the same everywhere. Keep your nose reasonably clean, do your job, and you're going to get promoted. This is good for us, since if you have a habit of stepping on your tallywacker and getting busted, it is pretty easy to get promoted back to your old rank again. This is especially true in a combat zone. Go get shot at, kill a bunch of folks, get promoted, go on R&R, beat up some MPs, burn down a building or two, get busted, go back to the war and repeat the process. Hendrick explains that it is like a great Mandala, whatever that is, some kind of eastern mystic circle jerk as far as I can determine.

But you have to go through the motions: show up with all your ribbons in the proper order, clean starched uniform, shined boots, haircut, sit in front of six senior NCOs and sometimes a colonel thrown in for good measure. They ask you real important questions like who the Secretary of the Army is, where you are from, and what the proper setting is for a back azimuth on such and such bearing. They look you over and, shazam, you are out of there. The only way to really screw up is to show up in your birthday suit with the sergeant major's daughter impaled on your instrument.

I hope someday they let me sit on one of these boards. I will make it a point to ask some real questions. When is Hitler's birthday? How deep was Burnside's line at

Fredricksburg? If you have one prophylactic, and you have the opportunity to get laid by a doxy that you know has at least one serious venereal disease, but you need to keep the Fuzees (very large phosphorous matches) dry for your non-electrical blasting system, and it's in the middle of a downpour, how many lieutenants will you need to carry the rations? At least give the candidates something to go back with.

I am done in fifteen minutes and am dismissed. I will leave word for Peewee if he comes down as to where he can find us, and we will spend the next couple of days kicking back in Nha Trang. The last thing I do is go over to the head shed to ask if I can be put on the late list for the officer selection interview. That will be on the afternoon of the third day, which will ensure that we don't have to make an early flight back. No sense telling them now that I am not interested, as that is a sure way to get sent back north early. Then, easy, we will just miss showing up, be all apologetic. They will be, tsk, tsk, you missed the opportunity of a lifetime, then load us on a return flight to Da Nang with a letter about how disrespectful, AWOL, and disorderly we have been. Besides, if we don't show up, our nemesis won't have to sit there so long waiting to ambush us and he will get off early. Quid pro quo, he might even forget we tried to skunk his true love.

Peewee comes in the following day and we link up later in the afternoon. He is just a regular little gazette of information. It seems that his Nibbs is on the high watch for us and has a delicious little ambush planned when we get back for the selection interview. I am sure that he already suspects we aren't going to show up, so that leaves the flight back to Da Nang as the only danger area with him. But he can't afford to kill us or mess us up: that would mean that *he* would have to run the missions, hah! I am almost comfortable with the thought of just how slick we are. That's why the backbone of any good army is its NCOs. Officers command, and sergeants lead.

* * *

We organize a trip to the beach, taking our now blossoming crowd of female companions with us. There are a couple of nurses, one secretary from the consulate, and a whole bunch of Vietnamese and Cambodian, uh… ladies of the night. We have all the fixings for a barbecue: meat, charcoal, booze and even a couple of floatation devices. We also have enough guns to start a major skirmish. This is, after all, a war zone. We have gathered up a few helicopter pilots and taken them under our wing. They are brothers in arms after all, and if you rinse the little suckers off, they are almost lovable.

One of these stalwarts is a good-looking lad from Ohio. Well, he was at one time: he looks like the loser in a dogfight now. He was picked up the night before by the MPs and made the mistake of lipping off to the gendarmes. Now MPs are like cops anywhere: they assume that everyone is supposed to have a fearful respect for the thin blue line. So dispelling this delusion by telling the little pinheads off usually gets you a world-class ass-whipping after being handcuffed, which is easily explained as the results of resisting arrest. They all do it, a fact of life. Best thing to do is bite your lip and put up with their superiority crap until you can get one alone, or even two or three, and beat them to their senses, and they want to avoid you at all costs. Always pick your ground, and never, ever, let your temper get the better of you. Good sound advice, you would think. I should listen to it myself.

We feel for the poor guy, and we have some ideas about going MP hunting. All we need to do is to deploy a little ambush. And, what is our specialty in life, boys and girls? Well golly, ambushes are just our forte. It doesn't take us long to determine what the one thing is that will draw a crowd of MPs quicker than flies to a pile of warm feces: GIs, of course—GIs that are slovenly in appearance, and apparently intoxicated. No sir, we can't have that, it disgraces the uniform. But just being drunk in public will not get enough victims in the net. We need to have a few guys that are drunk *and* disorderly. Additionally, they must be able to keep their cool and hold their own against the first wave of detaining officers. In the end we pick Rick, a guy from some A camp with a nervous tic in his biceps, and a couple of the rotor heads who look like they can handle themselves.

We create a beautiful plan to set the playing field up, where we will come out the other end as non-indictable conspirators. We don't want to be involved in a head-on collision with these simians; we need to give them a little taste of humility without being special guests at the line-up later. And since we have established that they are simians, we need to get our own little band of simian guerillas.

Across from the beach is a sprawling market, where everything, from fresh fish to stereos, is for sale. The market has just what we require. It is a veritable menagerie of critters, so we send Hendrick's Nungs on a mission and they soon come back carting cages with six gibbons. Sweet Jesus, they also found a couple of adolescent orangutans. There is nothing like teenagers, full of piss and vinegar, no matter what species.

Our plan is actually very simple. We want to get the MPs to come and respond to something that fits their idea of disturbing reports. When they get here, however, we intend to confront them with an entirely new and terrifying set of circumstances. You want to get the fight out of someone real quick? Confront him with primal fears. We all hate two things, fangs and claws.

Now among certain monkey and gibbon species, there is one thing that will drive a male ape into a slobbering, testosterone snit. That is the presence of any kind of menstrual stimuli. It doesn't have to be their own species, either. Human discharge is also a sure-fire recipe for attention from the monkey tribe; the female monkeys also go all wacky and get very territorial.

One of the medics slips off to take care of our pheromone-based requirements. He comes back with two spray bottles full of a cloudy liquid. We don't ask. Instead, we run a taste test by spraying down a rag, then pulling it past the lads' cages. The reaction is swift and conclusive and soon the cages are a shrieking bedlam. All we need now are the other participants, who will provide the main source of entertainment.

We break into three groups. The first is the scout section, comprised of Reeves and two guys from the camps, here for the promotion board. Their job will be to mix in with the MPs as curious bystanders. This is a cover for them to surreptitiously spray the backs, legs and arms of the gendarmes in the process. Back at the cages, our assault forces are gradually working themselves into frenzy because Lamar keeps dragging the rag in front of them. No one seems to have told him that he has gotten enough of the scent on him to be the regular little hotspot himself. The third group, bait, goes over to the edge of the highway that runs by the beach and gets to work on being merrily and obviously out of order. The rest of us mingle in with the normal crowd in the area. Everyone left over has explicit instructions to not get into fisticuffs, unless it is absolutely necessary.

Sure enough, two MP jeeps pull Rick and his crew over and begin their little shakedown game. These guys don't even try and affect a normal DR stop. The first one whips out his night stick and walks up slapping it in his other palm, while his partner whacks one of the pilots right in the thigh with his night stick and the other two from the second jeep walk up to join the fun. The crowd begins to shout and make a fuss over their methods. The MPs are sure of themselves, however. This is their turf, and mere noise is only an incentive to show the crowd who is in charge here.

A bottle is thrown, and then some more trash, including some well-aimed, used sanitary napkins, all of which pepper the forces of the law. This little distraction gives Reeves and the other two a chance to slip in amongst the MPs and spray them down.

Seeing that this isn't going to be their usual roust with a quiet kick fest as dessert, the MPs call for backup. Within minutes, the side of the highway looks like the blue light special, as about a dozen jeeps, along with a three-quarter-ton troop hauler with ten MPs in the back, come screeching to a halt. Reeves and the other two waste no time dousing this crowd down with scent as well, some before they even get out of the truck. The trash bombardment increases in intensity. The Vietnamese are getting into the spirit of the event without knowing what it is all about. The area around the gendarmes is a litter field, with the odd rat scurrying for safety.

The lead MP is some SFC, who has the build and character of a pot-bellied Southern deputy. He gets out and goes over to start deploying the riot squad. So far no one has done anything other than verbally abuse the MPs and throw a little trash. They intend to settle this blatant breach of etiquette by breaking a few heads. This is glaringly apparent, as the SFC orders the rest of his troops into a wedge formation, ideal for hand weapons in a crowd. But what the helmet-liner crowd doesn't know is that we are going to do the same thing Caesar did to the Greek phalanx: we are going to disrupt that little press before it goes into action.

On signal, we all pull back until the MPs are in the middle of a clear area. Hendrick and the others manage to slip away and the assault force is released to follow their instincts to run amok. The gibbons and the two orangutans boil out of the cages in a rush, and there is only one place that smells ever so lovely to them. It is the recently sprayed gendarmes, and the litter field they are standing in.

From the other side, we release our *pièce de resistance.* We have purchased two female gibbons that are in heat. These are heaved out so that they land in and amongst the MP crowd. One leaps up and lands on some rawboned farm product, latching onto his helmet liner and back of his neck. He immediately goes berserk with his attempt to dislodge Ms. Gibbon. One thing is apparent and that is you have no friends when you have a shrieking ball of fur attached to you. The second gibbon does almost the same thing, except the MP that she jumps has the reflexes of the Flash, and he manages to snag her with one hand. This move is an example of incorrect procedure in handling simians, because she sinks her teeth into his hand. He yowls and shakes her loose, wherein she lands on her second victim.

The males are going zonkers, all this heady hormone stuff boiling their little action cells. Three of them bolt for the victim with the female attached to him. They land on the hapless fellow, and the female manages to bite, scratch and pummel her three amours and two adjacent MPs. By this time the troops are thinking only of their safety and are all trying to get into the closed cab of the truck and two nearby jeeps. The sergeant has his own problems in the form of an amorous orangutan, who has him in a tight embrace. The good Sarge is desperately trying to free his forty-five, but Herr Simian keeps pulling on the lanyard. It is a desperate struggle between the two. There is a gunshot, then another. You can hear the bullets ricochet off the pavement.

The crowd starts to ease away. The monkeys, seeing freedom within reach, start to disengage and head for high ground. It is time to go. There are a couple more shots and two of the MPs chase after a gibbon, which makes it to the top of a stall in the market. However, one of their shots must have hit a fuel container, because soon the entire row is starting to burn. Shrieks of panic rise above the bedlam and the crowd becomes a mindless mob. The bloody market is blazing now, as we make it to the jeeps and vans. There is no pursuit. The MPs are too busy regrouping and shouting to each other about rabies. They will have enough to do just reassuring themselves and congratulating each other on surviving. It won't stop their enforcement tactics, but it might give them notice, that two can play this game.

The night is spent in revelry with the great MP massacre told and retold, until we begin to realize that having our names attached to this when it gets back to Command is not a particularly good idea. By the end of the evening, I am going by the name of Budrow, and Hendrick is Manes. It is flimsy but it is the only thing we could come up with.

The fire in the marketplace, which was caused by one of the MPs lost shots, turned into a full-blown riot, which eventually took troops to disperse. It is that pesky little thing called collateral effect. That is one of those details you forget when you are being creative. Of course, the MPs didn't slow down a lick after the great embarrassment. Their pride wouldn't allow that. There were a few days of quiet, then they hit the streets with a vengeance. They got even more pushy, arrogant, and brutal. About a week after we left, they evidently picked the wrong guy to administer a little physical respect to. He got his M16 and a couple of grenades and shot up a place before they shot him down. I hear they have a new Provost Marshal now.

We are on the plane back to camp and it is reverberating at the end of the runway. I look up, and there is our character witness, and amor to the lovely Chai. He doesn't say anything; he just looks at Rick and me, and then grins evilly. He ought to thank us. Maybe we ought to charge for our services.

* * *

CHAPTER 17

In the Dark of the Night

Everyone knows about our escapades in Nha Trang. No one is directly pointing their fingers at us, but everyone knows. Still, we haven't been locked up, which is an indication that someone needs bodies more than they need justice. Our intelligence is more critical than ever, since they need to prepare the ARVN for the coming flood from the North. Tricky Dick has decided that the US must disengage and that the South Vietnamese are going to have to grow a spine. That will be the day that Old Scratch decides to install heaters in his domain because a cold wind is blowing.

Now there are plenty of hardcore ARVN; I have been on missions with them. The Rangers, Airborne, Marines, and some of their Infantry all have the will to fight and will kick some ass. The problem is with the upper staff and the oily little popinjays that are the political core of this country. They could give a shit for the idea of nationalism, or the betterment of the poor people. They have been lining their pockets for so long that many of them are multimillionaires...not that this disease is an indigenous one.

I have just finished reading Fitzgerald's *Fire in the Lake*. Nice little map of the reasons we can't win this war. It is all laid out, from the ethno-critical mistakes we have made to the underlying need to completely restructure the whole socio-political fabric. Well I am sure that none of those ninnies, including McNamara, has even bothered to give it passing notice. Nor have any of them picked up Bernard Fall or Larteguy's excellent books on the death throes of the French Army here two decades ago. That is one of the things I like about Taipei: no copyright laws, so every time someone goes over we buy a couple of boxes of books. I have a pretty good library developing, and when it gets too full, I box them up and send them home to my brother Ron, who probably uses them to level his fish house, but at least they are at home.

Saigon might as well be on the moon, for all the proximity the embassy has with reality. That bunch of Ivy League snits are too busy sipping their iced coffees and stealing from the USAID projects to be bothered with what's happening outside of Tu Doh Street. I am not high enough on the food chain to decipher what the war planners are up to, all I know is that we will be part of the enema Command will insert into the enemy's backside.

* * *

All good things must come to an end, and our time running classic Recon missions out of Marble Mountain ends with a vengeance. We are pulling more Bright Lights than usual because a team just can't stay in any longer than a few hours before the NVA masses on it. No more sneak and peek; we are bait, plain and simple. We go in, stir them up, and when they come like a horde of locusts to kill our little skinny asses, their maneuver elements will get on the radio. The secret squirrels will use radio direction finding and signal strength, and maybe sacrifice a few chickens in front of an altar, or whatever else they do, to locate the radio source. Then some cleanly starched techno-cherub will pick up the telephone in his air-conditioned office and ring up the Air Force, Navy, Marine Corps, and Star Fleet, who will then trundle out their aerial bomb chariots, and dash out there and bomb everything into scraps. Hopefully we will have been extracted by the time this fleet of over enthusiastic bomb jockeys arrives in the wild blue over the target area. If not, we will soon find ourselves on the receiving end of someone's misplaced ordnance. To be honest, we would never get in or out without air support. Their casualties and record of destroyed aircraft are a testimony to their courage and tenacity. The aircrews are like us; the cutting edge of the sword.

The NVA have become so adept at running us to ground that we can only last a few hours before we get the snot beat out of us. Now to the non-military mind this would be the end of the exercise because there are too many bad guys down there, "Well shucks, let's just carpet bomb the area and be done with it." As a matter of fact, count me, and all the rest of us, in with that mixed bag of dissenters. That sounds like a perfectly sound synopsis to me. In fact it is *logical*, which, in the hallowed halls of wherever they are running this charade, means nothing.

So we continue to go, we get shot to ribbons, we limp back, and they bomb it anyway. Why can't they just leave us out of the equation? That would be fine with us, well most of us anyway. There are a few glory hunters still pissing on the tall trees, but not many. In the meantime, my extension has been put on hold.

At last the Sergeant Major Waugh has had his way with the ninnies upstairs. The question is how do we infiltrate into the enemy strongholds, quietly and without attracting attention. Obviously parachuting would work if the conditions and terrain cooperate. The refined end of that exercise is High Altitude Low Opening or HALO. The concept is finally about to get its shakedown cruise. Command has agreed to trying out the great HALO experiment. You know, silent killers from above, dropping out of the sky into enemy territory in the black of night. Theoretically it is a very sound idea. Special Forces has been playing with the concept for a few years now. But dropping out of the sky over Raeford, North Carolina, is whole different pissing match than doing it for real. Billy is beside himself with glee. Saigon has gone along with the concept briefing and has given the go-ahead, which results in their stripping the teams for experienced One-Zeros that are HALO qualified.

That is a bunch of our best and whomever else they have uncovered that have ever fallen out of the night sky before. They are hoping to prove that we could get in without all those chattering noise-boxes with rotors on them. This would start a whole new era of infiltration techniques; we could go back to those heady days of the late sixties and run around like Apache scouts. But the gods of war are a fickle bunch.

HALO is based on the precept that the team is able to group in the air and, after that, all of them can land in close proximity. Unlike WWII, where you needed big open fields and meadows, we were looking for small clearings in the jungle. But, try and do this at night, in bad weather, over a combat zone. It looks good on film, sounds great in fictional works, but in reality, it is very hairy stuff indeed. The team lineup reads like the superstars of Recon. No, let me rephrase that: it's more like the Good, the Bad, and the Ugly. All of the volunteers are experienced One-Zeros, who by virtue of the fact they are even alive, attest to their skill levels. That is on the positive side of the grading sheet. Now, on the other side of the sheet is, first and foremost, the fact that they are willing to do this, which is right above the mark that one would receive if you were willing to do your own lobotomy to save money.

Manes and Billy Waugh are caught up in this madness and are the progenitors of this "new" technique. If adrenalin were a controlled substance, they both would be considered pushers. They have coaxed, cajoled, and blackmailed two full teams of Americans to do the missions. The whole group ships off to Long Than for a few weeks of practice, practice, practice.

The first mission has gone off, with the predictable result of being a total FUBAR. To the layman, this translates into "Fucked Up Beyond All Recognition." At the end of the mission, we manage to get all souls back, which is enough to show proof of concept. Even though Nguyen eventually ran their little asses out of there, and even though they were scattered all over the place on insertion, they are reasonably sure that the enemy still hasn't figured out how they got in there. This is comforting, at least to the near-brain-dead.

Everyone wants to be on the next one. Andre wants on, Wesley wants on; Billy, Trantanella, Gast, Newman Castillo, and Manes are already on it. I *don't* want on it and I wish that they would quit hanging little carrots like this in front of the Cookie, since he is loopy enough without the prospect of reliving the Normandy invasion. But the superstars need a backup team. That means someone that will have to ride to the rescue when their tits get pinched. That is where we come in, so while they are getting ready to put their knees in the breeze, we are sitting here, all primed and ready to come galloping to the rescue, should they need it. They are going to need it sure as a pig's ass is pork. I know it, they know it, everyone agrees. It is just a question of how much and when.

* * *

We had followed the first mission on the radio link. This is the one the tactically twisted are calling an "almost success." That's like almost getting laid. At the end of the exercise you are still scared and frustrated. They had exited the aircraft in a snarling storm and fallen into the night. Spider Trantenella and Gast had managed to link up in the air and had fallen holding hands until they opened. Then it was *Lost in Space*. Everyone was scattered all over hell's half-acre.

Spider and Gast ended up together. They landed close to each other, which was fortunate since Gast had armed a toe popper anti-personnel mine and placed it in the back pocket of his rucksack. When you free fall, the rucksack rests on the back of your legs, cinched up to your butt and tied down with leg straps. You are supposed to drop the rucksack on a twenty-foot line so that it lands before you do. That didn't happen. In fact, when Gast hit the ground, the mine exploded and blew the left cheek of his ass off.

As a result Spider linked up and stayed with him, administering first aid. Castillo and Manes were still able to carry out the mission, but they were separated by several kilometers and on opposite sides of a ridgeline. Cliff Newman, the team leader, was in the same shape; they were basically three separate one-man Recon elements at that point. Covey tried to link the elements up, but they all had run into NVA before they could link up. Everyone lasted until they got pressed too hard; then came extraction time. The Covey guided them individually to a pickup point, from where they were extracted one at a time.

The Cuban lasted longest. He was on the ground for three days before he finally ran out of water and had to dig for it in an open elephant-grass area. He was surrounded by NVA, which is natural since we are always surrounded by NVA. That is why they call it enemy territory. The decision was made to pull Castro out. They sent forth the mighty fleet to go drag his little keester out, but they couldn't find him. Covey told him to pop smoke, but all he had with him were a couple of those mini smoke grenades.

I can produce more smoke by setting fire to a tampon than one of those things can produce and Covey couldn't see the minuscule amount of smoke it managed to belch through the ground haze. He finally had to tape one to the barrel of his rifle and hold it over his head. That is great in Fort Bragg, but do that in the middle of a couple of thousand NVA and someone is going to mosey over and see who is making the smoke signals. The choppers finally spotted him and went in to pick him up, luckily before the NVA fire brigade got there.

Everyone is back from the first mission. Gast and Spider barely survived the rescue, having been dragged through concertina wire after being lifted out on the end of 120-foot ropes. The pilot made a small miscalculation and they were pulled through the perimeter wire of the firebase they put down on. Gast is missing half of his ass from the mine going off and both of them look like they were the losers in a straight razor confrontation.

* * *

Now here we are, getting ready to do the same thing again. The area is west of Da Nang, in the twisted terrain about 60 kilometers out there in Indian Country. Same drill: dark and stormy night, unable to group in the air completely, and the team is scattered. They had even tried some sort of luminous goop, smearing it on their helmets and the backs of their packs. Good stuff, but it was water soluble. When you jump out in the middle of a deluge, you can guess how long that lasted. Billy and Jesse are alright but separated by a couple of kilometers. Tubby and Stroh are both in bad shape and injured. Tubby wrenched his back when he landed and needs immediate extraction, and Stroh is hanging in his harness about forty feet up in a tree, maybe 800 meters to the southwest of Tubby's position.

We listened to the clusterfuck as it unfolded and were sitting on the pad ready to go do the "here comes the cavalry" bit. Stroh is in bad shape and it is decided to get him out first. Mac and Woody, the chase medic, are going to rappel in and retrieve Tubby, so they are en route already.

The rest of Habu has combined with Dirty Dave's team and are saddling up for an attempt to get Stroh before the enemy finds him. He is badly injured and he is getting weaker, hanging in his harness. We can follow his conversations with Covey and it doesn't look good.

Dave is the designated One-Zero, by virtue of the fact that he was familiar with working Spectre gunships and the rest of us will follow his lead. We are heavy in both numbers and armament. The enemy know something is afoot and are streaming into the area to find what they suspect is a Recon team. We will try and get Stroh out as quickly as possible. En route, we hear that they have Tubby, up and safe. At the last minute he saw a couple of guys walking towards him and thought it was Mac and Woody or Billy and Jesse, then realized that they were NVA. He saw them. They missed seeing him. Good fortune sometimes smiles on you. It is all past news to us because we are headed for the cauldron.

We get on the ground: sixteen people, including one guy from Recon who is a really close friend of Stroh. Wagy and Dave deploy their team and I get Habu tucked in with them. According to Covey, we are about three hundred meters from where Stroh is hanging in the trees.

Covey says that he has lost contact with Stroh. His last transmission was garbled, but he thinks that the NVA were looking for him, then nothing. We move as quickly as we can, topping the rise of the finger ridge and then stopping so Dave can talk to Covey. The area we are in is a stand of trees, which reach a height of forty to sixty feet. Directly to our front is a relatively open forest, which rises from a small depression, then starts to climb the ridge to our southeast. Dave and I decide to spiderweb out and see if we can find Stroh. According to Covey, we should be right in the general area.

I send two of the Yards off to reconnoiter ahead and to the right for a hundred meters, then return. I take the straphanger and one Yard and go the same distance to our front. Dave does the same to the left front with his team. We leave Wagy with the bulk of the team in a perimeter fighting formation. We move cautiously until we have covered nearly seventy-five meters. I keep getting wisps and traces of something chemical. It smells like one of our issue cooking tablets. These are blue affairs, the same consistency of those little cakes in better-class urinals, and they emit a smell you can detect quite easily. Now I know we aren't cooking, and I am sure that Stroh isn't cooking up a spot of tea, so it must be the bad guys. Shit, if he is in here, he is right in amongst them.

While looking for trail signs, anything that might have disturbed the dead foliage on the forest floor, I see something dark and linear. I move up and recognize it as a CAR-15 with a 203-grenade launcher. It has a damaged receiver from a round hitting it. It is Stroh's weapon. We check it for booby traps, and find none, so I sling it over to the straphanger to carry.

Again, I can still smell those damn cooking tablets. It's a faint smell, but I am sure that's what the odor is. Ti Ti points out another object about twenty meters away; we go over and find it to be the night vision device that Stroh was carrying. Next we find his map. All of the items are in a trail leading uphill.

This is too neat and orderly, and I cast back with the straphanger. Near where we first found the rifle, we find AK shells, and a couple of holes in the tree trunk about fifteen feet up. There are broken branches and foliage, as if someone had drug something down from the tree. As we are looking, Dave comes up with another Yard, and we begin to cast for sign. We find scuff and drag marks, where we are sure that they carried Stroh off after pulling him down from the tree. They have him as sure as the nose on your face. We can both smell the tablets now.

We return to the team position with the abandoned equipment. It has surely been left, in an attempt to lure us to pursue to a point where they can ambush us. The Yards that I had sent off to our right front report that they went about a hundred meters and noticed a lot of sign up toward the top of the ridgeline. All they will say is *beaucoup VC*. I believe them; this has all the earmarks of a classic ambush. They obviously have Stroh, and we have a choice: go balls to the wall to try and snap through them, and hopefully catch up with them before they get away, or get out. We still don't know if he is alive or dead. All we are certain of is that they have him.

Covey talks to Da Nang and the weather is closing in, so there is no way in hell they can get us out of here. We are going to have to find a hiding hole that we can fight from. Sure as shit, the NVA are going to realize that we aren't able to get out. If we get stuck on the ground, it won't take long for them to do the arithmetic and realize that they can maul us and maybe capture a couple of us as well. We are royally screwed unless we can find the right place, and even that might not save us. Covey is calling up Spectre and anything that can shoot through the clouds. But if the cloud cover gets too thick, they won't be able to see our ground marker.

We will have to find a real good patch of terrain, something that is well marked on a map so that Covey can pinpoint it and help direct fire for us. If we can find that, we can work Spectre around and not get chewed up at the same time. There is a small rise in the finger ridge, just before the elephant grass. Good tall trees, and we think we can work the guns by spotting, then adjusting. The forest is open in here so we can see them coming even in the dark if we are at ground level. We move back in that direction.

As we top the beginning of the rise, the light is beginning to fade under the trees. We can see what appear to be dark gashes in the floor of the copse we are entering. As we get closer we find that these are positions, dug to the depth of about four, maybe five, feet. Each one can hold three men standing side by side, and they are laid out in a semi-circle with two positions located at the tail, about forty meters across. We move the team into these. Jesus did we luck out. These are bomb shelters the NVA built in the event someone bombed this section of their complexes. They have foxfire or some other phosphorescent material smeared on the walls, so they glow in the dark just enough you could find them in the pitch black.

We get the claymores out and set up a defensive plan. It is going to be a long night, and probably a deadly fight for our survival. I am not feeling like Sergeant Rock here. I am about to have an accident in my britches. We are in a bad position, there is no doubt. All we can hope for is that we can get Spectre up and work him when the time comes. The weather is completely socked in, so working him with accuracy is going to be almost impossible.

After about an hour we can hear movement coming down the ridge and across our front. From the amount of clinking of metal on metal, there are a lot of them. Occasionally, over to the east of us, we hear a rifle shot. They do that to align their sweep formation, and sometimes to spook you into firing. We all hunker down and start praying that we can miraculously go invisible.

Occasionally we see a flashlight blink on, then off, in the trees. Again, they are arranging their formation, keeping it on line. They are coming slowly and working their way down to us. From the way it sounds and looks, they still think we are to the south and east of where we actually are. The line stops, then there is a rattle of automatic fire over about a hundred and fifty meters from where we are. Then a B40 crashes into the trees in that area, then silence.

There is some shouting, which Cuman, who is in the hole with me, interprets for me. It is their NCOs yelling for cease fire and kicking some incompetent butts to get back on line again. We see the lights again as they start moving. We can hear a bugle after about an hour, and then another blares out, north and east of us nearly three hundred meters. We can see flashlights now in that direction. They are moving away from us and working their way to the north and down slope from us. We hear what sounds like a cowbell being hit to our rear and then movement coming down the ridge toward us.

Amazingly the two arms of the sweep flow right around the little copse we are in. I guess they must have screwed up and either figured we weren't in their bunkers, or whoever was assigned this part of the line never linked up the two flanks. We see figures move across our front not forty meters out and down slope.

I hear someone yelling out in Vietnamese. From the sound of it, it is some NCO trying to dress the line. Cuman pulls me down so he can whisper in my ear.

"Ooosh, *Trung Si*, he *beaucoup* pissed off at VC *Tahan*." He chuckles.

The line passes off to the north, and is past us. About an hour later, we hear a hellacious firefight cook off almost a kilometer away. They must have run into each other and mistaken each other for us.

We hear more bugles, and the sound of metal banging on metal further out nearly two hours later, then it is quiet until dawn. No one sleeps more than fifteen minutes at a time. I don't want to take any Green Hornets to stay awake. I am too wired as it is.

As dawn breaks, the weather starts to clear. We are on the horn with Covey and he tells us that they are mounting up to come get us. We plan to blow the claymores just before the choppers start their final approach and move out to the small elephant-grass area to our north, maybe seventy meters. I will tie the formation to the wood line, just in case we run into trouble. They are going to use a Marine Chinook to get us; we are all going out on one ship. They are going to plaster the whole area around the LZ so we had better get our asses in the middle of that grass as soon as the guns get on station.

We can hear the Chinook coming; the slap of the blades is echoing and thumping in the canyons. Rescue is on the way. We see Covey break over us and he tells us to get moving. We blow the claymores and move out of the foxholes and down through the trees. We break out of the trees and into the elephant grass. We hear a fifty-caliber open up on the birds as they come in. Two Cobras come in and work the slope we just left with rockets and their chin turrets. We are pushing down the grass, making a clear area so the bird can see us.

There is no way that he can set down all the way, but he can hover and drop us a ladder. We are scrambling aboard. I can hear a rattle of small arms from the hillsides around us, but it is scattered and light. The Marine gunner is chopping up the area with a machine gun off the port side as I clamber aboard. Then Dave and the rest of the team are up and into the bird. The Chinook leaps up like it was rocket propelled, banks a bit to the downhill, and we are off.

The whole area we have just left is getting chewed into tossed salad by the guns. We climb up and away into the clean fresh air. I am never so grateful to be alive. We have survived by an incredible chain of circumstantial luck. I used up eight cat lives down there, I am sure. Poor Stroh, though; he is either a prisoner, or dead. There is no way of confirming his survival. The chances of our being able to find him in that warren of hills and hidden camps are virtually nil. We have lost a good man; as well, we have almost lost two teams in the attempt to rescue him. It is our way to find and recover our own.

We come back into the Da Nang area and land at the base. As we exit the aircraft and begin to walk over to the trucks that will take us back to isolation for the full debrief, the SMAJ and Manes waylay us and we give them a short recount of what we saw. I give them Stroh's weapon and the other stuff, then we load aboard the trucks and go up to do the official debrief.

One good thing is that we will get some time off before we have to go back in the batter's box. The second thing that is encouraging is that Saigon has apparently decided that HALO needs some refining. I am thinking, that's just marvelous, maybe they can ship all those experts from HALO School back in Fort Bragg over here to run these. They might not know how to run the missions but at least they will be able to group together so that all the victims are in one place. As for us, we can go back to dying the way we were before.

CHAPTER 18

The Peter Principle

The Sergeant Major has been replaced after the HALO program got scratched into the great beyond. The Colonel has also been replaced, and the new command structure has begun to establish its mark on the unit. We have a pep talk from the new commander at the theater, for once with Manes in the audience instead of stomping around the stage. All the Recon people that are not out on missions are gathered here, to meet and greet the new Grand Phoobah. All of us are wondering what great crime he has committed in the eyes of his superiors in order to get sent here, to be in charge of the Devil's children.

He is a great bull of a person; in fact he looks like a water buffalo in fatigues. He is short and concise in his statements, and praises the unit on its history and reputation. He also makes it clear that he will command, and that some things will change. This is normal protocol; the same speech was probably given by some Praetorian in the forest strongholds of Tiberius's legions a couple of millennia ago. We will see what those changes are as time goes by. The Colonel moves off the stage and heads up to the headquarters.

Manes, replaces him in front and glowers his best look that says, "I'm about to give an important speech," and then launches into the follow-up.

"Well the party time is over gents; this colonel is going to change some things. Not the important things, but your shenanigans downtown and during your off-time are under scrutiny. You degenerates had better get used to the idea that you are part of THEUNITEDSTATESARMEE." He runs the last part together in one long word. Someone from the back of the crowd quips up.

"Well, let the THEUNITEDSTATESARMEE come on up here and run some of these fucking missions then." This results in raucous laughter and several other offside remarks about the Army, the new Colonel, and the Midget's ass, all rolled into one chorus of the hidden. This doesn't faze Manes though; he looks the crowd over until it quiets down, then continues.

"Just keep it up, I know all of you by your voices. I have to listen to them enough, squeaking on the radio, about please come rescue me, or some other self absorbed demand, so whoever said those last remarks, remember, I know who you are."

Sure Dai Uy, and we know that you won't pursue this for long. You have to warn us. We have to see how much we can get away with. The new command will decide what an appropriate response is, and then everyone will adjust. The only question is, who will be the test case? The funny thing about this outfit is that every one of us is thinking about some really bizarre offense to commit, just for that honor. Manes places his hands behind his back. It doesn't have a slimming effect. He continues.

"I would like to introduce you degenerates to your new Sergeant Major. Some of you have probably already met him. He has been quietly observing this zoo for the last few days and has been tainted by already having to talk to the few of you tax burdens that he met during that period." He pauses, takes a breath, and starts in again. "We were NCOs together and he knows every excuse and sneaky trick your feeble little minds can conjure up, and if he may have forgotten some, I remember them."

"That's right, *Dai Uy*, probably because you were committing them as late as just last night," someone catcalls from the back again. Manes doesn't even break stride, he just glowers the Chunky Death Stare at the entire crowd and leaves the stage to the new SMAJ.

Here is absolutely the homeliest person that I have ever seen. He looks like a cross between Abe Lincoln and an abused coon hound. He strolls out front and center, and begins by fishing a pipe out of his side pocket and lighting it up. He looks over the crowd and starts in slowly.

"My name is Tom Jones. I have been around Special Forces a long time, at least as long as most of you here. I know some of you from Panama and some of you from other places in this swamp they call a country." He takes a pull on the pipe and exhales a blue-white cloud of smoke. "Those that know me, know that I am fair and impartial, until you try to screw with me. Most people don't do that twice." There are a few snickers in the crowd, from people that obviously have worked with him before. I look over at Hendrick; he nods that he knows this guy, then leans back and tells me in a stage whisper, "This is one good son of a bitch." I am thinking, Well that's good enough for me. Let's get to the club, it's hot out here. But the SMAJ isn't done quite yet.

"This isn't going to be a long rah-rah speech. I just want to tell you my door is always open. I'm not Billy, and I have my own ways. If you want to settle things man to man, bring a gun because you're going to need it. I stick by my people if you're right, and the only one that has the right to fuck with you, is me. NO ONE else." Oooh, I like this guy. He still is a homely son of a bitch though.

We are dismissed and everyone starts heading for the mess hall for lunch. Mac and Cookie and I are walking with Hendrick, when the new SMAJ comes walking by. He looks at Rick, gives himself a pull on his pipe, and smiles. Rick nods.

"Hey Top, been a long time. We're glad to have you." He says, and then grins like he has some private joke going on. The Sergeant Major looks at him and puffs on his pipe for a bit before he speaks.

"I remember that the last time I saw you, I was having to cover your ass for something about shot-up vehicles and blowing up someone's real estate" The pipe smoke curls up and away in the breeze, making him look like some jihn from *Arabian Nights.*

Shit, I knew it. Just our luck, he knows Rick. No, he *really* knows Rick, which means that we are automatically branded as associates. On top of all that, Hendrick has burned down or blown up the only bar somewhere. That for sure will get us a price on our heads, from both sides. We start to lag back as a defense mechanism, but Hendrick grabs all three of us and grins like the dog that ate the neighbor's cat.

"Hey Top, let me introduce you to some of my good friends here. This is the Mini Mac, he is the One-Zero of Habu; this here is Cook who is his One-Two and," he pauses to get a breath, which gives me the opportunity to break free. I get a couple of steps away and say to the crowd.

"Well it's been nice guys, but I have to get back to my job at the motor pool. Mister Fish, he goin' to be upset if I hangs around wif yo' boys from Recon." I give my best shuffling imitation and try to get free. But there is no pity in Combat City. Jones just smiles and looks at me with the oily pleasure of a Cajun looking at a crawdad.

"You must be Brokhausen. That would make you," he stabs the pipe in Mac's direction, "his One-One." Mac and Cookie are grinning like a couple of searchlights. Misery loves company.

Maybe if I pull out the Luger and shoot Rick, he might take that as an act of kindness. No time for reflection though because Wesley trots up, grins, looks at the three us and Rick, then pats Jones on the arm. Jones turns and smiles warmly at the Weasel. This is bad: this means that he also knows Wesley. Wes looks us over, grins again, and starts in. I want to throttle him.

"I see you have already identified the three biggest troublemakers in Recon, Tom. Good show. These three and him—" he nods in Rick's direction, "are the cause of all the trouble you may possibly encounter here." He does his little oily snicker bit, and then continues.

"The best policy would be to send them all into the A Shau with no radio, just to save your career." The ferret grins at us and sticks his chest out. The SMAJ knocks the ashes out of his pipe, and shakes his head slowly.

"You know that is exactly what Budrow said to me when I talked to him. Now why do you gentlemen think everyone has such a high opinion of your ability to wreak havoc, ruin careers, and commit general mayhem?" He smiles, but doesn't give us a gnat's chance to reply before he adds, "Oh and by the way, I'm not Larry. I have the sneaking suspicion that the three of you have been pulling the ether mask over Captain Manes's eyes, about the two of you—" he stabs the pipe stem in Cook's and my direction, "being so dim-witted you couldn't lead yourselves to the latrine." We have been trying to keep Habu together, so there have been rumors of my stuttering under pressure and Cook's derangement fueling why it was best to leave us be.

Where is that bloody Marble Mountain VC home guard unit that occasionally drops a mortar round into the camp anytime there is a crowd out in the open? We are a crowd! It's bloody daylight, you incompetents. Get the fucking mortar out and shoot it at us! Maybe it will actually hit near us, wound me, and kill the ferret, and that frigging thug Hendrick too, just for good measure.

"We are short on experienced One-Zeros here, and the time comes for all of us to move on." The SMAJ continues as he is looking at Cookie, and then in my direction. I have a sick feeling in my stomach as he continues. "We are going to all have to make adjustments to take up the slack. But...All in due time." He finishes and we start walking towards the mess hall. Wes and Rick are grab-assing and joking with the new SMAJ the entire way. I look over at the Mini Mac; he just shrugs and grins his "Don't worry about it" smile. The Cookie is still pumped up that we have been singled out right off the bat. That's the trouble with Rangers; their survival gene has been replaced with reruns of *The Guns of Navarone*.

After lunch we head over to the hootch for emergency planning. The Yards are there and it's the after-mission mugging for money, new fatigues, boots, and whatever else they can garnish. This procedure takes up most of the afternoon. Mac gets called down to the head shed and comes back in about an hour. There is good news and there is bad news.

The good news is that they aren't going to break us up completely, yet. Cook will stay with Habu. The bad news is that they want to move me over to take over as either the One-Zero of Crusader or the One-One slot. My extension papers have not been approved, so I will be on the short list soon if they disapprove it. They asked Mac if I could lead a team. He gave them the honest assessment since it was apparent that they had already made up their minds. I will go through the motions but in my mind it sucks. Meanwhile, we will adjust to the new command.

* * *

In the interim a whole batch of new guys arrive at Marble Mountain and are eventually assigned to Recon. I see a few familiar faces from Fort Bragg...one of them is a guy I always suspected was Intelligence or a CID agent. I never liked him in Bragg and I like him even less now that he is here. He is one of those guys with too many answers for questions you haven't asked yet. He gets assigned to Habu. I catch Mac and Cook when they are alone and tell them my misgivings about this guy. Mac says not to worry about it, that they will work it out. Cook, on the other hand, gets that grim look which spells trouble for the cherry. He won't do anything outright, but I know the Cookie: he will watch the cherry like a hawk. If he does one thing that endangers the team, there will be one less problem in the world.

For the life of me I can't figure why anyone would send this asshole up here in any kind of official capacity. Everyone in his graduating class went on levy to Vietnam… everyone except two guys assigned to the 10th Special Forces, and him. He got orders to report to Fort Meyers, with TDY in Fort Gordon. Fort Meyers is the Military Intelligence Center. Fort Gordon is where they train Military Police and Criminal Investigations Division. No reason for a young SF trooper to be going there unless he is more than that; like say a cop or an intelligence type masquerading as Special Forces. We will see just what he is when the time comes to go into the bush. If he suddenly has an excuse not to go or gets pulled at the last moment, well that will be the clincher. I am almost tempted to corner Manes about this, but more than likely he doesn't know.

I have more to worry about than that at any rate. I am about to get a new team and my days and nights in paradise will be full.

* * *

Mac and I sit down and go over the whole idea of me moving to Crusader. Since Kelly went back to the States, Crusader has just been filling in on other teams to beef up "heavy" teams. I like Crusader and the fact that they also have Bru as their little people. Peewee is coming to join me. Both he and the other American kid are good Recon folks. Shit, they should make Peewee the One-Zero, but some bright wit has decided that both of us need to go in there. I have two options: move over and get with the program, or quit. I can't see quitting, but shit, I don't want to leave Habu. We, as a team, are lucky together. We have survived these long months, returning from missions we should not have come through.

It looks like we will be launching from Quang Tri, instead of our southern launch site at Phu Bai. At least Pappy Budrow will be there to look over me and our new brood of chicks.

Our Yards on Habu know something is afoot by the fact that we all are hangdog about it. Cuman finds out the situation from Mac before long, and I have to go over and sit with the team and talk to them. When I get there, Cuman has two of the little people from Crusader there, and introduces me to them. We talk and Cuman gives me his blessing. The other two adopt me on the spot. The head of the Bru at Marble Mountain has vouched for me and given me to them; they are mine now. Peewee comes over and there is some more bonding, then Peewee and I go over to Crusader's hootch and I meet the rest of the team. I talk to Peewee and tell him as far as I am concerned that Crusader is and will continue to be our joint baby. We aren't going to last that long if my extension doesn't come through and he is within that ninety day window as well.

Around four I go to see Manes in the orderly room, He and Jones are professionally apologetic. Which is a study in my giving all the reasons that I would rather stay on Habu, and them acknowledging my whine and telling me that with the losses we just are too short of experienced personnel to have so many good people on one team. So quit whining. It is the kiss of death but that is it. I will just have to buck up and shoulder the load. I go by Habu for some odd trinkets I had forgotten, and while I am tossing their stuff for my property, they prattle on with their congratulations. I am now officially on Crusader. I can't help but feel like a bastard stepchild though. I am leaving my family and starting out anew.

My overriding concern is to pull this one off. We have new people, and it will take a couple of missions for us to actually get our timing together. That is the same no matter where you go or, for that matter, whatever war you're in. The problem is that you don't get much of a chance for a learning curve here. If you slip up even a pubic hair, good people are going to die. Being on a team is the best damned position in the Army, but it comes with a weight of responsibility that would make Atlas grunt. When we are ready, we will gather up our collective gonads and see if we can shine.

I figure if I keep giving myself these little pep talks, no one will notice all the doubts I have about being able to walk and chew gum at the same time. I will go and do. Now that the horrid event has happened and I am on my own, I actually am getting to like it. But I feel naked without Mac and the Cookie.

As the teams are going over to the club we run into Castro, who sees us and comes running up.

"I hear that they made you a One-Zero," he says to me. Looking at Peewee, he inquires: "What happened, do you still owe Billy money or something? You can't pay, so they give you Dr. Death here as a One-Zero? You know, don't you, that Habu hardly ever got shot at until he came along. Since then," he slaps his hands together for emphasis, "it's been-boom-boom city every time they go out." He giggles to himself then shoots off ahead, throwing a snide "Toooooo bad Peeeeweee" over his shoulder. Billy looks at Castro, then at me, as if he doesn't want to believe it but still suspects. Yup, I have arrived.

CHAPTER 19

St. Elmo's Day

As I start towards my team hut, I see Wesley whistling up the walk with a bag, and something that is obviously detonation cord hanging out of it. Wes is notorious for coming up with new and exciting ways to kill his fellow man. The only trouble is that his devices will most likely end your career at the same time. I start to ease by him in the hope I can avoid being victim number one, to no avail.

"You gotta see this. I have the perfect solution for trackers," he blurts out excitedly, and grabs me by my arm. Trapped! Maybe I can reason with him.

"Wes, in case you haven't heard, trackers are the least of our problems. They *know* we are there and *where* we are because there are so many of them. It's hard to land a helicopter without hitting a platoon of them."

He looks hurt but that passes quickly, as he fishes what looks like a mini ring main, with nails, a bolt, and rusted chunks of steel taped to the outside, out of the bag he has slung over one shoulder. The whole shebang is already primed and capped ready to go off.

"See here, I have rigged this up with a coat hanger inverted this way so you can toss it up in the trees as you are running. I have "S-rolled" this claymore wire and attached it to a clacker right here." Yes he has done all that, disregarding the obvious fact that if anyone keys the mike on any radio within a 100-meter area, there is a good chance that it might set the bloody thing off. There are only about fifty radios in the vicinity that might be the cause of that little oversight, but that doesn't deter Dr. Demento here.

"So you just sling it up in a tree as you're running and when you hit the end of the wire, just push the clacker and wham, no more tracking team." I am trying to think of all the incidences when I found myself running, trying to avoid trackers, and still having enough energy to even throw up, which total none. I try to remember how many trees are out in the AO where the resulting shrapnel from his death ray wouldn't also wipe me out when I got to the end of the 25 meters of wire. I think of a host of other don'ts that would occur to anyone with even a modicum of sense.

A door opens and it is Mac and Cookie coming out of Habu's team house. They spot us and turn to escape before the Weasel sees them. I don't give them the chance.

"Mac! Hey Mac! Come over here, you have to see this really *neat* thing that Wes has designed. It is just *perfect* for your troubles with handling those nasty little tracker teams that we were *just* discussing this morning." Wes turns and they aren't quick enough. I get a couple of steps moving in the right direction and bid a hearty goodbye to Wes over my shoulder. Cookie and Mac are staring daggers at me as I get out of range and around a building, putting some cover between me and Sergeant Dynamite.

I hear Wes start in.

"Hey, I'm going to the range to test fire this and you two need to come along so I can explain how to best use it. Come on, I have three more already made up, and they are in the jeep over there."

I hear protests and murmurs of deceit about how much they would like to go, but the Colonel wants them, or Cookie's mother died. It won't do any good; once the Weasel gets you in the zone, best thing to do is humor him and find a safe spot on the range to tuck yourself into.

Once back at my hootch I go through the motions of packing a clean set of Tropical Worsteds and get all my ribbons and stuff ready for the selection board. Peewee and I go over what has to be done before he joins me for the fun and frolic in Nha Trang. He will get there on the second day, which will give us a two-day in-country rest. Nha Trang is a beautiful place with beaches and restaurants galore and plenty of sights to see…sights like the inside of several dozen bars that we both know. I am polishing my boots and listening to some Iron Butterfly on the stereo when I hear a reverberating blast. I am thinking that it is a real close lightning strike, when something clunks on the metal roof. Now that isn't rain, so we look out the door. There is a dirty black smudge of smoke being dissipated by the rain, just about where the range is.

SMAJ Jones, has taken the place of Billy Waugh, who is headed for Bragg and retirement it is rumored. If they are merciful they will drive a stake through his heart before he bites too many people. Billy? Retired? That is a scary concept. Jones and Manes come boiling out of the office and head off in one of the jeeps without saying a word to anyone. There is a crowd over by the Yard mess hall, so I wander over. The crowd is looking at a bent and twisted piece of metal. It is the twisted remains of the windshield assembly of a M151 military jeep. Uh oh. Wes and the two grit-eating brethren were going to the range. I am starting to worry.

After fifteen minutes, Manes and Jones come rolling back, followed by a three-quarter-ton containing Wes, Cookie, Mac, and Woodham the medic. There are fresh bandages on Mac and Cookie, but Wes is the funniest sight. His clothes are still smoldering with a few burn spots in them. He has a big, beautiful black eye and his face looks a bit swollen. They all get out of the truck, Mac and Cookie being helped by Woody. None of them offer to help Wes. Mac and Cookie look at him, shake their heads and walk over to the club. We all follow, except Wes, who just sits in the back of the truck staring off into space. Manes and Jones go back into the orderly room and leave Wesley sitting there. Everyone gets a beer and waits for the tale to unfold.

Woody starts with news that there was a "training accident" at the range. He was called because they thought there might be some seriously wounded. He had gotten there, lickety split, to find Mac and Cookie sitting behind the remains of what had once been the target shed. Not much of a target shed in the first place, and there was even less of it now. In fact, except a few shattered uprights and splinters, it was all gone.

They had been sitting behind it with a poncho shelter rigged to the back of it, with a mound of dirt plus the wall of the shed between them and the source of the "accident." It had started raining and then the lightning came, so they had, like all good soldiers, decided it was best not to be playing around with explosives primed with electric blasting devices. They had decided to wait it out at the range, rather than drive in the rain and electric plasma, in a jeep full of the same, back to the company.

Mac had brought along his new Leica 35 mm camera but had forgotten it on the front seat of the open jeep, which was parked about seventy-five meters away. Wanting to retrieve it, he looked over around the corner of the shed, and saw the jeep bathed in some sort of blue halo. St. Elmo's fire is what the floating bathtub crowd calls it: an electrical phenomenon. They were just deciding that it wasn't a good idea to go over to the jeep when the jeep blew up, or rather some electrical discharge set off Wes's toys. The whole load went off almost simultaneously, knocking everyone ass over teacups, and blowing the flimsy shed into a year's supply of toothpicks. Wes had been hit just under the eye by the body of Mac's formerly new Leica camera, and they had all been peppered with burning, zinging debris. The jeep was a total destruction job. Little bits and pieces of it were scattered around the camp. All three had walked away fairly unscathed.

Manes and Jones arrived shortly after, assessed the scene and made sure that no one was seriously injured, then had everyone brought back here. Wes is on the shit list with both Captain Manes, and Mac. The Cookie is just amused by it. He keeps bringing up Mac's camera. How nice it was, how many gadgets it had on it, how difficult it would be to replace, on and on. Mac just looks at him in sullen silence.

Wes finally comes in, walks over with that ah shucks look, and apologizes to both of them. They just grunt, which is the signal for the ribbing to begin. This is directed mostly at Wes but soon extends to Mac and the Cookie. How could you two be so brain dead as to go to the range with Demento? That's when it happens. It is like the lights went on in Georgia. I can see them rerunning the chain of events through their feral little brains. It eventually replays itself to the part where they got trapped into it. They both look at me. Wes looks at me, and the crowd looks at me. Fucking Peewee, who had joined us at the last minute, shuffles away from my side, deserting me. Oh yes, naturally it is my fault! It's raining out, you have three southerners with a jeep full of nitro-laden substances, it blows up—naturally I am guilty by default.

Well, you aren't going to pin this on me, you rat-faced rejects from a swamp. Screw you. I'm going to Nha Trang for four days, so good luck trying to pin this on me. Peewee is trying to appear as if he doesn't know me. I think to myself, you my fine-feathered friend, who deserts his brother when you are needed most, I am going to feed a Mickey to, then sell you to a Turkish boys' club. Peewee was on that same list as I was, "too much talent on one team" and was scheduled to be moved to a new team as well. I get up and go to the bar; my thoughts are not on the chimps. I have four days to kick back in lovely Nha Trang, and nothing is going to spoil that.

CHAPTER 20

Baptism

I spend the next day moving all my personal stuff into the Crusader team house and getting the hang of my new teammates. I know the One-Two of the team: a kid from Indiana, or someplace, since he came along as a straphanger with Habu on that fun static road-watch mission. Although he has only been in country for about two months and run just a few missions, he is alright under fire. Peewee and I will work it, drill the team and ourselves to determine who is best talking to Covey and which one of us will fight the team as a unit. Usually the One-Zero or the One-One has the radio. Both of us have been One-Ones, so we know how to fight the team as a unit. The immediate task is to get the team so it fights like a well-oiled machine.

The team spends the next few days going to the range, as Peewee and I start to mold the team to the tactics and formations that we want to use. These are similar to what we used in Habu with a few modifications, little things that make us more effective. Crusader's Bru Thump gunner can fire the 203 so fast it sounds like he has a magazine full of 40 mm to feed from. We adjust our drills to take this into account. Thank God for Kelly; this is his doing, picking and nurturing this Yard's natural talent. That will come in real handy in a firefight. On top of that, the lad can hit anything he is looking at with the grenade launcher.

The clock starts ticking, when we get notified we will go into isolation in two days. We will draw the Bright Light when we go out the door as a complete team. The Mini Mac is looking out for me as usual. Habu is on the list for a target so we will be going up to the launch site together. I'm not nervous about it. Hell, by this time Peewee and I are like Mac and I were: we work like a single brain connects us.

We will be the primary Bright Light. If any of the insertions incur downed aircraft, in addition to rescuing the team, one of the other teams on rotation will fill in as our backup for Bright Light. This is a distinct possibility if the situation goes from suicidal to a desperate fight for survival. I have worked the northern targets so much that I know the terrain.

The area in which we are going to operate abounds in old growth forest and triple canopy wait-a-minute flora. As we prepare our equipment, we are also going to rig some ring mains in case we have to blow some daylight to get the choppers in.

Peewee comes dragging through the hootch door with a whole sack full of explosives and detonation cord and other little merry makers. We start sorting the charges into earmuff charges. That is where you put two charges equidistant on a sliding line of detonation cord so you can adjust it for the diameter of the tree. Once we are done, we can cap the earmuff with a claymore detonator and put it on a tree in a matter of seconds. It blows the base of the tree into matchsticks and it topples over, taking smaller trees with it, hopefully not on top of you. But you get pretty adept at the laws of gravity after awhile. Some guys will do it with a claymore, but that only works on trees of fairly medium diameter. What is the old formula? D squared over forty, that's the diameter of the tree squared then divide by forty, and it gives you the amount of TNT in pounds to use to blow it down. That's for hardwood; if you try to use the charge on palmetto or something soft, it blows it to splinters. It is amazing: all this education, and I wonder how many job openings in the landscape industry there are that require such expertise.

We might as well get the gear together now so we don't have to do it in isolation. I might even wrangle a couple of hours over on Monkey Mountain so I can blow one of the earmuff charges. This will give the new guys a chance to see and hear it. Might as well make that the last part of the string training. Tomorrow we are going to give the new guys some practice at dangling under helicopters on a swaying 120-foot rope. There isn't much to cover other than getting four guys on the strings quickly, snapping in, then getting ready to catapult up. The most important part is remembering to hook up your leg straps and hold your legs apart so that when it all tightens up you don't crush your BBs. You only make that mistake once. It is virtually impossible to correct in the air unless you are the lowest man, otherwise you have everyone else's combined weight making you shriek in soprano.

Wesley comes in and sits down at the table where we have the half-prepared charges. He fishes a beer out of the fridge and eyes the explosives with the leer of a pyromaniac.

"Whatcha making? Ring mains?" He starts to fiddle with the charges. I swear this boy needs to sleep with plastique; he is so addicted to nitro compounds.

"Don't mess with that stuff, Wes. You and accidents that go boom, seem to be common thread around here."

"Jesus, you make it sound as if I am the sort that acts like a mad bomber," he grins and continues to fondle the charges.

"No Weasel, you're the sort that gives *that* sort a nervous breakdown. What do you want here besides some free beer and conversation?" I motion at the fridge and he fishes me out a cold Ba Mi Ba.

"Are you running out of Quang Tri? I will be flying Covey out of there. Just thought I would drop in and let you know. I'm down here for a couple of days; let's go to the Pink House." And he takes another swig on his beer.

"That makes me all warm and comfortable, just knowing you are going to play momma hen to us poor unfortunates. I just want you to know that if I see the window or door on that plane open in mid-flight, I am personally going to take you under fire. In fact, we may just have to have a shakedown inspection to make sure you aren't carrying any unauthorized ordnance." I threaten him, but I know it will be of no use. I can see that in his boiling little cesspool that he calls a brain, he is already thinking about how he could rig a whole series of exotic charges and drop them on us from the air.

He stays for about an hour and he helps me finish rigging the charges. Peewee takes care of the little people, and I run up to the TOC and lay on the choppers for a quick run over to Monkey Mountain. We will stay in camp tonight. We have a lot to do tomorrow, and besides, I think Wes is on the permanently denied list at the Pink House for some sort of explosive incident.

We are up early and put in a long day on Monkey Mountain. About three, we move into an area with plenty of brush and trees. We do a couple of dry runs on placing the explosives, and then I call up the choppers for pickup. When they are ten out, I give the signal and the team puts the charges in place; I call the birds and tell them I will blow the LZ. The whole drill works perfectly: there is a loud crump, the right trees go down, everyone is uninjured and I give the clear for the choppers to come in.

When the first ship comes in, four little people dash over and hook up to the strings. As they are lifting out, I notice that two of them are holding something between them; I can't make it out before they are gone.

Peewee is next with three more little people; they also appear to have extra stuff with them. Not too uncommon because they are constantly foraging. With the way these little people eat, we should just tell them that communists taste like bush meat, and the war will be over in a matter of months.

I am the last to leave, with Sang and two others. The ship comes in and drops strings, and we run over, hook up and run a snap link to each other. As I give the thumbs-up to the crew chief, I feel my leg straps tighten up and, at the same time, notice that one of the Yards is holding on to what appears to be a dead rock ape. I say "appears to be." Being the heaviest, as soon as we get up higher I sink down until my head is at their boot level. About that time Herr Monkey comes to and kicks off a snarling pissing match above me.

The three Yards are fighting this thing with all they got. I keep yelling at them to sling it away and let it drop. No go there: either they want to eat it too bad, or the monkey understands English because he is holding on for dear life and fighting at the same time. He has bit all of them by the time one of the Yards hits him solid enough to stun him. Sang wrings his neck, then I notice that they are getting ready to tie him off with some suspension line. That's a NEGATIVE boy because that will put him right at my level. You thought he was dead when you got him on this carnival ride, remember. I make them keep the monkey up there with them, which they think is real funny. I hope you little monsters all get rabies.

It seems there had been a small troop of monkeys in the trees when we blew the charges. It killed or stunned them and they fell to the ground like clumps of fur-covered bush fruit. Never waste a free meal is the Yard guideline, so they managed to round up four of them, fairly big suckers as well. I will have to get the doc to stitch a couple of my guys up, but they are beaming in anticipation of the feast.

* * *

We will go into isolation tomorrow. Habu will be going up to Quang Tri with us, as well as Intruder and Indigo. We will load out to the airport in two days for transit by Caribou aircraft to Quang Tri.

We will replace three teams that are coming down. Two of those teams are coming back missing some people, and the third is shot to hell, with both Americans wounded so badly that the teams will have to be reconstituted. Because we are getting plenty of replacements, the teams will be rebuilt quickly. That is good, in a sense, since the more teams actually out there running, the fewer missions will fall on our shoulders. We have literally been running missions back to back, with as little as two days back at camp before we head out again.

The teams will act as the Bright Light backup for downed aircraft for each other. Intruder will launch first, and we will be their Bright Light backup. Then the next team will launch after Intruder comes out. Unless we get slammed and have too many wounded getting the first team out, we will continue to be their Bright Light rescue force.

Early morning on our mission day, we grab a short ride from Quang Tri to the launch site from the airfield. We go over to the TOC for our briefings from the launch site personnel. Wes is the Covey and brings us up to date on the target areas, which he has been flying for the last few days and checking for activity. They make a swing over, never getting too low so that Chuck doesn't get suspicious. So far it looks pretty good, although they had spotted some trucks in the southwest corner of the AO the day before yesterday. I get down to the mechanics of it all.

The area has a mixture of broadleaf forests and stands of bamboo near to the streambeds and the main river that traverses its axis. The area that they want to scour will be almost four kilometers from where the Covey reported seeing trucks. Command is pretty sure that they have a major staging area down there under the foliage.

Please don't let some dimwit decide to defoliate this place. I have already been on two targets like that. They come in with C123s in staggered trails, and dump Agent Orange on everything. It literally melts the trees and foliage. Of course, they have all kinds of weenies telling you that it's perfectly safe, that it wouldn't hurt animal life, yada, yada, yada. Well I have been in those areas; we found not one living thing that was healthy and a bunch more that were evil-looking, sick, and dying from something. I am sure they didn't get sick eating the bananas.

Mac and I were on a target once when they came by and dumped this stuff. We moved as fast as we could tactically, all the way to the river so we could get out of it and wash off. When we got there the river was filling up with Nguyens a half a mile downstream with exactly the same idea. It melts plants for Christ's sake, how good can it be for you? Of course, this is the same group that told all those GIs in the fifties that it was perfectly safe to be within five kilometers of the A tests, if they wore their little diddy glasses and didn't look at the fireball. Some of those guys actually glowed in the dark before they died of all kinds of exotic diseases and cancers. Good old Military Industrial Complex, you know that they are trustworthy. Better living through chemistry and all that....

Intruder will try to work their way from a primary landing zone partway up a steep complex of ridges that fall off into a fair-sized valley. At the mouth of the valley is where Covey spotted the trucks before they ducked under cover in the trees. There doesn't appear to be a road there, but that isn't unusual. I bet it is there, it's just under the trees is all. Those trucks were careless or they thought they could shortcut somewhere. What bothers me is the abundance of bamboo near the fringes of the valley and in spots where it doesn't make sense. Either it is an anomaly or they are disguising something. We will find out for sure tomorrow.

The dawn breaks; well over here it sort of jumps up on mornings like this. The plan is to do a false insertion to the northwest and throw out a Nightingale device. When it goes off it will sound like a firefight. It might draw folks in that direction long enough for us to skirt the tree tops, drop in on my little clear area and un-ass the birds in such a way they never appear to have landed. It is going to be a hot roll-in.

Just for funsies, the bombers are going to drop some ordnance near where the Nightingale device is cooking off, just as if they were providing close air support for a team in trouble. It might buy them some time in the target and Intruder might actually see something.

The first ship drops the Nightingale device off and pulls up. The lift package is skimming the trees, then drops over the ridgeline. As we orbit in the distance, the team rolls into the LZ with enough spacing that none of the birds has to hover and wait. To anyone listening it would just sound like three helicopters passing from higher up the valley and out the mouth, gaining altitude as they went. Unless some yokel was close enough and saw them, we might fool them. Quick as Jack they are on the ground. They get the team into a perimeter just off the LZ, give Wes a team okay and start moving. They are real careful to cover their track as best they can, then even more careful once they get into the tree growth.

It is hot down there. That is the first thing you notice after the sound and fury goes away. But it will be cold at night, if the team gets lucky and can stay that long. They are moving, then stopping and listening for an equal amount of time, then moving again, gradually trying to work their way lower by a circuitous route. There is a fine balance between getting down where they will have their concentrations and staying close to some ground that can be defended. The last place you want to get in is one of the numerous streambeds that run off the ridge. If they get jumped in there, the team will die real quick.

The woods are getting thick down here so Intruder is skirting the bamboo, trying to work its way down about seventy-five yards to where the trees get larger and run off towards the southeast on a small plateau. There is good ground to the left if they have to scramble, and in a real crunch, the bamboo can be cleared with bomb strikes. You are always looking for a place to run to and hold. During movement, the team designates the good ones as rally points in case they are hit before they find another one. That way, if the team gets hit and split, at least some of them can get back to one of these and get pulled out.

Intruder has been on the ground for three and a half hours, and I am starting to feel like we may have pulled the wool over their eyes. The team stops and gets into a defensive perimeter, with about half of them in the trees and a couple of the little people in the edge of the bamboo. They're trying to decide whether to try to find a RON site in the next hour, then lie up there until tomorrow before moving down in the valley. It would give them time to listen and see if anyone is looking for Intruder. The One-Zero is talking with Covey when the One-One starts clicking his finger and pointing out into the brush and undergrowth, and then holding his hand to his ear. The team leaders sign off with Covey and tells him we got something, so he won't break squelch and come up until called back. Everyone hunkers down and waits.

They are being hunted. The team can't get up and move very well without making a whole bunch of noise, so they wait and hope the NVA pass or when they get close enough to kill a bunch of them and try to claw their way to an area that can be defended. Sitting at the firebase listening on the radio as the events transpire, it had been such a good day so far; we had been lulled into actually thinking they could do a little sneaking and peeking out here, instead of being pop-up shoot-back targets for Nguyen.

I am looking at the map of where they are when the One-One opens up full auto and an NVA falls out of the brush right to his front. The One-Two pulls a grenade and slings it so it lands about a third of the way between them and where he heard the last noise to his front. It goes off with a sharp crump. The Yards fire a quick burst, then another. The Yard in the rear and one of his buddies let go full auto, up and to the right rear.

They don't want to go down, and can't go back up. There is one quick route out. The map showed a small rise in the terrain with sharp cliffs to the east of it and a gentle slope running off almost due north. The One-Zero reports into the radio to Covey that they're are in contact and give him the location. Our volume of fire picks up and so does theirs. Shit, the bamboo is the only route.

The team starts a standard immediate action. It sucks because the bamboo is usually thick, but you'd be surprised how fast you can move when your adrenalin is up. The hope is that this stand of bamboo isn't thick, and there isn't a line of NVA waiting for them on the other side. As the action unfolds on the radio I also wish fervently that I could be transported to Hawaii, instead of being their Bright Light. Your adrenalin starts to crest in anticipation of having to join the fight.

The automatic fire is chopping the bamboo above and around them, but they are all moving forward. Suddenly the bamboo gets bigger in diameter and it is clearing out. They bust out of the thick stuff and there are a couple of thatch shelters and about six NVA all strung out like they were on a line. They go down as four guns open up on them and the team can see a cluster of rocks and some trees ahead of them. There is a dull whomp behind the One-Zero and before he can wonder what it was, he feels a searing heat. Someone has set something off and the dry bamboo goes up like tinder.

The bloody fire is on top of them before one can blink. The One-One had just stooped to check one of the bodies when the One-Two goes past him like a shot. Everything is burning so fast that it sucks up all the oxygen. The One-One's lungs are on fire and so is his clothing. Everyone is running, trying to stay ahead of the flames. One of the little people passes the One-One his eyes real wide and his arms and legs pumping. It's pure chaos with every man for himself. He pours it on: you don't want to burn in here. Then two more figures pass him; one of them has burnt fatigues and his hair is partially burned off. Someone reaches over to help him when he notices it is an NVA, not one of his. No one is shooting at each other; everyone is trying to escape.

They get to the rocks, dive over them and roll down a small gully. More scattered shots and they all manage to make the unburned ground. They are counting heads as more figures run out of the bamboo and head off to the left front, downhill into the forest. Back in the wash and there are two bodies there. Obviously NVA. Someone on the team must have shot them. We are getting all this as we crank up and get ready to move to the orbit point for insertion.

I am following it all on the radio. I hear Covey come up on the air and we are getting both their transmissions back and forth. The team is scorched and burnt but no serious casualties. Covey is firing the birds up. He has two F4 fast movers that he has on station. The team asks him what they have and he says napalm. Well what the hell, there isn't much left of the bamboo to catch. To the front is a roaring inferno. It is burning so fast there is hardly any smoke on the ground, it must be too hot to even stare at for long.

Intruder grabs a little more terrain and they rig the ring mains to blow down two of the larger trees so the air assets can get a chopper in here. The trees go down and make a nice fort wall to get behind and cover uphill.

Since getting to their last position, the team has heard only a few shots and a whole lot of screaming down there in the fire. The One-Two tells the team leader that they started using tracers on him as he started to pull back; he figures they were trying to set the bamboo on fire and cook Intruder inside, or they just got sloppy because there were about thirty of them that followed them into the thatch. One of the Yards had tossed a white phosphorus grenade behind him. That was the whomp that set off the big fire. No one expected the whole shebang to incinerate so fast.

As we come up on station we can see the fast movers come in as Covey works them upslope, just in case the NVA try to flank uphill from where the team is. Choppers are ten out, then five, when the birds start to get some fire from down slope, light nuisance stuff but they are getting in there. Then a mortar round comes in and crumps to the left of the team and down. Shit, how did they get a mortar operating so quickly? That's not good, that's lots of folks, just more proof this was more than a local patrol. Two more rounds come in but they are still to the left. Covey is trying to figure out the gun target line from the shells coming in. He knows roughly that they are to the southwest. Two guns come on station, as the team hears the mortars thump as the rounds leave the tubes. They are still hitting to the left. The NVA don't know where the team is, but he will when the first bird comes in. I tell Covey to start putting some more air in here because our Crusader Bright Light is going to be needed if they don't get those guns.

My answer comes in the shape of two more fast movers that bomb the ridge to the southwest. The first helicopter comes in and four of Intruder get on it. They scramble aboard, and it lifts off. As it tilts and gains speed, I can see the door gunners burning up the slopes below them from where we are orbiting. The second bird comes in and as it lifts off, Covey tells the One-Zero that his ride is right on its ass. It comes in and settles with a skid on the trunk of the tree that had been dropped.

One of the trailing birds has taken major hits and slams into a clearing about three hundred meters up slope. It skewed in the air belching smoke, before setting down rough then rolled on its side with the blades thrashing up the vegetation. Covey has us moving to set down and recover the crew.

We cover the ground to the crash site quickly and set down about fifty meters from the now burning aircraft. We move our Bright Light team up quickly with one of us round eyes in front so the crew doesn't shoot first in nervous reflex. We come up on the wreck and find all four aviators shaken but not stirred. They are banged up from the crash, slightly bewildered and at the same time glad to see us. We are informed by Covey that there is movement coming up on us fast and he works the guns to suppress that activity. The birds come back and we load the crew on the chase ship then we start to disengage. I am on the last ship with the NVA right on our heels. We had taken hits in the aircraft and everyone that can see out to shoot does because the NVA are right there. I smell of fear, sweat and burning aircraft, We slip the surly bonds of terra firma and rise up into the cool and lead-free air above. Intruder found out there was a lot of activity in there, so Covey can call up the Air Force and go out and bomb the area into snot, hopefully.

Wes, our Covey rider, comes back and tells me what he saw from the air: a whole bunch of folks trying to run out below where the firefight started. It looks like the NVA may have had trackers on Intruder, and the troops that came up from the south were the right flank of a sweeping force. The NVA the Yards killed at the edge of the bamboo at the start of the fight were probably the tracker team. Intruder had let the two suckers they wasted get so close that the first one almost ran into a rifle barrel before someone fired.

The ones I could see when they tried to hit us on the LZ going out were NVA regulars. The NVA that passed everyone in the fire were all young but in good shape; they left no ass dragging in the dirt. They are the enemy, but I hope they made it. I don't wish that kind of death on anyone. It's a bad way to go. Fire is not your friend, no matter how timely.

It's a smooth transition back to the launch site. Team Crusader had performed well, with no wasted motion from start to finish.

CHAPTER 21

Sidelines

The Dragon's Beak is part of the target area designated as DM-9. No one has run this target since Sluggo ran up on a hillside and re-enacted Custer's last stand. Now, lucky Crusader, we get to go back in and see if anyone is using the area to stage something particularly nasty. Who knows, I might even find Sluggo's banana knife which he left on top of his hill. He still calls it *his* hill. Why not? It can *be* his hill. In fact, he can come up here and go back to *his* hill, instead of me, to look for his damn cutlery.

Command is the epitome of optimism. We, the carpenters of their madness, will sally forth and try to accomplish the impossible. If one was to be pragmatic, we are bait. There is not one wit of a chance that we can stay long enough to find their truck parks, strong points, capture a prisoner, do a wiretap or do anything more than fight for our lives. The weather will determine if we can do just that. Air support is how this war is being waged. They have the tools to hurt him even in this weather. The NVA come out of their defenses to run us out, they communicate, their anti-aircraft fires, and the guys upstairs, locate, mark then direct bombers onto the targets.

Everything going on in our sector is starting to smell like a major offensive by the PAVN. The peace talks in Paris haven't progressed further than agreeing on the shape of the table and the seating arrangements. Kissinger is up there tugging at his gold cufflinks, practicing his phony German accent, eating French pastries, and being full of himself. The North Vietnamese are full of lies and deceit, so they should get along famously. You have to give it to Ole Tricky Dick, he is the master of drama. When he had his hand on the tiller, the North knew that his patience level was marked by pushing the "Go Bomb" button if they weren't quick on the uptake. Somehow that process has been bogged down and the bad guys are pouring into the DM area and to the south and west. We are in the middle of pulling out troops and they are getting ready to deliver the deathblow to those pimps running Saigon.

I have just come back from flying a visual recon on the target area. I have been up in an OV10 with the Covey pilot, who is another frustrated fighter jock. Jesus, where do they get these guys? I have to give the Air Force credit, they have found where best to assign their version of us. They give them a prop-driven suicide machine and send them out as Forward Observers. We had slipped and skidded all over the area, trying not to appear interested in the particular patch of ground that represents my target box. We were fired on at all four points of the quadrant outside the box, so it stands to reason that inside the box are equally pissed-off Nguyens. No sense in calling that in, it would be a waste of breath. We will still have to take Crusader in there to find out who is home and find out what they are doing now that we know they are home and active.

The weather has turned to downpour, then a brief respite, then downpour again. This is the third time we have tried to do a visual to determine the primary and alternate Landing Zones for an insertion. The fact that the weather just wasn't going to cooperate adds a chilling note to our chances of survival if the weather closes in after we insert.

Bad weather is worse out in Indian Country because bad weather is an advantage for the enemy. We can't get air support for close-in action under the cloud base and Covey risks all every time they try to dive through a hole in the clouds and get below with enough altitude between them and the jagged terrain below.

We've been holding because of the weather and so far none of the teams have been able to get in. Even when it's clear over here on the coast the weather is socked in for most of the day out there in Indian Country. It sucks, and we are running out of rations at the launch site. Knowing the nature of how long we will be able to stay in the bush, I have started to have the Yards and ourselves eat only one meal a day as a PIR ration. We'll only need two if we go in, and those will probably be survival rations in the hope we get rescued. Everyone is prickly because of the delays. The weather gurus say there won't be clear air for probably another week.

I am sitting in the mess hall enjoying a packet of freeze dried coffee with Mac and Budrow and the two Americans on Mamba; the Sedang team. Pope the One-Zero is a stocky bulldog with all the charm of a leg breaker for the mob. His One-One is MacPhearson a tall dark stranger in the ethereal sense. He lisps slightly and is the perfect counterbalance for his teammate. Whatever is going on inside his head will someday make medical history. Both are extremely intelligent, but then with the exception of me, most of Recon is that way.

* * *

Mac starts in again on the Bomb Damage Assessment mission that he and the Cookie had completed in the box below the center of the target area a few weeks before.

The weather had cleared and Saigon wanted to punish the formations we had been uncovering for the last month or so. Mac had inserted on a clear day right on the ass end of an Arc Light bombing strike. Command estimated that there was a major command and logistic point under the canopy and had bombed it back into the dark ages then Habu had geared up and went to see what damage they had done. They inserted with no resistance from the ground.

Mac is coming up on the radio about every ten minutes with a report. They find a bunker complex just inside his target box and it takes them a while to sift through the ruins. He reports back shortly after that they find a bunch of bodies in a ravine, probably all killed by concussion; a couple more bodies are seen in the collapsed bunkers. They strip a few docs and equipment off the bodies. No enemy activity in his zone; looks like this is going to be a walk in the cemetery. The choppers with the Bright Light return to their refuel point and wait, listening as Mac picks his way through the devastation.

They find lots of pieces of people after that but no real intact bodies. They find a shoe with a foot in it, nobody around, just the shoe sitting there on top of the churned-up soil. They find broken pieces of weapons and kit, nothing really significant, until they top a small rise and there are the smoking ruins of a two-ton Russian truck. All the paint is stripped off and it has that charred look you get around high-explosives incidents. The rear tires have been blown completely off and the front ones are burning. Mac is taking photos of the devastation and recording, so Command can make an estimation of what was down there before the bombs started falling.

So far Habu has moved about a kilometer into the impact area. They are climbing over and around all the debris created by the bombs. It is hard to imagine the devastation one of these can create, until you have walked at ground level. Splintered trees and the confetti of shredded vegetation are everywhere, most of the bark has been stripped off any identifiable tree part, and everything is smoldering. It is a scene right out of a classic description of hell. Usually, there are pieces of equipment, but nothing is intact, although there might be the anomaly of a watch with the band still fastened, as if it was blown right off that way. I remember finding a flower swaying in the breeze behind the shattered trunk of a large tree once.

Mac comes across three more trucks and one of them is the twisted remains of a fuel truck. It looks more and more as if there was a truck park of some kind here. He is starting to count axles and major wreckage to see if they can piece together how many trucks there actually were. They haven't seen a single living being since they landed, only pieces and the few corpses that were in defilade from the rolling concussion waves. They come to a stream that is gray and choked with mud and debris, but it winds down through the complex. Here, they find a few more bodies, and parts to a whole bunch more. It looks like it may have been a mess area and the troops were just picking up their ration allotments.

They start to climb up when an NVA soldier stumbles out of the trench line. He is missing his web gear, and his clothes are half blown off and smoking. His left side is covered with blast contusions and blisters, and the concussion has blown one eye completely out of its socket; it is dangling by the optical nerve, bouncing against his left cheek. He is bleeding from the nose and ears, and his skin has that white-blue hue, splotched with red, of someone who has been in a major explosion event. One of the Yards puts a round into him, hitting him square in the chest and dropping him like a sack of wheat. No malice there; it is a mercy shot.

This is the first survivor they have found, which means that there just might be more who were in deep enough bunkers. Worse, there could be a tunnel complex up there that goes down several levels and a whole bunch were deep enough to have survived. Mac and the team deploy so they can use what little cover there is as they move up. They reach the trench and bunkers that the man emerged from. There is a small knot of bodies in a depression to the rear of them, and what looks like it had once been an opening leading back into the hillside. They can see tracks are leading into a hole that is just big enough for a man to have exited. This is a tunnel opening. How far it goes back or how deep it is cannot be determined. It could have been just an ammo storage area, or it could lead to a whole complex below. They pull up and deploy in a perimeter. Mac is relaying the situation to Covey. They are searching the surrounding terrain for indications of more openings. If this guy dug himself out, how many more survived, and how long before they emerged?

The birds are firing up, in case they have to go in and help Mac extract himself from some very pissed-off survivors. Covey and the launch site are talking about whether Mac needs to walk the whole box. In the end it is decided to pull Habu out and bring in a Recon bird to take some aerials over the next few hours, to see who digs themselves out and from where, and who might come in to assist. Not much chance of that happening in daylight, but they will scan the area before dark, then come back and do it again after nightfall. They might get lucky and catch the NVA with their knickers down.

Mac and the team are extracted without incident. They will probably come back in to the area and bomb any suspected tunnel complexes with delay-armed hard bombs in an effort to collapse the tunnels if there are any. After that it is just follow-up. The show will belong to the Air Force for the time being. They will close the door on the area by bombing it into dust and rock piles. All the intelligence they have gathered will be analyzed by Saigon, and from there the war planners will decide what is afoot. I can tell them what is bloody afoot. There are a whole bunch more of the enemy massing up here, and it isn't for a Norwegian Barn Dance.

Budrow is grousing about the expenditure of fuel assets and personnel going to Mai Lac. We had been discussing past successes in this our target areas and, of course, the possibilities of going to Mai Lac. It rounds back to Budrow again, telling us to hope we get in because he can't feed all of us for much longer even with one PIR meal a day.

"You Pencil dicks might want to start looking for the chubbiest Yard for sacrifice to the No Rations God", he suggests with a sneer. I am looking at Pope and thinking that he has enough muscle mass to feed us for at least three days if we make it an open competition. Besides, if you find a chubby Yard it's because he has consumed a whole monkey and a rock lizard, and his belly is distended.

With the withdrawal, the ration point we had been drawing from is no more. We are relying on rations from Danang and what we can purchase or barter for on the local economy.

The weather is clear enough for us to get to Mai Lac and back. Therefore, we have suggested we accompany two Bru, who have lost their lives, back to their clan for burial. Since two of the teams are Bru, and one is Sedang we all want to go over to pay respects, let the Bru have time with their clans, stuff ourselves and get mildly drunk from the jugs. The Sedang and the Bru are related. Both are short hardy people with a fierce warrior spirit. I have seen them endure the worst conditions, stoically accept pain with no complaint, and exhibit a loyalty to each other and us beyond compare.

It will also be a recruitment trip to fill out our ranks with new strikers. It's a respite from being cooped up here at the launch site on a razor wire of emotions and ennui. We are planning to go out in three lifts and come back on the same day. The weather is clearing, so we should start to leave in about an hour.

I remind Budrow that as all of us will be feasting with the Yards it relieves him of at least two meals per head for the day. He just looks at me with mirth and says, "Well that's just fine. You all go out there and stuff yourselves until your bellies look like a maternity ward. Then come back here and hope you can digest at least part of it before the weather clears and we insert you. Just hope you're not too fat to run off the LZ. Choppers will be here in an hour and fifteen, get your funerary ensemble and your bandits ready and out on the pad in order." He then smirks a laugh, rises and heads out the door. He stomps his way to the TOC splashing as he makes his way across the flooded grounds.

It is always a sad trip to return one of our little people in the simple wooden box that is supplied for their last voyage. The body has been kept refrigerated and has been prepared for transport. But this is the tropics and the corruption of death begins again as soon as it is taken out of the cold. We grab enough helicopters, with an escort of two gunships, and make the short hop over to Mai Loc, where most of the Bru are now living.

Our arrival is a mixture of grief for the fallen and a celebration of the return of the others, and us. The body will be prepared for burial, and the family will be given the customary death benefits, all of which we will arrange and handle personally. Our measure of respect to a trusted friend and brother is as old as the relationship between Special Forces and these rugged people.

The day is spent at the village, the first part in the burial preparation and dealing with the families, then with the tribal elders. Cuman is the center of attention, as befits his status as, for the lack of a better term, their war chief; we spend quite a bit of time with him and the other elders in the longhouse. As the afternoon drags on I slip out and wander around the village. We have been eating and sipping wine from the jars since we got here. At this point I would give up all my ammo and last pair of dry socks for an antacid.

Our last chore will be to recruit new warriors, which is never a problem. The entire male population, from nine-year-olds to the infirm, is trying to show their stuff at every opportunity. I am being followed by a gaggle of small boys, who are at my heels and dashing in and around my path as I wander around the village.

I love the Yards: the village and the people never fail to evoke a sense of belonging to something greater than I have ever found in our society. There is a sense of home and family; their history and resiliency as a people overwhelms you. They have such trust in us, though we bring so much suffering in the deaths of their men who are the bulk of our fighting force.

Everywhere I go, I am greeted by smiles and in some cases shy looks from the women. Cuman and the others are always after me to take a Bru wife. This is not just a sexual thing—well, it is in a way since it adds your genes to the tribe, and they respect a fighter. It is much more complex: a way of ensuring that you are part of them, that your heart will be Bru. I am sure anthropologists understand the motivation and the process, but to me it is a mark of deep respect on their part. I have avoided it by always insisting that I have a wife in America and her tribe would not allow such a thing. Not true, but the Yards accept it as plausible. It doesn't mean that they won't keep trying though.

The other factor in my saying no is that everyone chews betel nut here. It produces a mild numbing and narcotic effect, but it also turns your gums and teeth black. It is quite charming if you are a Bru, but I am not sure that I find it a mark of beauty.

I wander down to where some boys are practicing with crossbows near the edge of the village. My arrival makes the competition more intense as the boys line up to show their prowess. I am watching them do what all boys do no matter the culture, that is compete to be the alpha males, when I feel a tug at my subconscious and start getting that old feeling as if I am being watched.

Scanning around the area my eyes are drawn to a large tree that sits across from where the "Me Great Hunter" clash is. Ah, there it is: the diminutive figure of Bong is up there with another man who has to be twice his age. They are squatting in that age-old position of rest that a culture with no chairs to ruin their posture has adopted. Bong, our prescient Habu shaman, has the brass pipe in his mouth and a black plug of tobacco is burning its soul into the wind as he serenely puffs on the pipe.

I walk in their direction, slowly wandering, not in a straight line so as to give them the opportunity of making some sign that I am welcome to join them. I go over and examine some interesting grass-like plants, then watch a couple of birds doing the mating aerobatics, then look at the stream, all the while getting closer to the small hillock from which they are surveying the village. I come up from their right front and squat near them, looking off at the boys and their shooting game. Bong half looks in my direction and then says something to the old codger next to him, who politely covers a toothless giggle and rocks on his feet and haunches.

"I have been calling you for some time now, *Trung Si*. Why did you take so long looking at nothing?" Now I hadn't heard him shout or anything, so I suspect there is some sort of Bru ju-ju going on here.

"I was being polite, Bong, you know I no walk up when you talk with your papa san."

"He is not my father, he is my teacher." He lapses into German since he is more fluent in that than English, and continues. "He was beginning to think you were dull-witted, it took you so long." They are both looking at me with amusement. Okay, have your little ha-ha with me, you old coots, I am a big boy; I can handle all this primitive voodoo stuff.

"We are not laughing at you, *Trung Si*," Bong goes on. "And I don't like the pictures in your head," he finishes in a rebuke. Holy shit, what? I am trying to repress any further thoughts just in case it isn't a lucky guess, and he just chuckles to himself, and goes back to his pipe. Shit, these people are the real master race, they have survived for millennia with their tattoos and superstitions and way of life.

This is a scene right out of the Celtic Iron Age. If you remove all the modern trappings of guns and weapons of war, we could be squatting on a hillside in fifth-century Europe, discussing those awful Wends that keep pissing in the water upstream from us, and how we should go up there and cave in a few heads, steal their dogs and eat them.

Bong and the old man look at me with a bemused expression on both their faces, chuckle to themselves, and do a little rocking motion on their heels for good measure. Ah that's right fellas, have your fun with the city slicker. I can grab this game by the tail. I start thinking about Dracula, and Genghis Khan, and every other bad B-movie. Try this out if you can read my mind. The old man laughs again and says something to Bong. Bong mutters something back.

"Cuman is looking for you; it is time for you to go back down there," he announces. Just then I see Ti Ti come to the edge of the village; he spies us and waves, then yells something and starts hurrying over. Bong smiles at me smugly.

I begin to walk away in the direction of the village. Bong calls out to me.

"I told my master that you may act like a child, and you think like one sometimes, but he insisted that you do that to hide the way. Oh and *Trung Si*, we have a spirit that drinks blood too, but he lives by a stream."

This is too much for my feeble peanut to absorb, so I just turn and walk away with as much dignity as I can muster. I hear the old man's cackle of laughter as I walk away.

When I get to the longhouse, things are in full swing. The hopefuls are all standing outside and Cuman is giving them a speech of some sort. The selected candidates are beaming; the remainder look very dejected but brighten up a bit as Cuman winds up his talk. Then it's over to do a little drinking from the Mampei jars.

Our choppers will be coming back in about an hour to pick us up, with our special gift to the tribe. For the last year we can see that they—meaning those whores in Congress and the public themselves—are going to dump out of this ball game. We haven't been fighting a winning game here; all we are doing is containment. Sure as a pig's genitalia are pork, we are going to pull out all together and let Ho fight it out with that bunch of cowboys that represent Democracy's shining star in the Orient.

The problem is the Yards will get caught in the middle, with both sides eager to wipe them out as. The lowlanders on both sides see the Yards and their way of life as incompatible with the future they are crafting. There is so much similarity between the Yards and the native American culture—including their fate in the end. Both sides would willingly exterminate them as a people. The survivors would retreat deeper into the forest and cling to a way of life soon to be extinguished.

For the last few months we, and a lot of other Recon folks, have been "losing" equipment: not an odd hand grenade or belt of ammunition, but whole truckloads of stuff that we have been lifting out of the dumps being left behind as the regular units are being demobilized and going home.

We are leaving them not only ammunition, but weapons as well. Most of this stuff we have been getting before the South Vietnamese show up to take possession of the camps, warehouses, and dumps left by our units. In fact, the Fifth Mechanized Division is in the middle of that exercise right at that moment. So coming in with the choppers is everything we can load inside and sling underneath in the way of armaments and munitions. Add to that, medical supplies, rations and anything else we can manage. We are going to give them as much help as we can. Washington be damned because they would abandon us just like they are doing with our POWs. They don't give a rat's ass about these people. So we are giving them at least the ability to fight for their survival.

Budrow and Manes, and likely a bunch of others, probably know what we are doing and turn a blind eye to it. They can't condone it so we make sure that we never get caught. The chopper crews suspect, I am sure, but again, don't ask, don't tell is the policy.

As the birds come in the entire village pours out and as quickly as the stuff is unloaded, it disappears. Cookie and I had found two 81 mm mortars and three 60 mm mortars, and the rest is ammo and machine gun ammunition, along with some medical gear. There is enough stuff to arm a weapons platoon and enough ammo to resupply a couple of rifle companies.

We do the usual fare thee wells and get everyone onboard and loaded up. We begin to leave, one ship after another, and pass over the village. I look down as we turn to the east and notice that the old man is still squatting on the hillside. He never looks up as we pass overhead and I imagine that he is quietly humming to himself and dreaming about shape-shifting into a horny male howler monkey or some other bizarre thing. I feel a pang of longing as the village fades into the distance. I feel so at home there, it is tough to leave sometimes.

CHAPTER 22

Fare Thee Well, My Brothers

> These are the times that try men's souls. The summer soldier and the sunshine patriot will, in this crisis, shrink from the service of their country; but he that stands by it now, deserves the love and thanks of man and woman. Tyranny, like hell, is not easily conquered; yet we have this consolation with us, that the harder the conflict, the more glorious the triumph. What we obtain too cheap, we esteem too lightly; it is dearness only that give everything it's value.
>
> *THE CRISIS*, THOMAS PAINE

Though penned for another time and another struggle, these words have become our mantra. We are overwhelmed by the tasks being requested by Saigon. Our targets are even more crucial to the war effort, since we know, as does Command, that the North has no intention of letting us withdraw without their flooding in to seize the South.

While the President and his Disraeli are content that the peace talks are effectively restraining the North Vietnamese, we are finding more and more evidence that they are building up for something major. They are layering anti-aircraft in the target areas that are suitable places to mass weapons and men for an offensive, which make our insertions and extractions a nightmare of interlocking fires designed to knock down aircraft.

Through our efforts we have uncovered pipelines running south and west which are capable of bringing fuel south, which means tanks and armored vehicles being available for a push when we withdraw. American units are being pulled out and ARVN units are being assigned the areas they previously defended. Many are first-rate units with good leadership and frontline equipment. Many more are poorly led, poorly trained conscripts who are plugged into a less than cohesive defense strategy. The hope is that with US air power backing them, the ARVN can match the NVA. We still have advisors with the ARVN, to bolster their confidence and to work the air support in a combined arms strategy. It won't be enough.

* * *

The roads around Quang Tri are choked with ARVN military traffic dispersing to the north and west. The more astute among the civilian population are flooding into the city and moving south to escape the possibility that the North will attack.

I am sitting on the edge of the hardball in one of our jeeps, which has taken the opportunity to mechanically surrender. I am trying to get the carburetor to work. We have removed the jets and cleaned them and are reassembling the infernal device. I am watching the traffic to make sure we don't get a grenade in our knickers from the crowd of refugees streaming south. Most have faces of despair and panic, but some are giving us the skunk eye. There are Vietnamese MPs scanning the crowd and occasionally snatching deserters who haven't changed into civilian clothing. The troops moving north are a column of Vietnamese Marines. They are like miniature copies of their hamburger-eating cousins. These are hardcore combat troops: you can see by their faces and demeanor that they know they are going in for a fight and want to get to the business at hand.

The sixth and seventh Vietnamese Marine Regiments are the bulk of the line around Au Ti Combat base. The NVA have tried probing actions around the base and are moving artillery up in following classic Soviet Doctrine. In layman's terms, they are preparing for an offensive.

We get the jeep started; it belches in protest a couple of times then begins to run rough. Frank Pulley is with me, as his team is in the slot behind mine. He is his usual sardonic self with all sorts of country homilies to enhance his views. His voice carries from beneath the hood saying to turn it off as he is going to retard the timing. I am contemplating slamming the hood on his Mr. Mechanic act since we have been stalled here for over an hour. I want to ditch the jeep and hitch a ride with the Marines; we can always acquire a new jeep. This one looks like it barely survived a demolition derby.

Pulley finally says to start it and the jeep roars back to life, belching black smoke until it settles down to just occasionally backfiring. Frank does some sort of odd Tarheel magic and the engine smoothes out. We ease back into the traffic pattern, dodging the occasionally overloaded truck or minibus heading south. We are about two klicks from the turnoff to the launch site when we come up on a convoy comprised of ARVN tanks and M113 armored personnel carriers with Vietnamese Rangers clinging onto them and jammed inside like war fruit. They are stopped on the side of the road. I see an American walking down the side of the convoy towards us, and am pleased to recognize Josh, an old friend, who apparently has been snagged as an advisor. He is on his way to Au Ti where the MACV advisor command is co-locating with the Vietnamese.

We catch up on the day while we wait for the convoy to get started. His unit will be the quick reaction force and they expect that they will be facing armor. This is pretty much what we have been telling Saigon. At least someone was filtering it down to the user level. We tell him about finding tank tracks indicating medium tanks, not the little PT76 model used by the Soviet Airborne, but big muckaharras like T54s.

We say goodbye to Josh and he remounts one of the APCs. As we slide around a wide spot and turn towards the camp, he gives us the finger.

* * *

The war is starting to wind up. The NVA took Quang Tri, in what is now being called the Easter offensive. Then the ARVN airborne went back in and retook the city, and in the process got chewed into broken pieces of units. They were followed by the Vietnamese Marines, who eventually chased the remnants of the NVA out and back into the highlands. Sounds real good but in the process thousands died. Quang Tri is a broken ruin, from which the reports of what the NVA and VC had visited on the population are beginning to make the evening news. Worse, it is a harbinger of what will come.

A few days after we got back to Da Nang, we found Josh in the evacuation hospital. Of the force we had seen him ride off with that day, only a handful had survived. They had run head-on into the NVA battle formations in their effort to relieve the marine base and been chopped into pieces before they ever got anywhere near the position that had been described as the line holding the NVA out of the city.

The NVA had attacked in classic Soviet Doctrine: massive artillery bombardment, with their infantry right at the back of the screen. They had tanks with the first formations and had overrun anything that looked like it was organized resistance.

Josh's unit had fought, and fought bravely, until firepower had overcome human courage. The only thing left was to split up and make it to the line of resistance to the south. They, like us, had run into the trigger-happy crowd at the river and had lost people trying to get across to safety. He also told me about witnessing the same sort of conduct from the liberators that we had been hearing about. Working in close proximity with the assault forces were the VC death squads, out for revenge and to terrorize the population of the south. It had worked. The population was in panic and the Army was trying to contain the offensive while keeping its own troops from bolting.

Our operations now mostly center on directing air strikes, and trying to find spots where we can get some elevation and disrupt their supply lines to ease the pressure on the ARVN. Command is starting to explore the concept of B52s close in, along the main hardball, and that awesome firepower will finally break the back of the NVA pincer.

These are the same type of missions as before, in the great raid days. Pick a high spot where you can observe their logistics corridors, dig in and call in the Air Force to bomb anything you spot, or suspect, into snot. To do that we are running combined teams. We need the added firepower and we are slowly but surely chopping up Nguyen's ability to reinforce his fighting formations with men and material. It has come at a terrible cost though. We are losing people all the time. So far, thank

God, we haven't lost a full team again, but we have had some really decimated on these operations. Everyone is getting worn down to a frazzle. The Command can only keep us at this pace for so long before they use us into the ground.

I have listened to one too many "You men are doing a brilliant job" bullshit speeches. They know we are almost shot, and worse, so do we. I am not interested in the big picture. I am tired; so tired that dying actually looks appealing. I am down to nearly 140 lbs. I look like one of those survivors of the Death March in Bataan, and so does everyone else. You know how drawn tight and ready to snap you are when any kind of stimulant, even a few beers, puts you into a comatose state. Doc has cautioned most of us in using the amphetamines because we have no reserves to draw on. The only thing we will do at this point is permanently damage our internal organs.

The missions are the same: Recon and Bright Lights, or grab terrain, hold it, make them mass on you and run you out. In the process we will chew up their manpower. We still have some targets where we are doing traditional reconnaissance but they are more to the south and west. I Corp is already showing the cracks that will engulf the country. We are hurting them bad and both sides are stretched to breaking point. The ARVN get a few critical victories and all the politicians in Washington and Saigon are congratulating themselves on the theory of Vietnamization having worked. Now America can pull out her troops and rearm the Vietnamese, leaving only a skeleton of advisors. See folks, our gallant allies are able to defend democracy on their own.

Anyone with a fragment of logic understands that we may have whipped the NVA, but this is just the opening bout. They will learn from their mistakes and be back. They know they can win now. The Vietnamese cannot stand, and will fall without our backing. It isn't because they don't want to, or the troops are cowardly. It is merely that the North has the resolve, and the South doesn't. I can tell you for a fact that the ones here who have been bearing the load all these long years know it is coming. We and the Yards know that when we pull out the shit will hit the fan. We are continuing our program of secretly arming the Yards. At least when Kissinger and the rest of those hookers abandon the effort officially and go on to write their memoirs, maybe our friends will be able to hold their own and some of them will survive.

I know some of the tribes are planning to take the central highlands and try to hold there, or open a corridor to Thailand. All big hopes: they will be ground up and spit out on the landscape, as a bad aftertaste. I am struggling with my conscience. I cannot leave these people to die. I am a soldier and I have to obey my orders; I just don't know if I can. I am not alone; there are a number of us that feel the same way. I have been with these people so long that I have become Bru. I am of the people. Or am I? I am so tired, and to get back away from this spirit-grinding morass is so appealing, but my heart is sick with the prospect. On top of all this, my malaria is starting to flower again. I don't have any reserves to fight it off.

Then, one day, the decision is taken right out of my hands. Sickness, time in country, and Command decide it for me. My extension, along with the extensions of a bunch of others, is disapproved. I am off the roster and am ordered to begin out-processing. With me are a lot of other experienced guys. The clock just ran out for us. We have been getting a whole flock of replacements and they are filling up the ranks. One-Ones are being made One-Zeros, issued a couple of new guys, and the cycle begins all over again.

I feel as if I am a couple of centuries old; I need a break from this. They know it and more importantly I know it. I go through the motions of getting wound down from this place. The Cuban, Eldon, and that sawed-off little stump from Texas, Davidson, are all on the same orders. We are officially out of the game.

* * *

It is strange that when the time comes and you are relieved of that awful certainty that the next day could be your end, you are both relieved and in despair at the same time. I have been at this for so long, I know the culture shock we will experience in a few days. The military prepares you for it by gradually immersing you back into the chickenshit and regulations, as a preparation for that which is to come. We have a few days where we are part of the normal Recon activities, and then we will be shipped to Nha Trang for the out-processing. Then it is to Saigon to catch what everyone calls the Freedom Bird home.

Davidson and I wander over to the Yard hootches with Mac and the Cookie; it is an emotional goodbye with these amazing people. I spend the night, my last night, sleeping with the Yards in the SCU barracks. I still have half a mind to desert and go up into the hills with them. I think we all have that thought. I am heartsick at the prospect of leaving them.

They have seen so many of us come and go, and yet they will be here long after we are all gone. It doesn't make sense at all; my world is made up of conflicts. I am safe, I made it, and yet I don't want to leave. These are my people. And my friends are staying here too. Mac and Cookie, and men that I consider closer than my own brothers, will remain here and in danger.

I go outside, partly because I want to have some fresh air, and partly because the Yards have now gotten everything I own. Each one gets something personal of mine. I have saved my Luger for Bong. He comes out a short while after I go outside. I am sitting there with Xam Pat, who is a real primitive, having showed up in the beginning with his only possessions being his loincloth and bracelets. I have just given him my tomahawk, and he is overcome with his good fortune.

Bong comes over and says something to him. Xam Pat gets up, sniffs my cheek while he shoves my tomahawk into his belt, then strides into the room where the rest are feasting and drinking the beer I brought them. Bong settles down next to me and lights up his pipe. He puffs thoughtfully on it and speaks to me quietly.

"You go home, *Trung Si*, but you will always be Bru." He reaches over and squeezes my arm. Just like that, no oratory, no explanations, just a simple statement that says it all. I have saved my best possession for Bong. I pull the Luger out of my cargo pocket where I had put it before coming over here. It is wrapped in the orange FUHRO scarf; I unroll it and, with both hands, hand it to him. He looks at it and I can see the deep appreciation in his eyes.

It is my most prized possession; it is also a link with his past and youth. The time he spent with all those Germans, whose only escape from defeat and despair was the Legion. He had been a young striker with the French in the "54" conflict and had participated in those battles here in this place so very long ago. He doesn't say anything, he just rocks and puffs on his pipe. After a while he begins to hum a tune under his breath; softly it tugs at the peaceful feelings I have. All the turmoil I have been feeling for the last few weeks seems to melt away from me, as we sit together in the soft moonlight. The sounds of the others escape from inside, along with the soft yellow glow of the lights within. The sounds of men, comrades and soldiers, alive today and bonded by that bridge that only war can create. It is raucous, and tender, and full of being alive and who we are. It is the muffled backdrop for the last time I will see these men. It is fitting and proper and my path is clear to me now.

I pick up the tune that Bong hums, and then he softly begins to sing the lyrics as we sit there under the night skies. It is the song of the Legion, the one that only those Germans who joined to escape post-war Europe could sing, and their gift to that family of men so much like us. It is called *Kamerad.*

"*Ich hat' einen Kameraden, Einen bessern findst du nicht...*" Its tune is haunting and the words tell of loss, and death, and love.

"I had a brother, a better one you could not find." That's so perfect, so balanced, so precisely how I feel; but more importantly, this song is our parting, our way of saying fare thee well. I begin to sing with him until our voices drift across the night air together in farewell. The night wraps us in its soft embrace, with the smell of wood fires, and sets the stage for my last memories of this place and these people. I feel strong and full of life, and at the same time a tremendous sense of losing something of great import to my soul. Fare thee well my brothers. I will look for you on the other side someday.

APPENDIX

Definitions, Acronyms, and Army Terms/Slang

01, 02, 03	The numbering system for indigenous team members
292	Long-range antenna of sectioned metal poles
A1E	Korean War vintage propeller-driven close air-support craft, also called SPADS
AA coverage	Anti-aircraft coverage
AK	Standard Russian automatic weapon
ALPHA	Became CCN
APC	Armored Personnel Carrier
ARVN	Army of Vietnam (south)
AST	Part of the S2 section responsible for target folders
B40	Rocket-propelled grenade, PRG2
Blast wall	Sandbagged wall designed to protect against artillery
Bright Light	Code name for armed rescue units
CBU	Cluster bomb unit
CCC	Command and Control Central
CCN	Command and Control North
CCS	Command and Control South
Chin turret	Housing in the front of a Cobra aircraft for miniguns
Chuck	Nickname for the enemy
CID	Criminal Investigation Division
Covey	Aerial coordinator for ground teams
CS gas grenade	Grenade that causes tearing eyes and nausea
Dai Yui	Captain
DR	Disciplinary Report
Earmuff	Charges connected together with detonation cord, for either side of a tree

FAC	Forward Air Control (Covey without Special Forces personnel)
Hardball	Paved road
HE warhead	High Explosive
IR	Info-red
Jolly Green	CH53 helicopter
Klick	Kilometer
LSA	Lubricant oil for guns
MACSOG	Military Assistance Command, Studies and Observation Group
MACV	Military Assistance Command Vietnam
MACVSOG	Military Assistance Command Vietnam, Studies and Observation Group
Mikes	Minutes
Nightingale device	Construct of time fuse and explosive charges, like firecrackers or cherry bombs, designed to simulate the sounds of combat
NKP	Airbase in Thailand
OMEGA	Became CCC
One-One	Second American on a reconnaissance team
One-Two	Third American on a reconnaissance team
One-Zero	American team leader on a reconnaissance team
PAVN	People's Army Vietnam
PEN camera	Single-lens reflex camera; standard camera carried
PRC-25	FM Radio with a usual 5-mile range
RDF	Radio Direction Finding
Recon	Reconnaissance
Ring mains	Charges connected together with detonation cord
RON	Remain Overnight
RPG	Rocket propelled grenade
RT Habu	Reconnaissance Team Habu
S2	Intelligence personnel/section
S3	Operations personnel/section
S4	Supply personnel/section
SCU	Special Commando Unit
SIGMA	Became CCS
Slicks	UH1 helicopter
SMAJ	Sergeant Major
SOG	Studies and Observation Group
SOI	Signal Operating Instructions

Stabo rig	Standard web gear comprised of parachute harness with pistol belt; leg straps for airlifting out with strings
Straphanger	Someone who augments, for one mission, a team other than their own
Swag	Loot
TOC	Tactical Operations Center
Trung Si	Sergeant
TWs	Tropical Worsted: summer, polyester, tan uniforms
URC-10	Emergency radio communicator
WP	White phosphorous